The Digital Turn
in Architecture
1992–2012

READER

The Digital Turn in Architecture 1992–2012

Edited by
Mario Carpo

A John Wiley and Sons Ltd, Publication

ISBN 978-1-119-95175-9 (hardback)
ISBN 978-1-119-95174-2 (paperback)
ISBN 978-1-118-42591-6 (ebk)
ISBN 978-1-118-42597-8 (ebk)
ISBN 978-1-118-42606-7 (ebk)

Executive Commissioning Editor: Helen Castle
Project Editor: Miriam Swift
Assistant Editor: Calver Lezama
Design by Artmedia, London
Printed in China by Everbest

Front cover image: Marcos Novak, Warp Map
© Image courtesy Marcos Novak

Acknowledgements

Thanks are due to the authors who authorised the republication of their texts and images, often retrieving old originals; to Caroline Ellerby who collected, collated and researched the original illustrations; to Henry Ng who scanned and transcribed some of the texts and captions; to Megan Spriggs who edited my English; and to Helen Castle who patiently supervised the whole operation.

Research on the history of *Architectural Design* (*AD*), and on some of the *AD* essays republished here, was carried out by Joseph Clarke, Kyle Dugdale, Steven Lauritano, Masha Panteleyeva and Eduardo Vivanco during doctoral seminars I taught at the Yale School of Architecture in 2010 and 2011. I am grateful to them all, and special thanks are due to Kurt W Forster, Director of Doctoral Studies, and to Dean Robert AM Stern, Yale School of Architecture, for their support and advice.

Editorial Note on Presentation and Editing of Texts

With the exception of new introductions for each chapter, the texts in this anthology are verbatim reprints of published texts. Captions may not be identical to the originals, having been reformatted, and in some cases rewritten to reflect the current copyright status of the images, these include pages 21, 46, 83, 119, 121, 126 (t), 144, 167, 168, 171, 177 and 178. On page 159 the original image and caption have been replaced. Typographical and bibliographical errors have been corrected when discovered in the anthologised texts, but idiosyncrasies of spelling and punctuation remain unchanged. The bibliographic sources for all essays are in the copyright lines at the end of each chapter.

Contents

Introduction
Twenty Years of Digital Design

Building a multistorey car park these days typically involves more digital technologies than were available to Frank Gehry's office for the design of the Guggenheim Bilbao in the early 1990s. Yet few of today's car parks are hailed as examples of digitally intelligent design. In fact, in the first instance, a meaningful building of the digital age is not just any building that was designed and built using digital tools: it is one that could not have been either designed or built without them. Alert designers have ideas about what the new tools are and what they can do, and this intelligence – among many other things – inspires them to imagine unprecedented solutions.

Following from these premises, and looking for salient ideas, we scoured the last 20 years of *Architectural Design*, and chose 26 essays on digital design matters published from 1992 onwards. They are republished here unabridged and unedited (except for some typos), accompanied when possible by the original illustrations, and in chronological order, so the sequence illustrates the unfolding of digital design theory over time. For sure, not all that matters in digital design was published in *AD*; but a lot of it was. Since Andreas Papadakis's purchase of the magazine in the late 1970s, *AD* was for long the main venue for debate on architectural Post-Modernism, and at times almost the official organ of the movement. Fifteen years later, having mostly missed the Deconstructivist turn, and shortly before Papadakis's departure, *AD* started to embrace digital design with an enthusiasm almost equal to that of its pristine endorsement of the PoMos – a commitment to the digital cause that has continued unabated to this day.[1] The original footnotes of the articles included frequent references to other relevant titles on digital matters, and some bibliographic notes have been added in the introductions. All together, and in spite of evident limits to the range of sources and number of entries, this reader represents, we believe, a comprehensive synopsis of the recent history of digital design and its theory.

As some of the earlier essays evince (see in particular Eisenman, pages 16–22 and 23–7, and Frazer, pages 49–52), the beginnings of the digital turn in architecture were first and foremost a matter of inspiration – and perhaps fascination. Electronic technologies in the early 1990s were changing – some thought, revolutionising – society, economy, culture and almost every aspect of daily life. So much was changing and so fast that some architects started to think that design should change too. No one quite knew how back then, and the first design experiments, in the spirit of the time, assumed that virtual reality, and cyberspace, would represent a radical alternative to the physical space of phenomena, existence and building. Some also concluded that many activities and functions would soon migrate from physical space to cyberspace, and that the design of new electronic venues in bits and bytes would soon replace the design of traditional buildings in bricks and mortar. *AD* devoted two noted Profiles to *Architects in Cyberspace* (in 1995 and 1998; a third one, also guest-edited by Neil Spiller, was planned in 2002 but the title was eventually changed to *Reflexive Architecture*). However, even at a time when many young architects thought that their future would be in web design, the development of new digital tools for design and fabrication suggested that electronics would drastically change the making of physical buildings as well.

The emergence of a new digital tectonics in the early 1990s paralleled the technical development of spline modellers, a new generation of software that, thanks to the more general availability of cheap processing power, allowed the manipulation of curved lines directly on the screen, using graphic interfaces such as vectors and control points. The calculus-based parametric notations of the curves themselves thus became practically irrelevant, but two mathematical aspects of this spline-dominated environment have had vast and lasting design consequences: first, digital splines should be continuous (otherwise they could not be derived, mathematically, and the system would stop working); second, spline curves are variable within limits, as they are notated as parametric functions. Setting limits for the variations of one or more parameters is the crucial design choice that determines the instantiation of a family of curves (lines, or surfaces). In turn, the idea of a generic, open-ended, parametric notation (as in Deleuze and Cache's *Objectile*, on which more will be said below) implies the possibility that authorship may be split between more agents – on one side, the designers of the general function; on the other, its final customisers, or interactors (see Frazer, pages 53–6, and Cache, pages 146–51). This basic set of notions was and still is the warp and weft of digital design, and also the main reason why continuous lines and parametric variations remain to this day the hallmark of digitally inspired architecture.

Computers are famously versatile machines, and they do not express aesthetic preferences. One could use CAD/CAM technologies to mass-produce boxes and blobs, indifferently. However, unlike boxes, blobs cannot be mass-produced in the absence of digital tools (and in fact they were never mass-produced until recently). Would this simple argument: sheer technical supply – we make blobs because we can – be enough to explain the lasting tie between digital design and smooth curves? Probably not. The essays collected in this reader prove that curving folds emerged in the early 1990s as a design strategy internal to the architectural debate of the time – as a deliberate mediation or synthesis between Post-Modern unity of form and Deconstructivist fragmentation. Lynn's theory of folding, Allen's 'field conditions', and Foreign Office Architects' writing of the time, among others, reiterate with different nuances this statement of principle; computers, splines and animation software were seldom or never mentioned (see Lynn, pages 29–44; FOA, pages 58–61; and Allen, pages 63–79). In retrospect, this current of digital design does appear like a continuation of Deconstructivism with digital means, and indeed many of today's star architects came to the continuous folds of digital design after training in the angular fractures of Deconstructivism – a legacy that still shows in the work of many, from Zaha Hadid to Gehry to some works of Eisenman himself. But the so-called 'Deleuze Connection' (in architecture, the influence of Deleuze's theory of the fold, relayed to designers through Bernard Cache's technological interpretation of the Objectile: see pages 148–51) adds further layers to this story.

The immediate architectural fallout of Deleuze's fold, and most likely one reason for Eisenman's and Lynn's interest in the matter, was Deleuze's exegesis of Leibniz's mathematics of continuity, of calculus-based points of inflection (the 'fold') and parametric notations (the 'objectile'). But, through Deleuze, it was a whole post-modern universe of thinking that offered itself, sometimes covertly or inadvertently, to the then nascent theory of digital design. Deleuze was interested in calculus as a quintessentially modern language of differentiality: calculus describes variations of variations, and is of no use in cultures or societies that are foreign to that notion (such as most of classical antiquity, for example). But in an odd reversal of alliances, the modernity of calculus as a notation of variations also partakes in a generically post-modern pattern of rhizomatic variability, complexity and fragmentation (of narratives, 'récits' or 'strong referentials'). Deleuzian, post-modern variability was the cultural framework within which digital technologies were first put to task to design and produce variations (variations in form and variations in series, or mass customisation), and in this more general sense the digital turn in architecture can also be seen as a belated vindication of some of the principles of Post-Modern architecture itself: against Modernist standardisation, the PoMos had argued for differentiation, variation and choice; almost one generation later, digital technologies provided the most suitable technical means to that end. A philosopher and historian could even argue that, in a typical cultural-technical feedback loop, post-modern culture was the 'favourable environment' where digital technologies took root and to which they adapted to finally evolve in the way they did.

Be that as it may, the essays in this reader provide ample evidence of another, equally pervasive kinship between architectural Post-Modernism and digital design. Systems theory, complexity science and the so-called theory of self-organising systems were part of the legacy that early cybernetics had bequeathed to contemporary digital design,[2] but they were destined to an odd revival of sorts in the 1990s. These and related theories on indeterminacy, chaos, etc often merged with various morphogenetic metaphors which are particularly apt at describing the digital dialectic between script (code, genotype) and parametric variations (phenotypical adaptations). In the mid 1990s, Charles Jencks offered a comprehensive assessment of this notional field under the term of 'nonlinearity' (in science and in design: see Jencks, pages 82–7 and 88–107). His synthesis did not immediately catch on, but most of the ideas underpinning it did. Oddly enough for a purportedly high-tech subject, this current of digital design theory was marked from the start by a starkly anti-technological bias.

The theory of nonlinearity, or emergence, posits that, sometimes, nature 'jumps' from one state to another in sudden and unpredictable ways, which modern science can neither anticipate nor account for. The simile often invoked is that of a heap of sand, where new grains falling onto the top accrue in regular ways up to a catastrophic point when the heap collapses or, as some say, reorganises randomly (ie, the same experiment, repeated ad infinitum, always yields different results). This state of indeterminacy can in turn be interpreted in different ways: as a banal contingency, for example, due to a variety of factors (shortage of data, fallacy of modelling, external interference, etc); or as a general law of nature. The latter may not necessarily lead to animism, spiritism or black magic, but it does lead to endowing nature with some form of free will, opposite to modern science's determinism (or, in theological terms, predestination); and once indeterminacy is seen as a state of nature, it is easy to see how computers, by the fuzzy ways they seem to work, may in turn be seen as 'nonlinear' thinking machines – or something similar to that. The notion that an electrically operated abacus can emulate the workings of nature and the faculties of human thinking may appear as a long shot; yet this is what research in artificial intelligence (and a lot of science fiction) is often about.

Nonlinear arguments, often declined in tamer or more practical terms, are frequent within even mainstream digital design theory; they have occasionally acquired more controversial Nietzschean, Bergsonian, übermenschliche and vitalistic overtones (if the universe is 'dancing on the verge of chaos', the hero or the artist alone can bend it to serve their will); and in many ways they continue to underpin a robust romantic, often irrationalistic approach to digital design. In the early times of digital design, anti-mechanistic ideologies often inspired 'ethereal' and psychologistic notions of cyberspace and of digitally mediated, immersive environments (see Spuybroek, pages 109–16, and Oosterhuis, pages 117–23);[3] in more recent times, they have equally furthered a more spiritual approach to digital tectonics, to the magic of materials and to the uniqueness of craft (whether manual, digital or digitally enhanced). Similar ideas were in part revived, in a more technological and less spiritual form, by the 'emergence' theories of the early 2000s, which still inform various practices of contemporary (2012) digital design, particularly in the field of 'performative' design experimentation (see Hensel, Menges and Weinstock, pages 160–64, and Menges, pages 165–81). Even though direct reference to phenomenology is rare, this side of digital design theory can be seen as an apparently unlikely but extremely fertile technologising of architectural phenomenology – or as a new phenomenology for the digital age. This convoluted genealogy of ideas also warrants the frequent albeit often understated or tacit sympathy of many digital designers for all the foes of industrial modernity – from Romanticism to Expressionism to Organicism. Not without reason: by chance or by design, digital technologies mass-produce variations and customise non-standards; they are anti-industrial hence post-modern, both in the philosophical and in the architectural sense of the term, and perhaps anti-modern in general as well.

An enthusiastically anti-technological endorsement of new technologies is an improbable intellectual construction. Yet this dual, almost schizophrenic nature of digital theory was an essential component of digitally intelligent design from its very beginnings. It is embedded in, and derives from, the dual genealogy and double allegiance of digital architecture (kindred with Deconstructivism on one side, and with architectural Post-Modernism on the other), and its ambiguity is in many ways the ambiguity of post-modern thinking itself, at times a critique of the modernity from which it derived, at times a reactionary anti-modern stance in the political sense of the term. Not coincidentally, digital design theory was also the harbinger of and the training ground for much end-of-millennium post-critical thinking in architecture, and many digital designers in the 1990s (and sometimes beyond) professed a free-market, neoliberal political creed (albeit this aspect of digital design history is scantly represented in this anthology).

When the dotcom crash of 2000 and 2001 stifled the wave of technological optimism and 'irrational exuberance' which had accompanied the rise of digitally inspired architecture in the 1990s, all the basics of today's digital design theory – of digital theory as known to date – were already on the table. In the years that followed, as technology continued to evolve, digital design went through major theoretical developments alongside adaptions, fine-tuning and steady progress in practical implementation – almost all of which, however, occurred within the general theoretical ambit that was defined in the 1990s, or extrapolating from some of its trends.

The essays republished here bear vivid witness to the 'crisis of scale' which marked non-standard form-making around the turn of the century: digital mass customisation, which had been proven to work effectively at the small scale of industrial design and fabrication, did not perform well at the full scale of construction (see Lynn, pages 45–7 and 125–30; FOA, pages 58–61; SHoP, pages 132–34; and Cache, pages 152–57. The shift from form-making to process that ensued prompted the adoption of new software for information exchange and for the management of building and construction tasks; this family of software, known under the generic name of Building Information Modelling (BIM), has been taking on increasingly important design roles (see SHoP, pages 135–45, and Garber, pages 227–39). At the opposite end of the digital design spectrum, a new generation of digital blobmakers[4] offered new definitions of architectural curvilinearity, involving at times a rejection of their predecessors' theoretical stance, and at times, quite to the contrary, a new theoretical awareness of the aesthetic implications of formalism (see Rahim and Jamelle, pages 213–20, and Foster Gage, pages 221–25). The universality of digital curve-making has been posited, in the strongest terms ever, by Patrik Schumacher's theory of parametricism (see Schumacher, pages 243–57). But arguably the most significant digital development of the 21st century, the participatory turn in its multifarious manifestations, often generically known as the Web 2.0, has found but a feeble echo among the design professions. Interactivity and responsiveness have long been staples of electronically augmented environments, but automatic variations in most buildings are necessarily limited to non-constructive features, such as environmental controls, lighting, gadgetry or occasionally to moving parts of curtain walls or other surfaces. Participation in design is another story altogether.

Today, many technologically savvy designers use open-source software, or exploit other collaborative aspects of networked technologies (see Hight and Perry, page 189–200, and Morel, pages 201–07), but few or none envisage to develop open-sourceable architectural design – ie, design notations that others could use and modify at will. Design and building have always been participatory endeavours, as no one (except perhaps Henry D Thoreau, or Robinson Crusoe) can make a building all alone. Participatory authorship is inherent in the very idea of parametricism, from its Deleuzian beginnings, and BIM software was developed precisely to facilitate the exchange of digitised information among the many agents – human and technical alike – that must interact in large design and construction projects; not surprisingly, recent BIM software is increasingly fostering and facilitating collaborative and even collective decision-making strategies. Yet individual authorship has long been such an essential aspect of modern architecture that one can easily understand the mixed feelings of the design professions vis-à-vis a techno-social development that many feel might threaten or diminish the architect's traditional authorial role.

This reticence, however, is creating a gap between the digital environment at large, which is fast embracing generalised models of mass collaboration at all levels, with potentially huge intellectual, economic and social consequences, and the culture of digital design, which in this instance at least appears to have taken another path. This apparent decoupling is an ominous sign, as design theory used to be at the forefront of digital innovation: in the 1990s architects and architectural theoreticians were pioneers of the digital frontier – which is probably one reason why end-of-millennium digitally inspired architecture was so eminently and almost universally successful. The best digital architecture of that time was not only inspired by digital technologies – it was a source of technological and aesthetic education for all. Ten years later, it is difficult to be inspired by a *soi-disant* cutting-edge architectural style which has now been repeating itself, in a kind of precocious mannerism, for at least 15 years; much in the same way as young architects may find it difficult to be inspired by *soi-disant* cutting-edge design theories which are often recapitulating, rephrasing or revising ideas that have been around since the early 1990s. Not surprisingly, many in the design professions – including noted *AD* authors like Neil Spiller – have recently started to look elsewhere for the next big thing. In fact, *AD* itself has already tentatively inaugurated a new age of post-digital high-tech.[5]

Some of this gloom may be premature. This digital reader is not meant as an epitaph or obituary. The shift from mechanical to digital technologies is a major historical turning point, and the makings and unmakings of the digital age should be assessed in the long view of the history of cultural technologies. This is particularly true for architecture, because architecture itself, as we know it, is the fruit of the early modern techno-cultural invention of architectural notations and of authorial design, and follows from that bizarre Renaissance claim that a new kind of humanist author, called an architect, should make drawings, not buildings. Today's computers do not work that way and, after upending the Modernist tenets of mass production, economy of scale and standardisation – that was the easy part – digital tools for design and construction are now unmaking the Albertian, humanistic principles of allographic notation. The resulting shift, from mass customisation to mass participation, may be more disruptive for architectural production than the digitally induced dominion of the spline to which we are now almost getting accustomed: again, that was the easy part.[6] If history has something to teach – the digital history of the last 20 years, as well as the architectural history of the last 20 centuries – the best, or at least the most momentous days of the digital turn may still be ahead of us.

Notes

1   In 1992 Andreas Papadakis, the Editor and proprietor of *Architectural Design* (*AD*), sold *AD* as part of the Academy Group, the architectural and design publishers he owned, to VCH, a large German scientific, technical and professional publisher. Papadakis continued with VCH as Editorial Director of Academy until the end of 1994. On his departure, Maggie Toy took over as Editor of *AD*. In 1997 the American-owned scientific and professional publishers John Wiley & Sons acquired VCH and with it *AD* and the Academy architecture list; Helen Castle has been Editor of *AD* since 2000. Throughout the 1990s, under Papadakis and then Toy, while generously promoting the first steps of digital design, *AD* continued to feature Classicists and Post-Modernists, with sometimes bizarre juxtapositions: in 1993, Greg Lynn's seminal digital Profile, *Folding in Architecture*, was included in an *AD* issue mostly featuring Russian neoclassical architecture (*AD* Profile 102, *AD* 63, March–April 1993. Reprinted London: Wiley-Academy, 2004).

2   On the rift between early architectural applications of cybernetics, shape grammars and today's visually oriented spline modellers, see Frazer, pages 49–52, and McCullough, pages 183–87.

3   Among the first artists and theoreticians of virtuality, Marcos Novak contributed seminal essays and artwork to the *AD* 'cyberspace' issues of the 1990s, including the image reproduced on the cover of this book.

4   The architectural blob was famously invented by Greg Lynn in the 1990s: see his 'Blobs (or Why Tectonics is Square and Topology is Groovy)', *ANY* 14, May 1996, pp 58–62.

5   See Neil Spiller and Rachel Armstrong (guest-editors), *Protocell Architecture*, *AD* Profile 210, *AD* 81 March–April 2011, p 17, where the design of new materials (including, more esoterically, the design of living materials suitable for building) is presented as the new technological frontier of architecture.

6   See Mario Carpo, *The Alphabet and the Algorithm*, MIT Press (Cambridge, MA), 2011).

© 2012 John Wiley & Sons Ltd.

Architecture After the Age of Printing (1992)

Peter Eisenman

These two essays by Peter Eisenman inaugurate digital discourse in architecture in the 1990s, and highlight the continuity between Deconstructivism and the first age of digital design. The contrast between the photograph and the telefax, cited in both essays, refers less to image-making than to the different nature of mechanical and digital reproducibility: unlike mechanical copies, which once printed are fixed and stable, digital images derive from number-based notations, or files, that can morph and change all the time. In Eisenman's reading, the new paradigm of electronic mediation destabilises and 'dislocates' centuries-old habits of anthropocentric vision, rooted in the monocular, perspectival tradition and in the modern technologies of mechanical reproduction, and should inspire and prod architects to further contest 'the space of classical vision' and break 'the gridded space of the Cartesian order'.

In the first essay Eisenman also refers to Gilles Deleuze's theory of 'the fold' (from Deleuze's book *The Fold, Leibniz and the Baroque*, first published in French in 1988, and which would inspire a seminal issue of *AD*, guest-edited by Greg Lynn with major contributions by Eisenman himself: see pages 28–47). Folding, Eisenman argues, may provide a new 'strategy for dislocating vision', by subverting the hierarchy of interior and exterior and by weakening the notational correspondence between drawing and building. The second essay republished here, 'The Affects of Singularity', does not mention Deleuze but refers to 'singularity' as a new ontological condition of the subject – significantly, not of the object, yet, Eisenman suggests, equally opposed to the mechanical ideas of standardisation and repetition, and in sync with the new technical logic of electronics.

Both Deleuze's 'fold' and the notion of digital singularity will become topoi of digital discourse in the 1990s. Similar notions of 'singularity' also generally refer to the new post-modern differentiation of subjects and objects alike. But in 1992 the digital is not yet a tool for a new mode of design, or even less for building; the rise of electronics is seen here as a general techno-cultural shift that should inspire architects to engage with an unprecedented cultural environment and with a new view of the world. Electronics, in Eisenman's view, vindicate and corroborate the stance of all the historical enemies of the dominion of the classical eye. Deleuze's Folding is seen as a new Deconstructivist weapon of choice, and the forthcoming digital fold as a continuation of Deconstructivism by electronic means.

Visions Unfolding: Architecture in the
Age of Electronic Media AD September–October 1992

During the 50 years since the Second World War, a paradigm shift has taken place that should have profoundly affected architecture: this was the shift from the mechanical paradigm to the electronic one. This change can be simply understood by comparing the impact of the role of the human subject on such primary modes of reproduction as the photograph and the fax; the photograph within the mechanical paradigm, the fax within the electronic one.

In photographic reproduction the subject still maintains a controlled interaction with the object. A photograph can be developed with more or less contrast, texture or clarity. The photograph can be said to remain in the control of human vision. The human subject thus retains its function as interpreter, as discursive function. With the fax, the subject is no longer called upon to interpret, for reproduction takes place without any control or adjustment. The fax also challenges the concept of originality. While in a photograph the original reproduction still retains a privileged value, in facsimile transmission the original remains intact but with no differentiating value since it is no longer sent. The mutual devaluation of both original and copy is not the only transformation affected by the electronic paradigm. The entire nature of what we have come to know as the reality of our world has been called into question by the invasion of media into everyday life. For reality always demanded that our vision be interpretive.

How have these developments affected architecture? Since architecture has traditionally housed value as well as fact, one would imagine that architecture would have been greatly transformed. But this is not the case, for architecture seems little changed at all. This in itself ought to warrant investigation, since architecture has traditionally been a bastion of what is considered to be the real. Metaphors such as house and home, bricks and mortar, foundations and shelter attest to architecture's role in defining what we consider to be real. Clearly, a change in the everyday concepts of reality should have had some effect on architecture. It did not because the mechanical paradigm was the sine qua non of architecture; architecture was the visible manifestation of the overcoming of natural forces such as gravity and weather by mechanical means. Architecture not only overcame gravity, it was also the monument to that overcoming; it interpreted the value society placed on its vision.

The electronic paradigm directs a powerful challenge to architecture because it defines reality in terms of media and simulation; it values appearance over existence, what can be seen over what is. Not the seen as we formerly knew it, but rather a seeing that can no longer interpret. Media introduce fundamental ambiguities into how and what we see. Architecture has resisted this question because, since the importation and absorption of perspective by architectural space in the 15th century, architecture has been dominated by the mechanics of vision. Thus architecture assumes sight to be pre-eminent and also in some way natural to its own processes, not a thing to be questioned. It is precisely this traditional concept of sight that the electronic paradigm questions.

Sight is traditionally understood in terms of vision. When I use the term 'vision' I mean that particular characteristic of sight which attaches seeing to thinking, the eye to the mind. In architecture, vision refers to a particular category of perception linked to monocular perspectival vision. The monocular vision of the subject in architecture allows for all projections of space to be resolved on a single planimetric surface. It is therefore not surprising that perspective, with its ability to define and reproduce the perception of depth on a two-dimensional surface, should find architecture a waiting and wanting vehicle. Nor is it surprising that architecture soon began to conform itself to this monocular, rationalising vision – in its own body. Whatever the style, space was constituted as an understandable construct, organised around spatial elements such as axes, places, symmetries, etc. Perspective is even more virulent in architecture than in painting because of the imperious demands of the eye and the body to orient itself in architectural space through processes of rational perspectival ordering. It was thus not without cause that Brunelleschi's invention of one-point perspective should correspond to a time when there was a paradigm shift from the theological and theocentric to the anthropomorphic and anthropocentric views of the world. Perspective became the vehicle by which anthropocentric vision crystallised itself in the architecture that followed this shift.

Brunelleschi's projection system, however, was deeper in its effect than all subsequent stylistic changes because it confirmed vision as the dominant discourse in architecture from the 16th century to the present. Thus, despite repeated changes in style from the Renaissance through Post-Modernism and despite many attempts to the contrary, the seeing human subject – monocular and anthropocentric – remains the primary discursive term of architecture.

The tradition of planimetric projection in architecture persisted unchallenged because it allowed the projection and hence the understanding of a three-dimensional space in two dimensions. In other disciplines – perhaps since Leibniz and certainly since Sartre – there has been a consistent attempt to demonstrate the problematic qualities inherent in vision but in architecture the sight/mind construct has persisted as the dominant discourse.

In an essay entitled 'Scopic Regimes of Modernity', Martin Jay notes that 'Baroque visual experience has a strongly tactile or haptic quality which prevents it from turning into the absolute ocular centrism of its Cartesian perspectivalist rival.' Norman Bryson, in his article 'The Gaze in the Expanded Field', introduces the idea of the gaze (le regard) as the looking back of the other. He discusses the gaze in terms of Sartre's intruder in Being and Nothingness or in terms of Lacan's concept of a darkness that cuts across the space of sight. Lacan also introduces the idea of a space looking back which he likens to a disturbance of the visual field of reason.

From time to time architecture has attempted to overcome its rationalising vision. If one takes for example the church of San Vitale in Ravenna, one can explain the solitary column almost blocking the entry or the incomplete groin vaulting as an attempt to signal a change from a Pagan to a Christian architecture. Piranesi created similar effects with his architectural projections. Piranesi diffracted the monocular subject by creating perspectival visions with multiple vanishing points so that there was no way of correlating what was seen into a unified whole. Equally, Cubism attempted to deflect the relationship between a monocular subject and the object. The subject could no longer put the painting into some meaningful structure through the use of perspective. Cubism used a non-monocular perspectival condition: it flattened objects to the edges, it upturned objects, it undermined the stability of the picture plane. Architecture attempted similar dislocations through Constructivism and its own, albeit normalising, version of Cubism – the International Style. But this work only looked cubistic and modern, the subject remained rooted in a profound anthropocentric stability, comfortably upright and in place on a flat, tabular ground. There was no shift in the relationship between the subject and the object. While the object looked different it failed to displace the viewing subject. Though the buildings were sometimes conceptualised, by axonometric or isometric projection rather than by perspective, no consistent deflection of the subject was carried out. Yet Modernist sculpture did in many cases effect such a displacement of the subject. These dislocations were fundamental to Minimalism: the early work of Robert Morris, Michael Heizer and Robert Smithson. This historical project, however, was never taken up in architecture. The question now begs to be asked: why did architecture resist developments that were taking place in other disciplines? And further, why has the issue of vision never been properly problematised in architecture?

It might be said that architecture never adequately thought through the problem of vision because it remained within the concept of the subject and the four walls. Architecture, unlike any other discipline, concretised vision. The hierarchy inherent in all architectural space begins as a structure for the mind's eye. It is perhaps the idea of interiority as a hierarchy between inside and outside that causes architecture to conceptualise itself ever more comfortably and conservatively in vision. The interiority of architecture more than any other discourse defined a hierarchy of vision articulated by inside and outside. The fact that one is actually both inside and outside with architecture, unlike painting or music, required vision to conceptualise itself in this way. As long as architecture refuses to take up the problem of vision, it will remain within a Renaissance or Classical view of its discourse.

Now what would it mean for architecture to take up the problem of vision? Vision can be defined as essentially a way of organising space and elements in space. It is a way of looking at, and defines a relationship between a subject and an object. Traditional architecture is structured so that any position occupied by a subject provides a means for understanding that position in relation to a particular spatial typology, such as a rotunda, a transept crossing, an axis, an entry. Any number of these typological conditionals deploy architecture as a screen for looking at.

The idea of a 'looking back' begins to displace the anthropocentric subject. Looking back does not require the object to become a subject, that is to anthromorphise the object. Looking back concerns the possibility of detaching the subject from the rationalisation of space. In other words, to allow the subject to have a vision of space that no longer can be put together in the normalising, classicising or traditional construct of vision; an other space, where in fact the space 'looks back' at the subject. A possible first step in conceptualising this other space, would be to detach what one sees from what one knows – the eye from the mind. A second step would be to inscribe space in such a way as to endow it with the possibility of looking back at the subject. All architecture can be said to be already inscribed. Windows, doors, beams and columns are a kind of inscription. These make architecture known, they reinforce vision. Since no space is uninscribed, we do not see a window without relating it to an idea of window, this kind of inscription seems not only natural but also necessary to architecture. In order to have a looking back, it is necessary to rethink the idea of inscription. In the Baroque and Rococo such an inscription was in the plaster decoration that began to obscure the traditional form of functional inscription. This kind of 'decorative' description was thought too excessive when undefined by function. Architecture tends to resist this form of excess in a way that is unique amongst the arts, precisely because of the power and pervasive nature of functional inscription. The anomalous column at San Vitale inscribes space in a way that was at the time foreign to the eye. This is also true of the columns in the staircase at the Wexner Center, however most of such inscriptions are the result of design intention, the will of an authorial subjective expression which then only reconstitutes vision as before. To dislocate vision might require an inscription which is the result of an outside text which is neither overly determined by design expression or function. But how could such an inscription of an outside text translate into space?

Suppose for a moment that architecture could be conceptualised as a Moebius strip, with an unbroken continuity between interior and exterior. What would this mean for vision? Gilles Deleuze has proposed just such a possible continuity with his idea of the fold. For Deleuze, folded space articulates a new relationship between vertical and horizontal, figure and ground, inside and out – all structures articulated by traditional vision. Unlike the space of classical vision, the idea of folded space denies framing in favour of a temporal modulation. The fold no longer privileges planimetric projection; instead there is a variable curvature. Deleuze's idea of folding is more radical than origami, because it contains no narrative, linear sequence; rather, in terms of traditional vision it contains a quality of the unseen.

Folding changes the traditional space of vision. That is, it can be considered to be effective; it functions, it shelters, it is meaningful, it frames, it is aesthetic. Folding also constitutes a move from *effective* to *affective* space. Folding is not another subject expressionism, a promiscuity, but rather unfolds in space alongside of its functioning and its meaning in space – it has what might be called an excessive condition or affect. Folding is a type of affective space which concerns those aspects that are not associated with the affective, that are more than reason, meaning and function.

In order to change the relationship of perspectival projection to three-dimensional space it is necessary to change the relationship between project drawing and real space. This would mean that one would no longer be able to draw with any level of meaningfulness the space that is being projected. For example, when it is no longer possible to draw a line that stands for some scale relationship to another line in space, it has nothing to do with reason, of the connection of the mind to the eye. The deflection from that line in space means that there no longer exists a one-to-one scale correspondence.

My folded projects are a primitive beginning. In them the subject understands that he or she can no longer conceptualise experience in space in the same way that he or she did in the gridded space. They attempt to provide this dislocation of the subject from effective space; an idea of presentness. Once the environment becomes affective, inscribed with another logic or an ur-logic, one which is no longer translatable into the vision of the mind, then reason becomes detached from vision. While we can still understand space in terms of its function, structure, and aesthetic – we are still within the 'four walls' – somehow reason becomes detached from the affective condition of the environment itself. This begins to produce an environment that 'looks back' – that is, the environment seems to have an order that we can perceive even though it does not seem to mean anything. It does not seek to be understood in the traditional way of architecture yet it possesses some sense of 'aura', an ur-logic which is the sense of something outside of our vision. Yet one that is not another subjective expression. Folding is only one of perhaps many strategies for dislocating vision – dislocating the hierarchy of interior and exterior that pre-empts vision.

The Alteka Tower project begins simultaneously with an 'L' shape drawn both in plan and section. Here, a change in the relationship of perspectival projection to three-dimensional space changes the relationship between project drawing and real space. In this sense, these drawings would have little relationship to the space that is being projected. For example, it is no longer possible to draw a line that stands for some scale relationship to another line in the space of the project, thus the drawn lines no longer have anything to do with reason, the connection of the mind to the eye. The drawn lines are folded with some ur-logic according to sections of a fold in René Thom's catastrophe theory. These folded plans and sections in turn create an object, which is cut into from the ground floor to the top.

When the environment is inscribed or folded in such a way the individual no longer remains the discursive function; the individual is no longer required to understand or interpret space. Questions such as what the space means are no longer relevant. It is not just that the environment is detached from vision, but that it also presents its own vision, a vision that looks back at the individual. The inscription is no longer concerned with aesthetics or with meaning but with some other order. It is only necessary to perceive the fact that this other order exists; this perception alone dislocates the knowing subject.

The fold presents the possibility of an alternative to the gridded space of the Cartesian order. The fold produces a dislocation of the dialectical distinction between figure and ground; in the process it animates what Gilles Deleuze calls a smooth space. Smooth space presents the possibility of overcoming or exceeding the grid. The grid remains in place and the four walls will always exist but they are in fact overtaken by the folding of space. Here there is no longer one planimetric view which is then extruded to provide a sectional space. Instead it is no longer possible to relate a vision of space in a two-dimensional drawing to the three-dimensional reality of a folded space. Drawing no

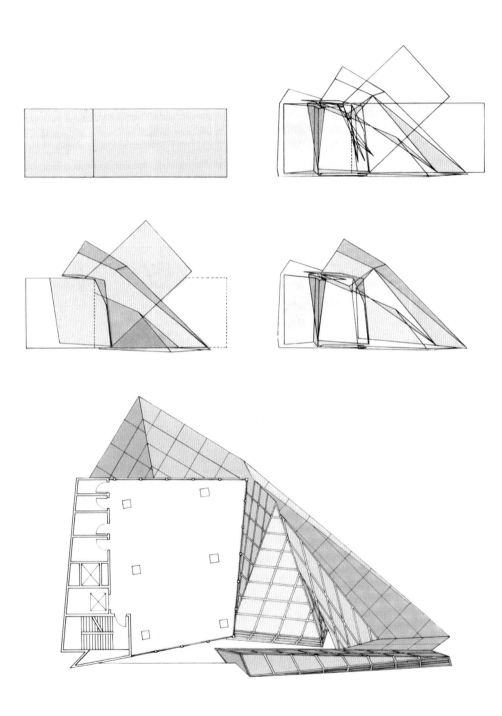

Eisenman Architects, Alteka Office Building, Tokyo, 1991;
folding diagrams and plan, levels five to seven. Courtesy
of Eisenman Architects. © Peter Eisenman.

longer has any scale value relationship to the three-dimensional environment. This dislocation of the two-dimensional drawing from the three-dimensional reality also begins to dislocate vision, inscribed by this ur-logic. There are no longer grid datum planes for the upright individual.

Alteka is not merely a surface architecture or a surface folding. Rather, the folds create an affective space, a dimension in the space that dislocates the discursive function of the human subject and thus vision, and at the same moment creates a condition of time, of an event in which there is the possibility of the environment looking back at the subject, the possibility of the *gaze*.

The gaze according to Maurice Blanchot is that possibility of seeing which remains covered up by vision. The gaze opens the possibility of seeing what Blanchot calls the light lying within the darkness. It is not the light of the dialectic of light/dark, but it is the light of an otherness, which lies hidden within presence. It is the capacity to see this otherness which is repressed by vision. The looking back, the gaze, exposes architecture to another light, one which could not have been seen before.

Architecture will continue to stand up, to deal with gravity, to have 'four walls'. But these four walls no longer need to be expressive of the mechanical paradigm. Rather they could deal with the possibility of these other discourses, the other affective senses of sound, touch and of that light lying within the darkness.

The Affects of Singularity *AD* November–December 1992

There are two English words, 'affect' and 'effect', that sound alike but mean quite different things. *Effect* is something produced by an agent or cause. In architecture it is the relationship between some object and its function or meaning; it is an idea that has dominated Western architecture for the last 200 years. Since the French Revolution, architecture, in its political, social and economical sense, has dealt with effect. If it is good it is effective: if it is good it serves more people. The clearest example of effect is the utilitarian creed of modern architecture; form follows function. This argued that a socially viable programme, properly elaborated, would provide good architecture. Affect, on the other hand, has nothing necessarily to do with good. *Affect* is the conscious subjective aspect of an emotion considered apart from bodily changes. Affect in architecture is simply the sensate response to a physical environment.

Effect can be contrasted with the word affect in many different contexts. This is particularly true when it comes to mediated environments. For example, when I lecture in a foreign country, everyone listens with headphones to a technical translation of my words. This experience is different from the here and now of a physical place: the earphones diminish the affect of my live voice; its emotion, animation and spirit. At the same time the translator desperately tries to tell the audience what I mean. And what I mean is precisely what is at issue. The audience feels it must understand what I say – it must have an effective response to my presence. But I want them to feel my presence, my affect. Like the audience at my lecture, people all over the world are also walking around with headphones listening to rock music, losing the affect of being in space. The loss of the individual response to unmediated stimuli is one consequence of the phenomenon.

The same loss of affect appears when we watch television. For example, for sporting events there is something called instant replay which allows you to watch the play over again in slow motion. Now, in the actual arenas there is also instant replay because people are so attuned to watching the slow motion they can no longer see because of the speed of the actual event; they begin to cheer only after they have seen the instant replay. This is because we have all become junkies of simulated reality to the detriment of the reality of the event itself. For example, after the kick off, in a recent Super Bowl of American football, the players all piled up but the referee blew his whistle and said, 'No play'. What was wrong? The television camera was not ready, so they had to go back and kick off again. The question arises: 'Is this real or is it a mediated event?' And the effect of this non-human mediation is very real; it has become another kind of affect in itself.

The same thing happened at a wedding a year ago. As the bride was coming down the aisle (they were filming for home video use), suddenly the producer said, 'Cut, OK, go back. We need this again.' And so the bride stops, walks back and comes down the aisle again. This continued through the whole service: the exchanging of rings, the 'I do's' and the kiss. The question, again, was whether there was ever a real event because it looked rather like a rehearsal for a video tape. Perhaps the only time the real wedding would be seen would be on the edited video tape, in which case the edited video tape would become the reality. In a similar sense, just this year, in a beauty contest being taped for airing later, they had to shoot two different endings with two different contestants making acceptance speeches and pretending to be happy about winning. This was done because the judging had not taken place. Again the affective reality of the event lay in the video tape.

Another agency that contributes to this loss of affect seeping into our homes is the *1984*-like creature called CNN, which is everywhere on the globe bringing 'instant' news. I remember one night at home before dinner two years ago when I was suddenly watching the bombardment of Baghdad. This action was interspersed with soft drink and travel commercials. I remember the grotesque paradox of watching people being annihilated live, as if for television, only to be interrupted by 'normal' life: buy a car, have a beer. Sitting in front of the CNN television news, one is practically anaesthetised to an affect. Does one believe the commercials or the live bombing? Is it possible to know what is real in such a situation and, therefore is it possible to have any affective response to such a juxtaposition? That is not to say that simulation is not a form of reality. It would be ingenuous to say that what is on television is not real, that it is some form of child's nightmare, a Grimms' fairy tale brought up to date. But if this is the case, that we are uncertain today what reality is, then it is also difficult to understand what architecture is, because architecture has traditionally been seen as the home of reality.

This is addressed by Walter Benjamin in his essay, 'The Work of Art in the Age of Mechanical Reproduction'. Benjamin says that a photograph is clearly an original, although a different kind of original from that which, let us say, is crafted by hand. In one sense the art or the craft product, such as, a handmade piece of furniture or a handmade book is different from a book that is made on a mechanical press or a piece of bentwood furniture – which is reproduced many times. But in another sense they are both original, the craft product being individual and the bentwood furniture multiple.

Now there is a difference between repetition in mechanical reproduction and repetition in electronic reproduction: this is the difference between a photograph and a telefax.

The photograph is mechanically produced: it is a product of repetition. It is not a unique handmade artefact: that is, it is not an object of art as craft. The mechanical paradigm dealt with the shift in value from the individual hand, as in the hand of a painter as an original maker, to the value of the hand as intermediary, as in the developer of raw film: from the creation of an individual to the meditation of the multiple. The photograph can be manipulated by an individual to have more contrast, more texture, more tone. Thus, there remains within the mechanical repetition of a photograph a unique, individual quality: it remains a particular object even within the idea of the multiple. And within the process, the individual subject is still able to effect as well as affect.

In electronic repetition, that is the telefax, there is less human intervention, a less value-added dimension by the individual. Further, the condition of the original is thrown into question. Whereas one can agree that there is an original negative plate for a photograph and that this plate can be reproduced, there is no negative plate in a telefax. The original that may be on a disk in a computer: it is no longer an object but rather a series of electronic impulses stored in a matrix. Even the disk original is often modified by corrections, and thus a unique individual original is hardly ever kept. And in fact now, with telefax, the original may not even ever be sent so as not to confuse the reception with the reception of the telefax.

The nature of both repetition and originality changes from mechanical reproduction to electronic reproduction. The change in the nature of originality effects a definition of singularity. Thus, it is difficult to know what reality is, the reality as the former notion of reality, as the scientific, the organic, the anthropocentric notion of reality that existed in the mechanical paradigm. But if it can be said that it only by virtue of the relationship of media to reality that reality is no longer homogeneous but rather heterogeneous, then there are possibilities for conceptualising architecture.

Within the mechanical paradigm the subject's relationship to the object was clearly understood since the mechanical paradigm evolved from the classical anthropocentric, organicist paradigm. There was a continuity; that is, with every change there was a homogeneity within each paradigm. The individual knew how to react to the object, even though the individual became clearly displaced from his or her centric position. It can be argued that architecture, even though it deals with the same physical individual with the same functional needs and the same need for an affective response to a physical space, no longer produces the same affect because of the shift of the human subject's relationship to the paradigm, that is, the shift from the mechanical to the electronic.

From the beginning of the mechanical paradigm, that is from the beginning of the 15th century, architecture was considered strong media. There is no question that architecture was the *sine qua non* of the mechanical paradigm in that it was the embodiment of the material resistance to natural forces. In its sheltering and enclosing function it provided not only a metaphorical image but an actual physical image of statics: architecture stood against natural forces. Architecture, in order to shelter and enclose, was therefore not only actually but metaphorically a symbol of a mechanical paradigm.

For example, in the late Middle Ages, in the Gothic cathedrals and even in the early Renaissance wall churches, the symbolic evocation of a town was in the church, was articulated in the body of the church itself; in the facades, the side chapels, the carvings, etc. The discourse of the mass was the discourse of the structure and organisation and decoration of the Gothic church. Now obviously this all changed in the 15th century, with the change from Theocentrism to Anthropocentrism.

Another important change occurred in the 18th century when new functions and new political institutions began after the French Revolution. With the rise of the social and economic state, there was a new demand for architecture to make apparent these institutions through new forms. New building types, for example the library, the prison, the hospital, the public school and social housing were introduced into architecture. Because of this, architecture of necessity became more effective: there was a primary relationship between the object of architecture and the physical programme, rather than with the mediating or symbolic functions. Because of this, architecture began to lose its condition as strong media. While it housed and provided for the functions of society, it began to symbolise these functions less. The more the effective nature of the mechanism became important, the less the affective nature of both the medium and the message: the social and political type replaced the metaphorical or the affective type. As the public recognition of these building types became more important, little distinction was made between the type and the unique instance of the type in the individual building. As architecture became more of a public, collective concern, it naturally began to deal with the question of repetition and standardisation.

Throughout the 19th century, there is a development of architecture for a mass society parallel to the development of the new political state. It is not without interest that the modern political state of the late 18th and the early 19th century corresponded with the rise of social and economic institutions and with the beginning of the change of architecture from strong media to weak media. While strong media as architecture was about affect, strong media today in terms of commercial television and journalism, is basically concerned with effect: how quickly, compactly and distinctly can the message get across?

But crucial to this argument, is the fact that the mediated behaviour of today does not come from any personal or individual form of behaviour: it is collective behaviour. Media not only sets out to destroy the possibility of individual affect in order to be affective itself, but also must substitute effect for affect. Media assumes that an affective message must be an effective one and this influence alone has entirely altered our concept of affect as well as individual behaviour. For example, media cannot tolerate the possibility of mistake, the misgotten message, error and untruth, all of which are part of the possibility of affect.

Architecture not only does not deal with affect, but it no longer deals with effect as well as strong media. Then how does architecture stand in the face of media, and specifically with the loss of the affecting aspect of individual expression. A possible way of returning architecture to the realm of affect may not be through the idea of the individual or the expressive, or through any kind of standardisation or repetition of a norm but, in fact, through an idea of singularity.

Architecture — now operating as weak media — needs to regain the possibility of an affective discourse. The term singularity begins to explore the possibility of a discourse which brings to the electronic paradigm what particularity, individuality, personal expression was to the mechanical paradigm. That is a general context for exploring the possibility of an architecture of affect. It begins to suggest a contemporary notion of how architecture which is seen as singular can operate as weak media in an affective way within the electronic paradigm.

One way to approach the question of affect in architecture is by looking at the difference between singularity and individual expression, and to answer the questions: 'Why is individual expression no longer valid?' and 'Why is singularity not merely a form of expressionism?' The difference is at the heart of the idea of singularity.

Singularity, as the Japanese critic, Kojin Karatani, suggests is the difference between 'I' the individual subject and the 'I' which belongs to the general category of everybody.

It is precisely the difference between a 'this I' and all 'I'-s that must be distinguished. The attachment of the 'this' to the 'I' does not mean that 'this I', the 'me' is special. Rather the reverse, it is taking the ego, the individual subjectivity, the persona, out of the 'me' which is in this 'I'. This begins to distinguish the idea of singularity from the idea of particularity and individuality. In other words, Karatani is trying to take the idea of the special 'me'. Even though I know that I am like everyone else, I am not anyone else. What is at stake here is the 'this' in 'this I' and not the 'I' as consciousness. It is the qualification of 'I', the naming of the 'this I', that is important in this context. What is the this of 'this I'? This applies equally for Karatani from the subject, to the object thing and to 'this thing'. Karatani says that 'this-ness' of the subject and object, 'this I' or 'this thing' has nothing to do with its formal or physical features and characteristics. The 'this-ness' of a 'this I' or a 'this dog' is singularity, it distinguishes it from particularity. So it is the 'ness' of this — the 'this-ness' — that is the condition of singularity as opposed to the 'I'. Singularity does not mean that a thing is unique. As opposed to particularity and individuality, which are seen as unique when seen in relationship to generality, singularity is an individuality no longer able to belong to the realm of generality. The attempt is to move the question of 'I' and the individual outside a metaphysical discourse. The singularity of a thing is inseparable from the act of calling it by a proper noun. Thus the nomination of 'this thing' also begins to separate singularity from particularity.

Peter Eisenman, 'Visions Unfolding: Architecture in the Age of Electronic Media', *Domus* 734 (January 1992), pp 17–24; *AD* 62, September–October 1992, pp xvi–xviii; Ole Bouman and Roemer van Toorn (eds), *The Invisible in Architecture*, Academy Editions (London), 1994, pp 144–9; Kate Nesbitt (ed), *Theorizing a New Agenda for Architecture: an Anthology of Architectural Theory 1965–1995*, Princeton Architectural Press (New York), 1996, pp 554–61; Eisenman, *Written into the Void, Selected Writings 1990–2004,* Yale University Press (New Haven), 2007, pp 34–41. © Eisenman Architects.

Peter Eisenman, 'The Affects of Singularity', Andreas C Papadakis (ed), *Theory + Experimentation*, *AD* Profile 100, *AD* 62, November–December 1992, pp 42–5; Eisenman, *Written into the Void, Selected Writings 1990–2004,* Yale University Press (New Haven), 2007, pp 19–24. © Eisenman Architects.

Folding in Architecture (1993)

Greg Lynn

'Architectural Curvilinearity', Lynn's keynote essay in *AD* Profile 102, *Folding in Architecture*, heralds the age of round shapes and smooth, intricate surfaces that flourished during the second half of the 1990s and that to this day are seen as the most visible expression of digital making in architecture. Lynn himself would eventually term these forms 'blobs', and some of the most iconic buildings of the digital age, first and foremost Gehry's Guggenheim Bilbao, are often related to this formal tendency – in spite of Gehry's very different technological approach and design processes.

Yet, seen in its context, this essay is also a chapter in the 'long history' of Deconstructivism – albeit a chapter that, in hindsight, appears to have been a turning point. Computers did not play a major role in the invention of the digital fold. Lynn's theory of curvilinearity emerges from the internal and autonomous discourse of architectural theory itself. Lynn defines the new style of 'smooth transformations' as the almost inevitable, Hegelian resolution of the dialectical opposition between Post-Modernism (classical composition, unity and order, or contextualism) and Deconstructivism (angularity, disjunctions, conflict and oppositions). Lynn also claims that this stance, unlike that of the precedents he cites, is not formalist; but he does not discuss the more general implications or meaning of a new style of visual compliance and fluid accommodations. The success of Lynn's theory proves that it was in the spirit of the time.

Possibly the first instance of digital mass-customisation in design theory, Lynn's brief presentation of Shoei Yoh's roof for a sports hall at Odawara, Japan is a prescient anticipation of the formal and tectonic potentials of a non-standard space-frame truss (but even the term 'non-standard' was not yet in use at the time). The 'differentiated smoothness' of the truss enables the roof to ply in response to programme requirements; Lynn also explains that the variations in the production of the structural components are made possible by the 'computerisation of design, construction and fabrication processes'.

Architectural Curvilinearity: The Folded, the Pliant and the Supple *AD* March–April 1993

For the last two decades, beginning with Robert Venturi's *Complexity and Contradiction in Architecture*,[1] and Colin Rowe and Fred Koetter's *Collage City*,[2] and continuing through Mark Wigley and Philip Johnson's *Deconstructivist Architecture*, architects have been primarily concerned with the production of heterogeneous, fragmented and conflicting formal systems. These practices have attempted to embody the differences within and between diverse physical, cultural and social contexts in formal conflicts. When comparing Venturi's *Complexity and Contradiction* or *Learning from Las Vegas* with Wigley and Johnson's *Deconstruction Architecture*, it is necessary to overlook many significant and distinguishing differences in order to identify at least one common theme.

Both Venturi and Wigley argue for the deployment of discontinuous, fragmented, heterogeneous and diagonal formal strategies based on the incongruities, juxtapositions and oppositions within specific sites and programmes. These disjunctions result from a logic which tends to identify the potential contradictions between dissimilar elements. A diagonal dialogue between a building and its context has become an emblem for the contradictions within contemporary culture. From the scale of an urban plan to a building detail, contexts have been mined for conflicting geometries, materials, styles, histories and programmes which are then represented in architecture as internal contradictions. The most paradigmatic architecture of the last 10 years, including Robert Venturi's Sainsbury Wing of the National Gallery, Peter Eisenman's Wexner Center, Bernard Tschumi's La Villette park and the Gehry House, invests in the architectural representation of contradictions. Through contradiction, architecture represents difference in violent formal conflicts.

Contradiction has also provoked a reactionary response to formal conflict. Such resistances attempt to recover unified architectural languages that can stand against heterogeneity. Unity is constructed through one of two strategies: either by reconstructing a continuous architectural language through historical analyses (Neo-Classicism or Neo-Modernism) or by identifying local consistencies resulting from indigenous climates, materials, traditions or technologies (Regionalism). The internal orders of Neo-Classicism, Neo-Modernism and Regionalism conventionally repress the cultural and contextual discontinuities that are necessary for a logic of contradiction. In architecture, both the reaction to and representation of heterogeneity have shared an origin in contextual analysis. Both theoretical models begin with a close analysis of contextual conditions from which they proceed to evolve either a homogeneous or heterogeneous urban fabric. Neither the reactionary call for unity nor the avant-garde dismantling of it through the identification of internal contradictions seems adequate as a model for contemporary architecture and urbanism.

In response to architecture's discovery of complex, disparate, differentiated and heterogeneous cultural and formal contexts, two options have been dominant; either conflict and contradiction or unity and reconstruction. Presently, an alternative smoothness is being formulated that may escape these dialectically opposed strategies. Common to the diverse sources of this post-contradictory work – topological geometry, morphology, morphogenesis, Catastrophe Theory or the computer technology of both the defence and Hollywood film industry – are characteristics of smooth transformation involving the intensive integration of differences within a continuous yet heterogeneous system. Smooth mixtures are made up of disparate elements which maintain their integrity while being blended within a continuous field of other free elements.

Smoothing does not eradicate differences but incorporates[3] free intensities through fluid tactics of mixing and blending. Smooth mixtures are not homogeneous and therefore cannot be reduced. Deleuze describes smoothness as 'the continuous variation' and the 'continuous development of form'.[4] Wigley's critique of pure form and static geometry is inscribed within geometric conflicts and discontinuities. For Wigley, smoothness is equated with hierarchical organisation: 'the volumes have been purified – they have become smooth, classical – and the wires all converge in a single, hierarchical, vertical movement'.[5] Rather than investing in arrested conflicts, Wigley's 'slipperiness' might be better exploited by the alternative smoothness of heterogeneous mixture. For the first time perhaps, complexity might be aligned with neither unity nor contradiction but with smooth, pliant mixture.

Both pliancy and smoothness provide an escape from the two camps which would either have architecture break under the stress of difference or stand firm. Pliancy allows architecture to become involved in complexity through flexibility. It may be possible to neither repress the complex relations of differences with fixed points of resolution nor arrest them in contradictions, but sustain them through flexible, unpredicted, local connections. To arrest differences in conflicting forms often precludes many of the more complex possible connections of the forms of architecture to larger cultural fields. A more pliant architectural sensibility values alliances, rather than conflicts, between elements. Pliancy implies first an internal flexibility and second a dependence on external forces for self-definition.

If there is a single effect produced in architecture by folding, it will be the ability to integrate unrelated elements within a new continuous mixture. Culinary theory has developed both a practical and precise definition for at least three types of mixtures. The first involves the manipulation of homogeneous elements; beating, whisking and whipping change the volume but not the nature of a liquid through agitation. The second method of incorporation mixes two or more disparate elements; chopping, dicing, grinding, grating, slicing, shredding and mincing eviscerate elements into fragments. The first method agitates a single uniform ingredient, the second eviscerates disparate ingredients. Folding, creaming and blending mix smoothly multiple ingredients through repeated gentle overturnings without stirring or beating in such a way that their individual characteristics are maintained.[6] For instance, an egg and chocolate are folded together so that each is a distinct layer within a continuous mixture.

Folding employs neither agitation nor evisceration but a supple layering. Likewise, folding in geology involves the sedimentation of mineral elements or deposits which become slowly bent and compacted into plateaus of strata. These strata are compressed, by external forces, into more or less continuous layers within which heterogeneous deposits are still intact in varying degrees of intensity.

A folded mixture is neither homogeneous, like whipped cream, nor fragmented, like chopped nuts, but smooth and heterogeneous. In both cooking and geology, there is no preliminary organisation which becomes folded but rather there are unrelated elements or pure intensities that are intricated through a joint manipulation. Disparate elements can be incorporated into smooth mixtures through various manipulations including fulling:

'Felt is a supple solid product that proceeds altogether differently, as an antifabric. It implies no separation of threads, no intertwining, only an entanglement of fibres obtained by fulling (for example, by rolling the block of fibres back and forth). What becomes entangled are the microscales of the fibres. An aggregate of intrication of this kind is in no way homogeneous: nevertheless, it is smooth and contrasts point by point with the space of fabric (it is in principle infinite, open and uninhibited in every direction: it has neither top, nor bottom, nor centre: it does not assign fixed or mobile elements but distributes a continuous variation).'[7]

The two characteristics of smooth mixtures are that they are composed of disparate unrelated elements and that these free intensities become intricated by an external force exerted upon them jointly. Intrications are intricate connections. They are intricate, they affiliate local surfaces of elements with one another by negotiating interstitial rather than internal connections. The heterogeneous elements within a mixture have no proper relation with one another. Likewise, the external force that intricates these elements with one another is outside the individual elements' control or prediction.

Viscous Mixtures

Unlike an architecture of contradictions, superpositions and accidental collisions, pliant systems are capable of engendering unpredicted connections with contextual, cultural, programmatic, structural and economic contingencies by vicissitude. Vicissitude is often equated with vacillation, weakness[8] and indecisiveness but more importantly these characteristics are frequently in the service of a tactical cunning.[9] Vicissitude is a quality of being mutable or changeable in response to both favourable and unfavourable situations that occur by chance. Vicissitudinous events result from events that are neither arbitrary nor predictable but seem to be accidental. These events are made possible by a collision of internal motivations with external forces. For instance, when an accident occurs the victims immediately identify the forces contributing to the accident and begin to assign blame. It is inevitable, however, that no single element can be made responsible for any accident as these events occur by vicissitude; a confluence of particular influences at a particular time makes the outcome of an accident possible. If any element participating in such a confluence of local forces is altered, the nature of the event will change. In *A Thousand Plateaus*, Spinoza's concept of 'a thousand vicissitudes' is linked with Gregory Bateson's 'continuing plateau of intensity' to describe events which incorporate unpredictable events through intensity. These occurrences are difficult to localise, difficult to identity.[10] Any logic of vicissitude is dependent on both an intrication of local intensities and the exegetic pressure exerted on those elements by external contingencies. Neither the intrications nor the forces which put them into relation are predictable from within any single system. Connections by vicissitude develop identity through the exploitation of local adjacencies and their affiliation with external forces. In this sense, vicissitudinous mixtures become cohesive through a logic of viscosity.

Viscous fluids develop internal stability in direct proportion to the external pressures exerted upon them. These fluids behave with two types of viscidity. They exhibit both internal cohesion and adhesion to external elements as their viscosity increases. Viscous fluids begin to behave less like liquids and more like sticky solids as the pressures upon them intensify. Similarly, viscous solids are capable of yielding continually under stress so as not to shear.

Viscous space would exhibit a related cohesive stability in response to adjacent pressures and a stickiness or adhesion to adjacent elements. Viscous relations such as these are not reducible to any single or holistic organisation. Forms of viscosity and pliability cannot be examined outside the *vicissitudinous* connections and forces with which their deformation is intensively involved. The nature of pliant forms is that they are sticky and flexible. Things tend to adhere to them. As pliant forms are manipulated and deformed, the things that stick to their surfaces become incorporated within their interiors.

Curving Away From Deconstructivism

Along with a group of younger architects, the projects that best represent pliancy, not coincidentally, are being produced by many of the same architects previously involved in the valorisation of contradictions. Deconstructivism theorised the world as a site of differences in order that architecture could represent these contradictions in form. This contradictory logic is beginning to soften in order to exploit more fully the particularities of urban and cultural contexts. This is a reasonable transition, as the Deconstructivists originated their projects with the internal discontinuities they uncovered within buildings and sites. These same architects are beginning to employ urban strategies which exploit discontinuities, not by representing them in formal collisions, but by affiliating them with one another through continuous flexible systems.

Just as many of these architects have already been inscribed within a Deconstructivist style of diagonal forms, there will surely be those who would enclose their present work within a Neo-Baroque or even Expressionist style of curved forms. However, many of the formal similitudes suggest a far richer logic of curvilinearity[11] that can be characterised by the involvement of outside forces in the development of form. If internally motivated and homogeneous systems were to extend in straight lines, curvilinear developments would result from the incorporation of external influences. Curvilinearity can put into relation the collected projects in this publication, Gilles Deleuze's *The Fold: Leibniz and the Baroque* and René Thom's catastrophe diagrams. The smooth spaces described by these continuous yet differentiated systems result from curvilinear sensibilities that are capable of complex deformations in response to programmatic, structural, economic, aesthetic, political and contextual influences. This is not to imply that intensive curvature is more politically correct than an uninvolved formal logic, but rather, that a cunning pliability is often more effective through smooth incorporation than contradiction and conflict. Many cunning tactics are aggressive in nature. Whether insidious or ameliorative these kinds of cunning connections discover new possibilities for organisation. A logic of curvilinearity argues for an active involvement with external events in the folding, bending and curving of form.

Already in several Deconstructivist projects are latent suggestions of smooth mixture and curvature. For instance, the Gehry House is typically portrayed as representing materials and terms already present within, yet repressed by, the suburban neighbourhood: sheds, chainlink fences, exposed plywood, trailers, boats and recreational vehicles. The house is described as an 'essay on the convoluted relationship between the conflict within and between forms ... which were not imported in but emerged from within the house'.[12] The house is seen to provoke conflict within the neighbourhood due to its public representation of hidden aspects of its context. The Gehry House violates the neighbourhood from within. Despite the dominant appeal of the house to contradictions, a less contradictory and more pliant reading of the house is possible as a new organisation emerges between the existing house and Gehry's addition. A dynamic stability develops with the mixing of the original and the addition. Despite the contradictions between elements, possible points of connection are exploited. Rather than valorise the conflicts the house engenders, as has been done in both academic and popular publications, a more pliant logic would identify, not the degree of violation, but the degree to which new connections were exploited. A new intermediate organisation occurs in the Gehry House by vicissitude from the affiliation of the existing house and its addition. Within the discontinuities of Deconstructivism there are inevitable unforeseen moments of cohesion.

Similarly, Peter Eisenman's Wexner Center is conventionally portrayed as a collision of the conflicting geometries of the campus, city and armoury which once stood adjacent to the site. These contradictions are represented by the diagonal collisions between the two grids and the masonry towers. Despite the disjunctions and discontinuities between these three disparate systems, Eisenman's project has suggested recessive readings of continuous nonlinear systems of connection. Robert Somol[13] identifies such a system of Deleuzian rhizomatous connections between armoury and grid. The armoury and diagonal grids are shown by Somol to participate in a hybrid L-movement that organises the main gallery space. Somol's schizophrenic analysis is made possible by, yet does not emanate from within, a Deconstructivist logic of contradiction and conflict. The force of this Deleuzian schizoanalytic model is its ability to maintain multiple organisations simultaneously. In Eisenman's project the tower and grid need not be seen as mutually exclusive or in contradiction. Rather, these disparate elements may be seen as distinct elements co-present within a composite mixture. Pliancy does not result from and is not in line with the previous architectural logic of contradiction, yet it is capable of exploiting many conflicting combinations for the possible connections that are overlooked. Where *Deconstructivist Architecture* was seen to exploit external forces in the familiar name of contradiction and conflict, recent pliant projects by many of these architects exhibit a more fluid logic of connectivity.

Immersed in Context

The contradictory architecture of the last two decades has evolved primarily from highly differentiated, heterogeneous contexts within which conflicting, contradictory and discontinuous buildings were sited. An alternative involvement with heterogeneous contexts could be affiliated, compliant and continuous. Where complexity and contradiction arose previously from inherent contextual conflicts, present attempts are being made to fold smoothly specific locations, materials and programmes into architecture while maintaining their individual identity.

This recent work may be described as being compliant; in a state of being plied by forces beyond control. The projects are formally folded, pliant and supple in order to incorporate their contexts with minimal resistance. Again, this characterisation should not imply flaccidity but a cunning submissiveness that is capable of bending rather than breaking. Compliant tactics, such as these, assume neither an absolute coherence nor cohesion between discrete elements but a system of provisional, intensive, local connections between free elements. Intensity describes the dynamic internalisation and incorporation of external influences into a pliant system. Distinct from a whole organism – to which nothing can be added or subtracted – intensive organisations continually invite external influences within their internal limits so that they might extend their influence through the affiliations they make. A two-fold deterritorialisation, such as this, expands by internalising external forces. This expansion through incorporation is an urban alternative to either the infinite extension of International Modernism, the uniform fabric of Contextualism or the conflicts of Post-Modernism and Deconstructivism. Folded, pliant and supple architectural forms invite exigencies and contingencies in both their deformation and their reception.

In both *Learning from Las Vegas* and *Deconstructivist Architecture*, urban contexts provided rich sites of difference. These differences are presently being exploited for their ability to engender multiple lines of local connections rather than lines of conflict. These affiliations are not predictable by any contextual orders but occur by vicissitude. Here, urban fabric has no value or meaning beyond the connections that are made within it. Distinct from earlier urban sensibilities that generalised broad formal codes, the collected projects develop local, fine grain, complex systems of intrication. There is no general urban strategy common to these projects, only a kind of tactical mutability. These folded, pliant and supple forms of urbanism are neither in deference to nor in defiance of their contexts but exploit them by turning them within their own twisted and curvilinear logics.

The Supple and Curvilinear

> 1 supple\ *adj* [ME *souple*, fr OF, fr L *supplic-*, *supplex* submissive, suppliant, lit, bending under, fr *sub* + *plic-* (akin to *plicare* to fold) – more at PLY] 1a: compliant often to the point of obsequiousness b: readily adaptable or responsive to new situations 2a: capable of being bent or folded without creases, cracks or breaks; PLIANT b: able to perform bending or twisting movements with ease and grace; LIMBER c: easy and fluent without stiffness or awkwardness.[14]

At an urban scale, many of these projects seem to be somewhere between contexturalism and expressionism. Their supple forms are neither geometrically exact nor arbitrarily figural. For example, the curvilinear figures of Shoei Yoh's roof structures are anything but decorative but also resist being reduced to a pure geometric figure. Yoh's supple roof structures exhibit a logic of curvilinearity as they are continuously differentiated according to contingencies. The exigencies of structural span lengths, beam depths, lighting, lateral loading, ceiling height and view angles influence the form of the roof structure. Rather than averaging these requirements within a mean or minimum dimension they are precisely maintained by an anexact yet rigorous geometry. Exact geometries are eidetic; they can be reproduced identically at any time by anyone. In this regard, they must be capable of being reduced to fixed mathematical quantities. Inexact geometries lack the precision and rigour necessary for measurement.

Anexact geometries, as described by Edmund Husserl,[15] are those geometries which are irreducible yet rigorous. These geometries can be determined with precision yet cannot be reduced to average points or dimensions. Anexact geometries often appear to be merely figural in this regard. Unlike exact geometries, it is meaningless to repeat identically an anexact geometric figure outside the specific context within which it is situated. In this regard, anexact figures cannot be easily translated.

Jeffrey Kipnis has argued convincingly that Peter Eisenman's Columbus Convention Center has become a canonical model for the negotiation of differentiated urban fringe sites through the use of near figures.[16] Kipnis identifies the disparate systems informing the Columbus Convention Center including: a single volume of inviolate programme of a uniform shape and height larger than two city blocks, an existing fine grain fabric of commercial buildings and network of freeway interchanges that plug into the gridded streets of the central business district. Eisenman's project drapes the large rectilinear volume of the convention hall with a series of supple vermiforms. These elements become involved with the train tracks to the north-east, the highway to the south-east and the pedestrian scale of High Street to the west. The project incorporates the multiple scales, programmes and pedestrian and automotive circulation of a highly differentiated urban context. Kipnis' canonisation of a form which is involved with such specific contextual and programmatic contingencies seems to be frustrated from the beginning. The effects of a pliant urban mixture such as this can only be evaluated by the connections that it makes. Outside specific contexts, curvature ceases to be intensive. Where the Wexner Center, on the same street in the same city, represents a monumental collision, the Convention Center attempts to disappear by connection between intervals within its context; where the Wexner Center destabilises through contradictions the Convention Center does so by subterfuge.

In a similar fashion Frank Gehry's Guggenheim Museum in Bilbao, Spain covers a series of orthogonal gallery spaces with flexible tubes which respond to the scales of the adjacent roadways, bridges, the Bilbao River and the existing medieval city. Akin to the Vitra Museum, the curvilinear roof forms of the Bilbao Guggenheim integrate the large rectilinear masses of gallery and support space with the scale of the pedestrian and automotive contexts.

The unforeseen connections possible between differentiated sites and alien programmes require conciliatory, complicit, pliant, flexible and often cunning tactics. Presently, numerous architects are involving the heterogeneities, discontinuities and differences inherent within any cultural and physical context by aligning formal flexibility with economic, programmatic and structural compliancy. A multitude of *pli* based words – folded, pliant, supple, flexible, plaited, pleated, plicating, complicitous, compliant, complaisant, complicated, complex and multiplicitous to name a few – can be invoked to describe this emerging urban sensibility of intensive connections.

The Pliant and Bent

> pliable\ *adj* [ME fr *plier* to bend, fold – more at PLY] 1a: supple enough to bend freely or repeatedly without breaking b: yielding readily to others. COMPLAISANT 2: adjustable to varying conditions: ADAPTABLE *syn* see PLASTIC *ant* obstinate.[17]

John Rajchman, in reference to Gilles Deleuze's book *Le Pli*, has already articulated an affinity between complexity, or *plex*-words, and folding, or *plic*-words, in the Deleuzian paradigm of 'perplexing plications' or 'perplication'.[18] The plexed and the plied can be seen in a tight knot of complexity and pliancy. Plication involves the folding in of external forces. Complication involves an intricate assembly of these extrinsic particularities into a complex network. In biology, complication is the act of an embryo folding in upon itself as it becomes more complex. To become complicated is to be involved in multiple complex, intricate connections. Where Post-Modernism and Deconstructivism resolve external influences of programme, use, economy and advertising through contradiction, compliancy involves these external forces by knotting, twisting, bending and folding them within form.

Pliant systems are easily bent, inclined or influenced. An anatomical 'plica' is a single strand within multiple 'plicae'. It is a multiplicity in that it is both one and many simultaneously. These elements are bent along with other elements into a composite, as in matted hair(s). Such a bending together of elements is an act of multiple plication or multiplication rather than mere addition. Plicature involves disparate elements with one another through various manipulations of bending, twisting, pleating, braiding and weaving through external force. In RAA Um's Croton Aqueduct project a single line following the subterranean water supply for New York City is pulled through multiple disparate programmes which are adjacent to it and which cross it. These programmatic elements are braided and bent within the continuous line of recovered public space which stretches nearly 20 miles into Manhattan. In order to incorporate these elements the line itself is deflected and reoriented, continually changing its character along its length. The seemingly singular line becomes populated by finer programmatic elements. The implications of *Le Pli* for architecture involve the proliferation of possible connections between free entities such as these.

A plexus is a multilinear network of interweavings, intertwinings and intrications; for instance, of nerves or blood vessels. The complications of a plexus – what could best be called complexity – arise from its irreducibility to any single organisation. A *plexus* describes a multiplicity of local connections within a single continuous system that remains open to new motions and fluctuations. Thus, a plexial event cannot occur at any discrete point. A multiply plexed system – a complex – cannot be reduced to mathematical exactitude, it must be described with rigorous probability. Geometric systems have a distinct character once they have been plied; they exchange fixed co-ordinates for dynamic relations across surfaces.

Alternative Types of Transformation

Discounting the potential of earlier geometric diagrams of probability, such as Buffon's *Needle Problem*,[19] D'Arcy Thompson provides perhaps the first geometric description of variable deformation as an instance of discontinuous morphological development. His Cartesian deformations, and their use of flexible topological rubber sheet geometry, suggest an alternative to the static morphological transformations of autonomous architectural types. A comparison of the typological and transformational systems of Thompson and Rowe illustrates two radically different conceptions of continuity. Rowe's is fixed, exact, striated, identical and static, where Thompson's is dynamic, anexact, smooth, differentiated and stable.

Both Rudolf Wittkower – in his analysis of the Palladian villas of 1949[20] – and Rowe – in his comparative analysis of Palladio and Le Corbusier of 1947[21] – uncover a consistent organisational type: the nine-square grid. In Wittkower's analysis of 12 Palladian villas, the particularities of each villa accumulate (through what Edmund Husserl has termed variations) to generate a fixed, identical spatial type (through what could best be described as phenomenological reduction). The typology of this 'Ideal Villa' is used to invent a consistent deep structure underlying Le Corbusier's Villa Stein at Garches and Palladio's Villa Malcontenta. Wittkower and Rowe discover the exact geometric structure of this type in all villas in particular. This fixed type becomes a constant point of reference within a series of variations.

Like Rowe, Thompson is interested in developing a mathematics of species categories, yet his system depends on a dynamic and fluid set of geometric relations. The deformations of a provisional type define a supple constellation of geometric correspondences. Thompson uses the initial type as a mere provision for a dynamic system of transformations that occur in connection with larger environmental forces. Thompson's method of discontinuous development intensively involves external forces in the deformation of morphological types. The flexible type is able to both indicate the general morphological structure of a species while indicating its discontinuous development through the internalisation of heretofore external forces within the system.[22] For instance, the enlargement of a fish's eye is represented by the flexing of a grid. This fluctuation, when compared with a previous position of the transformational type, establishes a relation between water depth and light intensity as those conditions are involved in the formal differences between fish. The flexing grid of relations cannot be arrested at any moment and therefore has the capacity to describe both a general type and the particular events which influence its development. Again, these events are not predictable or reducible to any fixed point but rather begin to describe a probable zone of co-present forces; both internal and external. Thompson presents an alternative type of inclusive stability, distinct from the exclusive stasis of Rowe's nine-square grid. The supple geometry of Thompson is capable of both bending under external forces and folding those forces internally. These transformations develop through discontinuous involution rather than continuous evolution.

The morphing effects used in the contemporary advertising and film industry may already have something in common with recent developments in architecture. These mere images have concrete influences on space, form, politics and culture; for example, the physical morphing of Michael Jackson's body, including the transformation of his form through various surgeries and his surface through skin bleaching and lightening. These physical effects and their implications for the definition of gender and race were only later represented in his recent video *Black or White*. In this video multiple genders, ethnicities and races are mixed into a continuous sequence through the digital morphing of video images. It is significant that Jackson is not black *or* white but black *and* white, not male *or* female but male *and* female. His simultaneous differences are characteristic of a desire for smoothness; to become heterogeneous yet continuous. Physical morphing, such as this, is monstrous because smoothness eradicates the interval between what Thompson refers to as discriminant characteristics without homogenising the mixture. Such a continuous system is neither an assembly of discrete fragments nor a whole.[23] With Michael Jackson, the flexible geometric mechanism with which his video representation is constructed comes from the same desire which aggressively reconstructs his own physical form. Neither the theory, the geometry or the body proceed from one another; rather, they participate in a desire for smooth transformation. Form, politics and self-identity are intricately connected in this process of deformation.

A similar comparison might be made between the liquid mercury man in the film *Terminator 2* and the Peter Lewis House by Frank Gehry and Philip Johnson. The Hollywood special effects sequences allow the actor to both become and disappear into virtually any form. The horror of the film results not from ultra-violence, but from the ability of the antagonist to pass through and occupy the grids of floors, prison bars and other actors. Computer technology is capable of constructing intermediate images between any two fixed points resulting in a smooth transformation. These smooth effects calculate with probability the interstitial figures between fixed figures. Furthermore, the morphing process is flexible enough that multiple between states are possible. Gehry's and Johnson's Peter Lewis House is formulated from multiple flexible forms. The geometry of these forms is supple and can accommodate smooth curvilinear deformation along their length. Not only are those forms capable of bending to programmatic, structural and environmental concerns, as is the roof of Shoei Yoh's roof structures, but they can deflect to the contours and context of the site, similar to Peter Eisenman's Columbus Convention Center and RAA Um's Croton Aqueduct project. Furthermore, the Lewis House maintains a series of discrete figural fragments – such as boats and familiar fish – within the diagrams of D'Arcy Thompson, which are important to both the morphing effects of Industrial Light and Magic and the morphogenetic diagrams of René Thom, Gehry's supple geometry is capable of smooth, heterogeneous continuous deformation. Deformation is made possible by the flexibility of topological geometry in response to external events, as smooth space is intensive and continuous. Thompson's curvilinear logic suggests deformation in response to unpredictable events outside the object. Forms of bending, twisting or folding are not superfluous but result from an intensive curvilinear logic which seeks to internalise cultural and contextural forces within form. In this manner events become intimately involved with particular rather than ideal forms. These flexible forms are not mere representations of differential forces but are deformed by their environment.

Folding and Other Catastrophes for Architecture

> 3 fold vb [ME *folden*, fr. OE *foaldan*; akin to OHG *faldan* to fold, Gk di *plaisos* twofold] v1 1: To lay one part over another part, 2: to reduce the length or bulk by doubling over, 3: to clasp together: ENTWINE, 4: to clasp or embrace closely: EMBRACE, 5: to bend (as a rock) into folds, 6: to incorporate (a food ingredient) into a mixture by repeated gentle overturnings without stirring or beating, 7: to bring to an end.[24]

Philosophy has already identified the displacement presently occurring to the Post-Modern paradigm of complexity and contradiction in architecture, evidenced by John Rajchman's *Out of the Fold and Perplications*. Rajchman's text is not a manifesto for the development of new architectural organisations, but responds to the emergence of differing kinds of complexity being developed by a specific architect. His essays inscribe spatial innovations developed in architecture within larger intellectual and cultural fields. Rajchman both illuminates Peter Eisenman's architectural practice through an explication of *Le Pli* and is forced to reconsider Deleuze's original argument concerning Baroque space by the alternative spatialities of Eisenman's Rebstock Park project. The dominant aspect of the project which invited Rajchman's attention to folding was the employment of one of René Thom's catastrophe diagrams in the design process.

Despite potential protestations to the contrary, it is more than likely that Thom's catastrophe nets entered into the architecture of Carsten Juel-Christiansen's Die Anhalter Faltung, Peter Eisenman's Rebstock Park, Jeffrey Kipnis' Unité d'Habitation at Briey installation and Bahram Shirdel's Nara Convention Hall as a mere formal technique. Inevitably, architects and philosophers alike would find this in itself a catastrophe for all concerned. Yet, their use illustrates that at least four architects simultaneously found in Thom's diagrams a formal device for an alternative description of spatial complexity. The kind of complexity engendered by this alliance with Thom is substantially different from the complexity provided by either Venturi's decorated shed or the more recent conflicting forms of Deconstructivism. Topological geometry in general, and the catastrophe diagrams in particular, deploy disparate forces on a continuous surface within which more or less open systems of connection are possible.

'Topology considers superficial structures susceptible to continuous transformations which easily change their form, the most interesting geometric properties common to all modification being studied. Assumed is an abstract material of ideal deformability which can be deformed, with the exception of disruption.'

These geometries bend and stabilise with viscosity under pressure. Where one would expect that an architect looking at catastrophes would be interested in conflicts, ironically, architects are finding new forms of dynamic stability in these diagrams. The mutual interest in Thom's diagrams points to a desire to be involved with events which they cannot predict. The primary innovation made by those diagrams is the geometric modelling of a multiplicity of possible co-present events at any moment. Thom's morphogenesis engages seemingly random events with mathematical probability.

Thom's nets were developed to describe catastrophic events. What is common to these events is an inability to define exactly the moment at which a catastrophe occurs. This loss of exactitude is replaced by a geometry of multiple probable relations. With relative precision, the diagrams define potential catastrophes through cusps rather than fixed co-ordinates. Like any simple graph, Thom's diagrams deploy X and Y forces across two axes of a gridded plane. A uniform plane would provide the potential for only a single point of intersection between any two X and Y co-ordinates. The supple topological surface of Thom's diagrams is capable of enfolding in multiple dimensions. Within these folds, or cusps, zones of proximity are contained. As the topological surface folds ever and into itself, multiple possible points of intersection are possible at any moment in the Z dimension. These co-present Z-dimensional zones are possible because the topological geometry captures space within its surface. Through proximity and adjacency, various vectors of force begin to imply these intensive event zones. In catastrophic events there is not a single fixed point at which a catastrophe occurs but rather a zone of potential events that are described by these cusps. The cusps are defined by multiple possible interactions implying, with more or less probability, multiple fluid thresholds. Thom's geometric plexus organises disparate forces in order to describe possible types of connections.

If there is a single dominant effect of the French word *pli*, it is its resistance to being translated into any single term. It is precisely the formal manipulations of folding that are capable of incorporating manifold external forces and elements within form, yet *Le Pli* undoubtedly risks being translated into architecture as mere folded figures. In architecture, folded forms risk quickly becoming a sign for catastrophe. The success of the architects who are folding should not be based on their ability to represent catastrophe theory in architectural form. Rather, the topological geometries, in connection with the probable events they model, present a flexible system for the organisation of disparate elements within continuous spaces. Yet, these smooth systems are highly differentiated by cusps or zones of co-presence. The catastrophe diagram used by Eisenman in the Rebstock Park project destabilises the way that the buildings meet the ground. It smooths the landscape and the building by turning both into one another along cusps. The diagrams used by Kipnis in the Briey project, and Shirdel in the Nara Convention Hall, develop an interstitial space contained simultaneously within two folded cusps. This geometrically blushed surface exists within two systems at the same moment and in this manner presents a space of co-presence with multiple adjacent zones of proximity.

Before the introduction of either Deleuze or Thom to architecture, folding was developed as a formal tactic in response to problems presented by the exigencies of commercial development. Henry Cobb has argued in both the *Charlottesville Tapes* and his *Note on Folding* for a necessity to both dematerialise and differentiate the massive homogeneous volumes dictated by commercial development in order to bring them into relation with finer grain heterogeneous urban conditions. His first principle for folding is a smoothing of elements across a shared surface. The facade of the John Hancock Tower is smoothed into a continuous surface so that the building might disappear into its context through reflection rather than mimicry. Any potential for replicating the existing context was precluded by both the size of the contiguous floor plates required by the developer and the economic necessity to construct the building's skin from glass panels. Folding became the method by which the surface of a large homogeneous volume could be differentiated while remaining continuous. This tactic acknowledges that the existing fabric and the developer tower are essentially of different species by placing their differences in mixture, rather than contradiction, through the manipulation of a pliant skin.

Like the John Hancock Building, the Allied Bank Tower begins with the incorporation of glass panels and metal frames into a continuous folded surface. The differentiation of the folded surface, through the simultaneous bending of the glass and metal, brings those elements together on a continuous plane. The manipulations of the material surface proliferate folding and bending effects in the massing of the building. The alien building becomes a continuous surface of disappearance that both diffracts and reflects the context through complex manipulations of folding. In the recent films *Predator* and *Predator 2*, a similar alien is capable of disappearing into both urban and jungle environments, not through cubist camouflage[25] but by reflecting and diffracting its environment like an octopus or chameleon. The contours between an object and its context are obfuscated by forms which become translucent, reflective and diffracted. The alien gains mobility by cloaking its volume in a folded surface of disappearance. Unlike the 'decorated shed' or 'building board' which mimics its context with a singular sign, folding diffuses an entire surface through a shimmering reflection of local adjacent and contiguous particularities. For instance, there is a significant difference between a small fish which represents itself as a fragment of a larger fish through the figure of a large eye on its tail, and a barracuda which becomes like the liquid in which it swims through a diffused reflection of its context. The first strategy invites deceitful defection where the second uses stealth to avoid detection.

Similarly, the massive volume of the Allied Bank Tower situates itself within a particular discontinuous locale by cloaking itself in a folded reflected surface. Here, cunning stealth is used as a way of involving contextual forces through the manipulation of a surface. The resemblance of folded architecture to the stealth bomber results not from a similarity between military and architectural technologies or intentions but rather from a tactical disappearance[26] of a volume through the manipulation of a surface. This disappearance into the fold is neither insidious nor innocent but merely a very effective tactic.

Like Henry Cobb, Peter Eisenman introduces a fold as a method of disappearing into a specific context. Unlike Cobb, who began with a logic of construction, Eisenman aligns the fold with the urban contours of the Rebstock Park. The repetitive typologies of housing and office buildings are initially deployed on the site in a more or less functionalist fashion; then a topological net derived from Thom's Butterfly net is aligned to the perimeter of the site and pushed through the typological bars. This procedure differentiates the uniform bars in response to the global morphology of the site. In this manner the manifestation of the fold is in the incorporation of differences – derived from the morphology of the site – into the homogeneous typologies of the housing and office blocks. Both Eisenman's local differentiation of the building types by global folding, and Cobb's local folding across constructional elements which globally differentiates each floor plate and the entire massing of the building are effective. Cobb and Eisenman 'animate' homogeneous organisations that were seemingly given to the architect – office tower and *siedlung* – with the figure of a fold. The shared principle of folding identified by both Eisenman and Cobb, evident in their respective texts, is the ability to differentiate the inherited homogeneous organisations of both Modernism (Eisenman's *siedlung*) and commercial development (Cobb's tower). This differentiation of known types of space and organisation has something in common with Deleuze's delimitation of folding in architecture within the Baroque. Folding heterogeneity into known typologies renders those organisations more smooth and more intensive so that they are better able to incorporate disparate elements within a continuous system. Shirdel's use of Thom's diagrams is quite interesting as the catastrophe sections do not animate an existing organisation. Rather, they begin as merely one system among three others. The convention halls float within the envelope of the building as they are supported by a series of transverse structural walls whose figure is derived from Thom's nets. This mixture of systems, supported by the catastrophe sections, generates a massive residual public space at the ground floor of the building. In Shirdel's project the manipulations of folding, in both the catastrophe sections and the building envelope, incorporate previously unrelated elements into a mixture. The space between the theatres, the skin and the lateral structural walls is such a space of mixture and intrication.

With structure itself, Chuck Hoberman is capable of transforming the size of domes and roofs through a folding structural mechanism. Hoberman develops adjustable structures whose differential movements occur through the dynamic transformation of flexible continuous systems. The movements of these mechanisms are determined both by use and structure. Hoberman's structural mechanisms develop a system of smooth transformation in two ways. The Iris dome and sphere projects transform their size while maintaining their shape. This flexibility of size within the static shape of the stadium is capable of supporting new kinds of events. The patented tiling patterns transform both the size and shape of surfaces, developing local secondary pockets of space and enveloping larger primary volumes.

So far in architecture, Deleuze's, Cobb's, Eisenman's and Hoberman's discourse inherits dominant typologies of organisation into which new elements are folded. Within these activities of folding it is perhaps more important to identify those new forms of local organisation and occupation which inhabit the familiar types of the Latin cross church, the *siedlung*, the office tower and the stadium, rather than the disturbances visited on those old forms of organisation. Folding can occur in both the organisations of old forms and the free intensities of unrelated elements, as is the case with Shirdel's project. Likewise, other than folding, there are several manipulations of elements engendering smooth, heterogeneous and intensive organisation.

Despite the differences between these practices, they share a sensibility that resists cracking or breaking in response to external pressures. These tactics and strategies are all compliant to, complicated by, and complicit with external forces in manners which are: submissive, suppliant, adaptable, contingent, responsive, fluent, and yielding through involvement and incorporation. The attitude which runs throughout this collection of projects and essays is the shared attempt to place seemingly disparate forces into relation through strategies which are externally plied. Perhaps, in this regard only, there are many opportunities for architecture to be effected by Gilles Deleuze's book *Le Pli*. The formal characteristics of pliancy – anexact forms and topological geometries primarily – can be more viscous and fluid in response to exigencies. They maintain formal integrity through deformations which do not internally cleave or shear but through which they connect, incorporate and affiliate productively. Cunning and viscous systems such as these gain strength through flexible connections that occur by vicissitude. If the collected projects within this publication do have certain formal affinities, it is as a result of a folding out of formalism into a world of external influences. Rather than speak of the forms of folding autonomously, it is important to maintain a logic rather than a style of curvilinearity. The formal affinities of these projects result from their pliancy and ability to deform in response to particular contingencies. What is being asked in different ways by the group of architects and theorists in this publication is: how can architecture be configured as a complex system into which external particularities are already found to be plied?

Notes

1   Robert Venturi, *Complexity and Contradiction in Architecture*, Museum of Modern Art Papers on Architecture (New York), 1966.
2   Two ideas were introduced in this text that seem extremely relevant to contemporary architecture: typological deformation and the continuity between objects and contexts. Both of these concepts receded when compared with the dominant ideas of *collision cities* and the dialectic of urban *figure/ground* relationships. Curiously, they illustrate typological deformations in both Baroque and early modern architecture: 'However, Asplund's play with assumed contingencies and assumed absolutes, brilliant though it may be, does seem to involve mostly strategies of response; and, in considering problems of the object, it may be useful to consider the admittedly ancient technique of deliberately *distorting* what is also presented as the *ideal* type … So the reading of Sant Agnese *continuously fluctuates between* an interpretation of the building as *object* and its reinterpretation as *texture* … this type of strategy combines local concessions with a declaration of independence from anything local and specific.' p 77.
3   See Sanford Kwinter and Jonathan Crary, 'Foreword', *Zone 6: Incorporations*, Urzone Books (New York), 1992, pp 12–15.
4   Gilles Deleuze, *A Thousand Plateaus: Capitalism and Schizophrenia*, University of Minnesota Press (Minneapolis), 1987, p 478.
5   Mark Wigley, *Deconstructivist Architecture*, Museum of Modern Art (New York), 1988, p 15.
6   Marion Cunningham, *The Fannie Farmer Cookbook*, Alfred A Knopf (New York), 13th edition, 1990, pp 41–7.

7 Deleuze, *Thousand Plateaus*, pp 475–6.

8 An application of vicissitude to Kipnis' logic of undecidability and weak form might engender a cunning logic of nonlinear affiliations. This seems apt given the reference to both undecidability and weakness in the definition of vicissitudes.

9 Ann Bergren's discussions of the *metis* in architecture is an example of cunning manipulations of form. For an alternative reading of these tactics in Greek art also see Jean-Pierre Vernant.

10 Deleuze, *Thousand Plateaus*, p 256.

11 This concept has been developed by Leibniz and has many resonances with Sanford Kwinter's discussions of biological space and epigenesis as they relate to architecture and Catherine Ingraham's logic of the swerve and the animal lines of beasts of burden.

12 Wigley, *Deconstructivist Architecture*, p 22.

13 See 'O-O' by Robert Somol in the Wexner Center for the Visual Arts, special issue of *Architectural Design*, Academy Editions (London), 1990.

14 *Webster's New Collegiate Dictionary*, G&C Merriam Company (Springfield, MA), 1977, p 1170.

15 Edmund Husserl, 'The Origin of Geometry' *Edmund Husserl's Origin of Geometry: An Introduction*, by Jacques Derrida, University of Nebraska Press (Lincoln), 1989.

16 See Sarah Whiting, Edward Mitchell and Greg Lynn (eds), *Fetish*, Princeton Architectural Press (New York), 1992, pp 158–73.

17 *Webster's*, p 883.

18 Rajchman describes an inability in contextualism to 'Index the complexifications of urban space'. John Rajchman, 'Perplications: On the Space and Time of Rebstock Park', *Unfolding Frankfurt*, Ernst & Sohn (Berlin), 1991, p 21.

19 A similar exchange, across disciplines through geometry, occurred in France in the mid-18th century with the development of probable geometries. Initially there was a desire to describe chance events with mathematical precision. This led to the development of a geometric model that subsequently opened new fields of study in other disciplines. The mathematical interests in probability of the professional gambler Marquis de Chevalier influenced Comte de Buffon to develop the geometric description of the *Needle Problem*. This geometric model of probability was later elaborated in three dimensions by the geologist Dellese and became the foundation for nearly all of the present-day anatomical descriptions that utilise serial transactions: including CAT scan, X-ray and PET technologies. For a more elaborate discussion of these exchanges and the impact of related probable and anexact geometries on architectural space refer to my forthcoming article in *NY Magazine* no 1, Rizzoli International (New York), 1993.

20 Rudolf Wittkower, *Architectural Principles in the Age of Humanism*, WW Norton & Co (New York), 1971.

21 Colin Rowe, *Mathematics of the Ideal Villa and Other Essays*, MIT Press (Cambridge, MA) 1976.

22 For an earlier instance of discontinuous development based on environmental forces and co-evolution, in reference to dynamic variation, see William Bateson, *Materials for the Study of Variation: Treated with Especial Regard to Discontinuity in the Origin of Species*, Johns Hopkins University Press (Baltimore), 1894.

23 Erwin Panofsky has provided perhaps the finest example of this kind of heterogeneous smoothness in his analyses of Egyptian statuary and the Sphinx in particular: 'three different systems of proportion were employed – an anomaly easily explained by the fact that the organism in question is not a homogeneous but a heterogeneous one'.

24 *Webster's*, p 445.

25 In Stan Allen's introduction to the work of Douglas Garofalo forthcoming in *Assemblage 19*, MIT Press (Cambridge, MA), 1992, a strategy of camouflage is articulated which invests surfaces with alternatives to the forms and volumes they delimit. The representation of other known figures is referred to as a logic of plumage. For instance, a butterfly wing representing the head of a bird invites a deceitful detection. This differs from the disappearance of a surface by stealth which resists any recognition.

26 This suggests a reading of Michael Hays' text on the early Mies van der Rohe Friedrichstrasse Tower as a tactic of disappearance by proliferating cacophonous images of the city. Hays' work on Hannes Meyer's *United Nations Competition Entry* is perhaps the most critical in the reinterpretation of functional contingencies in the intensely involved production of differentiated, heterogeneous yet continuous space through manipulations of a surface.

Shoei Yoh, Prefectura Gymnasium *AD* March–April 1993

Shoei Yoh describes his Prefectura Gymnasium and Odawara Complex buildings as examples of aquatic architecture. Along with Kisho Kurokawa's logic of symbiosis, this project contributes to a movement towards more fluid and open systems of aqueous urban space, presently being formulated in Japan. Like Kurokawa, Yoh proposes unpredicted connections between programmatic, structural and cultural contingencies and form. Such a logic of *viscosity* develops stability by exploiting differential and fluctuating forces. The relations of spaces are extremely complex, rigorous and precise, yet irreducible to any single or holistic organisation. This complex resistance to reduction either to unity or contradiction distinguishes Yoh's sensibility from either the universal spaces of Modernism or the arrested formal conflict of Deconstruction. This irreducible complexity is engendered by the supple transformation of *an exact yet rigorous geometry* of the Prefectura Gymnasium roof structure.

The structural members cannot be reduced to any single uniform dimension. Their particular lengths and contours present an image which is seemingly between geometric exactitude and arbitrary figuration. This simultaneity of both figure and structure differs from a more familiar contradiction between decoration and structure. The roof of Yoh's project employs a particularised, 'diffeomorphic' and supple topological surface capable of fluid transformations. The precision and clarity of the continuous yet heterogeneous roof system should be distinguished from the reducible homogeneity of Mies van der Rohe's Berlin National Gallery. Similarly, this project is not merely driven by structural necessity but becomes involved with a multiplicity of subsystems including lighting, acoustics, programme and aesthetics. The roof structure employs affiliations between disparate programmatic, structural and mechanical systems; a supple rather than rigid geometry which is capable of sustaining the differences which result from unpredicted connections; and finally a resistance to arresting these complex relations in either fixed points of resolution or contradiction. Although Yoh, along with several others, could be inscribed within an expressionist style of curved forms, the specific and specialised roof structure responds to the smooth and intensive internalisation of outside forces. This differentiated smoothness results from an adherence to the pragmatic contingencies of structure, programme and cost.

Surprisingly, the plexing roof form spans a more or less straightforward grid of programme. The athletic fields determine specific span lengths and ceiling heights. A uniform snow load establishes the variable beam depths and roof heights. Finally, the internal surface is adjusted for lighting and acoustical concerns. Rather than averaging these requirements as a single mean dimension, their differences are maintained. These disparate forces become involved with this flexible system without revision to the global organisation. Yet, the entire organisation fluctuates subtly with every local adjustment. The savings on material costs, through this sustained precision and particularisation, outweighed the fabrication costs of the various structural members. These developments are now possible given the new technologies which can sustain multiplicity and complexity through the computerisation of the design, construction and fabrication process.

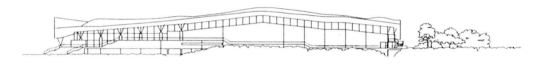

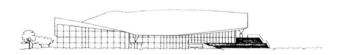

Shoei Yoh, Odawara Gymnasium proposal, Odawara, Kanagawa Prefecture,
Japan, 1991. Dissected axonometrics (top and opposite), East elevation
(centre), south elevation (above). © Shoei Yoh, Hamura.

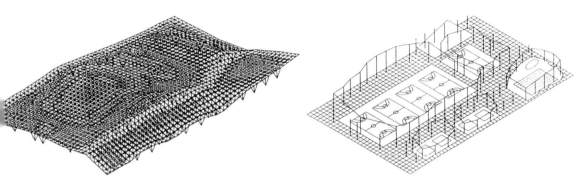

It is the discontinuity between part and whole and the smooth fluidity with which external forces are compliantly involved with internal requirements which gives Yoh's project its complex character. Both the structure and the figure of the roof are generated through the unpredicted connections between a multiplicity of plexing and pliant subsystems. In this sense, the form of the roof is constructed by vicissitude. The roof structure proposes a pliant architecture of surface and field relations. Yoh's aqueous paradigm results in an involved and intense system of connections between structure, use, economy and form.

Greg Lynn, 'Architectural Curvilinearity: The Folded, the Pliant and the Supple', Greg Lynn (guest-editor), *Folding in Architecture*, *AD* Profile 102, *AD* 63, March–April 1993, pp 8–15; *Folding in Architecture*, facsimile reprint of *AD* Profile 102, *AD* 63, March–April 1993, with new introductions by Greg Lynn and Mario Carpo, Wiley-Academy (London), 2004. Greg Lynn, *Folds, Bodies & Blobs: Collected Essays*, La Lettre Volée (Brussels), 1998, pp 109–34; Giuseppa Di Cristina, *AD: Architecture and Science*, Wiley-Academy (Chichester), 2001, pp 26–33; Krista Sykes (ed), *Constructing a New Agenda: Architectural Theory 1993–2010*, Princeton Architectural Press (New York), 2010, pp 32–61. © 2012 John Wiley & Sons Ltd.

Greg Lynn, 'Shoei Yoh, Prefectura Gymnasium', Greg Lynn (guest-editor), *Folding in Architecture*, *AD* Profile 102, *AD* 63, March–April 1993, pp 78–81. © 2012 John Wiley & Sons Ltd.

The Architectural Relevance of Cyberspace (1995)

John Frazer

The title of this essay by John Frazer refers to an article by Gordon Pask, 'The Architectural Relevance of Cybernetics', published in the *AD* issue *Design Augmented by Computers* in September–October 1969 (guest-edited by Royston Landau and with contributions from, among others, Imre Lakatos, Nicholas Negroponte, Karl Popper and Cedric Price.) In the late 1960s, cybernetics, system theory and electronic computers were seen primarily as tools to facilitate the logic of problem solving and decision making in architectural design. But in the early 1990s the sudden irruption of a new wave of computer-based information and communication technologies seemed to be subverting the anthropological and cultural foundations of daily life. Computers had begun to provide instantaneous, cheap and ubiquitous communication; the Internet promised to despatialise all kinds of functions and activities, removing social interaction and commerce from physical space to 'cyberspace', and virtual reality offered a revolutionary alternative to the Western canon of mimetic, perspectival images. As Frazer concluded, such pervasive cultural and technical changes 'are reshaping our understanding of the world', call into question our established notions of space and place, and will inevitably affect the way we design architecture and cities.

The coda to the essay documents a pioneering experiment exhibited at the Architectural Association in London in January 1995 (see John Frazer, *An Evolutionary Architecture* (London: Architectural Association, 1995)). An algorithm for 'form generation' is coded to respond to feedback received from given environments or to instructions given by participants (on site or via the Internet). The resulting evolution of visual shapes mimics, through computational means, the self-selective evolution of organic life. John Frazer's experiments may have been the first to explore the design potentials of the morphogenetic metaphor – a powerful and pervasive source of inspiration for digital designers to this day.

The Architectural Relevance of Cyberspace AD November–December 1995

A new consciousness – a new mode of thinking – is emerging with profound implications for architecture. The parallel world of cyberspace, created and sustained by the world's computers and communication lines is just one manifestation of deep cultural and technical changes which are reshaping our understanding of our world. This shift of perception from a universe of objects to one of relationships is the characteristic paradigm shift of the century. With this goes a shift from specialisation to generalisation, from the self-conscious to the unselfconscious, from linear relationships to complex webs. Our emerging new worldview is characterised as decentralised, desynchronised, diverse, simultaneous, anarchic, customerised … Key concepts are information, sustainability, participation, emergent properties …

In this context, the cyberspace of the Internet is also described as '… self-regulating, anarchic, decentralised, federated, very resilient and capable of a high degree of rapid evolution and growth. Partly by design and partly because up to now it has been operated by loose federations of like-minded, well-intentioned and very intelligent people'. This alone makes a fascinating socio-technological phenomenon working in quite the reverse manner to normal political decision making.

The term cyberspace is used loosely to describe the invisible spatial interconnection of computers on the Internet and it is also applied to almost any virtual spatial experience created in a computer. But tangible space and physical structure have already taken on a new significance as a result of the growth of cyberspace. Virtual reality has caused us to reassess reality. A shift in our perception of the old world has resulted from our developing perceptions of the new. The instantaneity and spontaneity of communications in cyberspace cause us to revalue the significance of contact in the old world. Meetings with colleagues are now more highly valued (but less frequent), they celebrate physicality … more handshaking, kissing, embracing, touching, a more frank and sensual enjoyment of the aromas … All major paradigm shifts have the effect of not only changing the way we see the future but they change the way we see the past. Old world architecture has achieved a new physicality just as the new architecture of process starts to transcend physicality and achieve ephemeralisation. An ancient goal with strongly spiritual overtones. Old space has become so tangible it takes physical force to penetrate it … quite literally compared with the cerebral effort of cyberspace.

Virtual worlds should not be seen as an alternative to the real world or a substitute, but as an extra dimension which allows us a new freedom of movement in the natural world. In other words, the transcendence of physicality in the virtual world allows us to extend our mode of operation in the physical world. A new means of travel, a new form of communication, a new way of operating, a new medium for expression.

No wonder the enthusiasts for cyberspace behave as if they have had a mystic experience – they have. It is not just that they have seen a new world, but have also seen the old world from a new perspective.

Contemporary science fiction concentrates on the coexistence of the real world and the metaworld of cyberspace. In Stephenson's *Snow Crash*, the real and meta worlds of Hiro Protagonist converge as the drama heightens, the transition between the two worlds becomes more frequent and the distinction more blurred until the two worlds become one for the hero (but unfortunately not necessarily for the reader). But for the reader of classic literature this experience is not new at all, for in reading any novel there is a simultaneous understanding that one is only in a prosaic world of reading words printed words on paper, yet simultaneously transported into a virtual world of the author's imagination and the real emotions of the reader.

Every theatregoer or opera lover has already experienced the simultaneous existence of two worlds in a more physical sense (the illusion is so strong it can work in the cinema or even on television). We are aware in the theatre of the sounds and smells around us (irritated if they become obtrusive) and yet transported to distant realms in time and space by the magic of bright lights, exaggerated sets, fantastic costumes, excess make-up and larger-than-life voices. All disbelief is suspended and however unreal the plot, the music and the setting and the emotions are powerfully aroused. We can be aware that we know the soprano and that she is very much alive (if a little overweight), but simultaneously we believe in her as a young and beautiful dying princess and the tears we cannot restrain are very real indeed.

I think I stole the idea of this analogy with the theatre from Woolley's *Virtual Worlds* where I think he also makes the point about soap operas. The front page of *The Independent*, 18 May, carried an item about how women's charities had been inundated by calls about the prison sentence received by Mandy Jordache for murdering her violent and abusive husband in the British television fictional serial *Brookside*. Real people calling real agencies about virtual characters and virtual events, real reactions and real emotions in response to virtual, but only too real, echoes of real events and memories. To echo TS Eliot, 'Human kind cannot bear too much reality.'

The realisation gradually dawns that we have been living in a virtual world all along. Kant produced an extravagant construction for the problem of agreeing that the virtual models inside our heads are a shared construct of reality. Our eyes transmit to our brains poor resolution, upside-down, mainly monochrome, moving two-dimensional images which the brain converts into a three-dimensional coloured model which moves with us but is static relative to our eye movements. The brain censors out our obtrusive nose, fills in the gaps where the bundle of optic nerves leaving our eyes causes a blind spot, employs a rich repertory of tricks such as size constancy which prevents someone appearing to shrink as they move away, is easily deceived by false perspective and other illusions. Then the ultimate trick is played and the brain gives us the feeling that this virtual model in our brains is actually 'out there' and incorporates other information from the senses such as vibration in the air which it conveniently converts into sounds also 'out there'.

The illusion is so complete that we happily take this very hypothetical model of what might be out there to actually be what is out there. In other words, from birth we confuse at least one form of virtual reality with some other shared idea of reality. Fortunately, by and large, this works until put to the test of conflicting evidence in a court of law or the more commonplace experience of having 'lost' the book which everyone else can see is in front of you. The mental model leaves out the commonplace (your nose, the rims of your glasses) and concentrates on what is new or moving in the mental model (still good at spotting predators – the piece of paper blowing in the wind that for a split second is seen as an animal). Due perhaps to over familiarity, the 'lost' book has got left out of a recent update of your mental model and it is pointless to 'look' for it – it has actually disappeared from the virtual world in your head – it is simply not there.

The concept of comprehensive ephemeralisation and the need to take a global view were pioneered by Buckminster Fuller earlier this century and the concepts are coming of age with the technical realisation of a cyberspace which simultaneously achieves both dematerialisation and global communication. But perhaps the greater impact will be on the reflected effect on our physical environment and its relationship to the virtual worlds ...

In the *Foundations of Modern Art*, Ozenfant talks of the effect of '... seeing oneself for the first time in a good mirror'. The introduction of any new technology gives cause for reflection, and the success of the Internet in establishing a rich anarchic net of invisible communication and intercourse should encourage us to think about the reasons for visible and physical contact. The electronic network is heterogeneous, location independent, informal, active (and not to mention again – simultaneous, customerised, decentralised, diversified, desynchronised): the exact opposite of the architecture of our current cities and this has led some to predict the death of the city, certainly the city as we know it. But the current decline of the nation state, hastened by communications and the realisation of the global village, has exposed other needs and aspirations currently indicated by an aggressive rise in nationalism.

In a sense the supranational companies have already transcended national politics. Democratic politics will be replaced by participation, not in the crude sense of voting for a pre-selected and very limited set of options, nor in the participatory sense of direct action or demonstration, but simply by putting in place an alternative meta scenario to which people are drawn and can associate with and simply act in accordance with a greater collective will. Not a kind of passive resistance as with Gandhi's *Satyagraha*, but a new kind of active positive movement which simply ignores the fatigued status quo.

The term cyberspace is derived from cybernetics which was a major architectural preoccupation of the '60s. In a historic edition of *Architectural Design* in September 1969, guest-edited by Royston Landau there appeared an article by Gordon Pask entitled 'The Architectural Relevance of Cybernetics', to which the title of this essay pays tribute.

In his article, Pask claims that architecture and cybernetics share a common philosophy of architecture in the sense that Stafford Beer had shown it to be the philosophy of operational research. The argument rested on the idea that architects were 'first and foremost system designers who had been forced to take an increasing interest in the organisational system properties of development, communication and control'. Pask identified a significant vacuum in architectural theory and claimed cybernetics as 'a discipline that fills the bill in so far as the abstract concepts of cybernetics can be interpreted in architectural terms (and, where appropriate, identified with real architectural systems) to form a theory (architectural cybernetics, the cybernetic theory of architecture)'. Thus cybernetics in architecture was advanced as a new theoretical basis and as a metalanguage for critical discussion. Cyberspace is just an aspect of this new theory concerned with our requestioning fundamental issues about space and the contemporary relevance of place.

Perhaps the symbolic function of the new architecture is to make the invisible visible, not by the monumentalisation and formal expression of the function or shape of these invisible networks, but as an essential part of their function. Architecture as an essential organ of interaction with the environment providing antennae for both sensing and transmitting information.

A new architecture is being conceived in cyberspace by the global cooperation of a world community evolving new ideas by modelling ecologically responsible environments and using the computer as an evolutionary accelerator. This movement is reinforced culturally by similar thinking in music and other art forms. The emphasis has moved from product to process as Buckminster Fuller, John Cage and Marshall McLuhan all foresaw: and it has moved from forms, to the relationship between forms, to forms in their environment, to the relationship between forms and their users. This paradigm shift will change our understanding and interpretation of past architecture as surely as it will change the way we conceive of the new.

Architectural Experiments *AD* November–December 1995

Evolution of a Virtual Space by Global Participation on the Internet

On 25 January 1995, an experiment was launched to involve global participation in the evolution of a virtual environment. The experiment was at the centre of an exhibition entitled *An Evolutionary Architecture* which was the work of the author, his wife and their students at the Architectural Association and the School of Design and Communication at the University of Ulster. This exhibition charted explorations of the fundamental form-generating processes in architecture. In an attempt to achieve in the built environment the symbiotic behaviour and metabolic balance that are characteristic of the natural environment, it proposed the evolutionary model of nature as the generating process for architectural form. The profligate prototyping and awesome creative power of natural evolution are emulated by creating virtual architectural models which respond to changing environments. Successful developments are encouraged and evolved as a form of artificial life, subject, like the natural world, to principles of morphogenesis, genetic coding, replication and selection.

Architectural concepts are expressed as generative rules so that their evolution and development can be accelerated and tested by the use of computer models. Concepts are described in a genetic language which produces a code script of instructions for form-generation. Computer models are used to simulate the development of prototypical forms which are then evaluated on the basis of their performance in a simulated environment. Very large numbers of evolutionary steps can be generated in a short space of time and the emergent forms are often unexpected.

Previously limited to easily quantified engineering problems, it is only now becoming feasible to apply them to the complex problems associated with our built environment. To achieve this it is necessary to consider how structural form can be coded for a technique known as a genetic algorithm, how ill-defined and conflicting criteria can be described, how these criteria operate for selection, and how the morphological and metabolic processes are adapted for the interaction of built form and its environment. Once resolved, the computer can be used not as an aid to design in the usual sense, but as an evolutionary accelerator and a generative force.

Genetic techniques for design model inner logic, rather than external form, and the exhibition afforded a glimpse of a future architecture as yet evolving only in the imagination of a computer.

The Internet Experiment

In making this evolutionary model accessible via Internet, the intention was to encourage wide participation, thus creating biodiversity in the genetic design pool on which the model is dependent. Central to the physical exhibition was a working demonstration of an evolving virtual environment based on a simplified version of the theoretical model described in *An Evolutionary Architecture*. This special demonstration version of the model, known as the Interactivator, was developed so that interaction was easy and results were

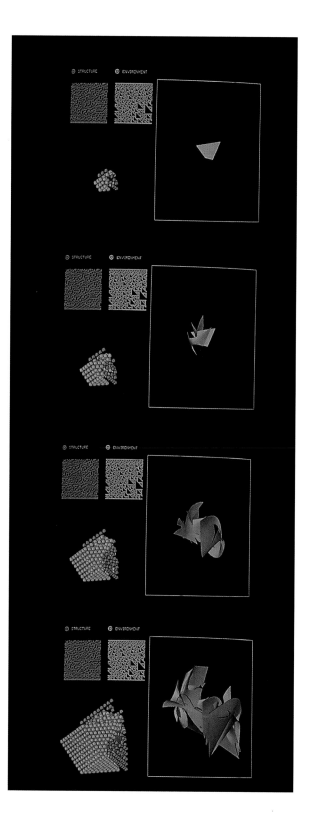

right: Manit Rastogi, negotiation of an interface surface between structure and environment, Architectural Association Diploma Unit 11, London, 1994. Cells representing structure (green) negotiate in the same dataspace as cells representing the environment (white) to define a boundary surface (yellow). In this case the rules for development of the three-dimensional (spherically close packed) automata are defined by two sets of evolving two-dimensional automata; technically described as a hierarchical multidimensional negotiated automata.

opposite: (left) Manit Rastogi, evolving virtual environment, Architectural Association Diploma Unit 11, London, 1994. A prototype sequence testing the development, evolution and mapping of an experiment in the collaborative evolution of a virtual environment by global participation on the Internet. (right) John Frazer, Julia Frazer, Manit Rastogi, Patrick Janssen and Peter Graham. An experiment in global cooperation to evolve a virtual environment on the Internet, Architectural Association Diploma Unit 11, London, 1994. All images © Manit Rastogi.

relatively quick. Although the theoretical model had been simplified, all the key elements were represented. Participation in the evolution of the model could be achieved either in the exhibition or in virtual form on the Internet. The exhibition travelled globally by replicating itself in other host computers where, under different environmental conditions, the model is still diversifying. New genes developed on other sites could be fed back to the host computer in London which now holds a pool of biodiversified genetic material.

This evolutionary model works by expressing the architectural concept in a simplified form of genetic language by switching genes in a string on and off to make them active or inactive. This genetic code script is packed into a seed which is developed in an environment, in accordance with instructions encoded in the genes so that the cells multiply. Information is absorbed from the environment into the evolving structure and travels through the model in a series of logic fields. Successful genes are identified by a process analogous to natural selection using a computer technique known as a genetic algorithm. The criteria for selection can also be adjusted. All genetic material is maintained in the gene pool but there is a higher probability of successful genes being selected for breeding. Genetic development takes the form of crossover between genes in an analogy with sex in nature, but small random mutations also occur.

Installation and Virtual Visitors

Three interlinked computers were used. The central machine handled the evolving model, displayed a rendered visualisation of the developing cell structure and a representation of the landscape of the genetic search space. One computer handled communication with the outside world and received input from the environmental sensors in the exhibition space, input from gene switches for visitors to experiment with, output sound generated by the system and was directly connected to the Internet to receive and transmit genetic information. The third computer generated images of the emerging forms and provided an animation of the growth and development of the model.

Virtual visitors could view the current state of the model and receive an explanation, or they could participate by providing genetic or environmental information. For real enthusiasts, copies of the software were available for downloading. Feedback from remote copies of the software also affected the source model.

Many thousands of virtual visitors and their comments have led us to develop the concept much further and a new experiment will be launched soon.

John Frazer, 'The Architectural Relevance of Cyberspace', Martin Pearce and Neil Spiller (guest-editors), *Architects in Cyberspace*, AD Profile 118, *AD* 65, November–December 1995, pp 76–7. © 2012 John Wiley & Sons Ltd.

John Frazer, 'Architectural Experiments', Martin Pearce and Neil Spiller (guest-editors), *Architects in Cyberspace*, AD Profile 118, *AD* 65, November–December 1995, pp 78–80. © 2012 John Wiley & Sons Ltd.

The Digital and the Global (1996)

Foreign Office Architects

Published between two seminal issues of *AD* dedicated to digital matters (*Architects in Cyberspace*, 1995, and *Architecture after Geometry*, 1997), *AD* Profile 122, *Architecture on the Horizon*, included some works in the new curvilinear, blob-like style of the time, and prominently featured FOA's (Foreign Office Architects: Farshid Moussavi and Alejandro Zaera-Polo) prize-winning entry in the competition for the Yokohama International Port Terminal (1994–95).

FOA's essay reiterates some key arguments of the new theory of curvilinearity: continuous lines create 'coherent differentiations' which bypass the formal conundrums of post-modernity, and dialectically resolve the opposition between classical unity and anti-classical (Deconstructivist) fragmentation. But FOA also suggests a new and powerful metaphor for the architectural style of sinuosity and pliancy, as they argue that the seamless articulation of 'local specificities' within or by dint of 'global processes' responds to the challenges of late-capitalist globalisation, and offers a new, universal language that is, by its own nature, permanently flexible, adaptable and variable.

The project presentation emphasises the designed variations in the continuous fold of the building in response to functional constraints and structural requirements. Well before its completion in 2002, the Yokohama Port Terminal was acclaimed as one of the most meaningful architectural achievements of the digital age, but its authors never mention here either computers or digital technologies.

Yokohama International Port Terminal *AD* July–August 1996

'Foreign' is defined as from outside; it attempts a definition by stating a position in space. Today, occupying a spatial position might be as important as adopting a political position was for the Modernist avant-garde. The production of vast amounts of information in the late-capitalist era has devalued representation as a vehicle of communication. Systems of signification, whether languages or value systems, are increasingly being replaced by material and spatial organisations as the basis of communication, exchange and consensus.

In the last seven years the map of the world has changed more than it did in the intervening years since the Second World War. Whether they address the reunification of Germany, the break-up of the former Yugoslavia, the GATT Agreement, or the accord between Israel and Palestine on the Gaza Strip, negotiations are now concerned primarily with roads and rivers, connections to cities and seas. There is no more significant action than the production of space, no deeper meaning than a material organisation. Architecture no longer needs to embody concepts, symbols and ideologies. This is why we are interested in a *performative* approach to material practices, in which architecture is an artefact within a concrete assemblage rather than a device for *interpreting* or *signifying* material and spatial organisations. Ultimately, any action or form of knowledge is motivated by a desire to modify or create our environment, not to explain or signify it.

In their efforts to construct difference, the movements that coincided with the onset of the late-capitalist era – historicism, regionalism, Deconstructivism – were essentially an escape from the rigidities of the Modernist, colonialist, enlightened project of universal rationality. But the fragmented spatial models produced by such movements are unable to account for the very fact that had produced them: the process of globalisation which originated in the need to disperse and absorb the over-accumulation of commodities. The other main concern of our research is the construction of a model which is capable

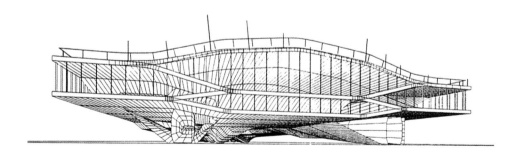

FOA, Yokohama International Port Terminal, Japan, 1994–95. View of sea approach, perspectival rendering (above). Plaza, civic exchange and leisure levels, axonometrics (opposite). © Alejandro Zaera-Polo.

of integrating differences into a coherent system. The problem is to discover how the spatial coherence which characterises globalised late-capitalist regimes can inform local differences, to approach the production of space as the articulation of *global* processes with *local* specificities, where global does not mean empty and local does not mean disconnected. As an architectural statement *after* Post-Modernism, *after* critical regionalism, *after* Deconstructivism, our strategy is to articulate the production of space which is coherently differentiated.

The Modernist techniques of erasure and homogenisation no longer seem appropriate as a way of achieving integration, nor is the identification of historical, regional and linguistic types or figures of any use in achieving differentiation – precisely because of their dependence on codes and systems of representation. We try to develop techniques that are capable of operating outside existing codes, to exploit the potential of a foreign operativity, to operate by migration, displacement, estrangement, not by seeking out origins or essences, developing genealogies, defining boundaries, assigning capacities or inventing languages. This is the origin of our interest in *de-territorialisation* and *re-territorialisation,* as processes in which specific domains and organisations are devoid of limits, origins, destination or significance: decoded, unbounded landscapes rather than overcoded, delimited places – and yet precise, specific, concrete.

A *nomadic* operativity does not imply a lack of control, but rather the development of specific modes of determination. Similarly, to engage in economic, social and urban processes of greater complexity does not imply an inability to determine, but an ability to become more sophisticated; to respond with complex orders rather than linear determinations, to redefine the limits of our control. The need for planning within material practices arises from the need to control the production of our environment. Any indeterminacy or inconsistency in the process is therefore simply the result of our lack of ability as planners.

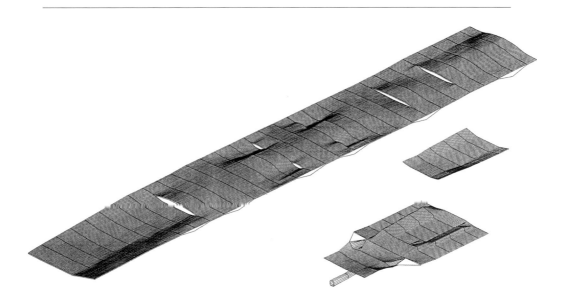

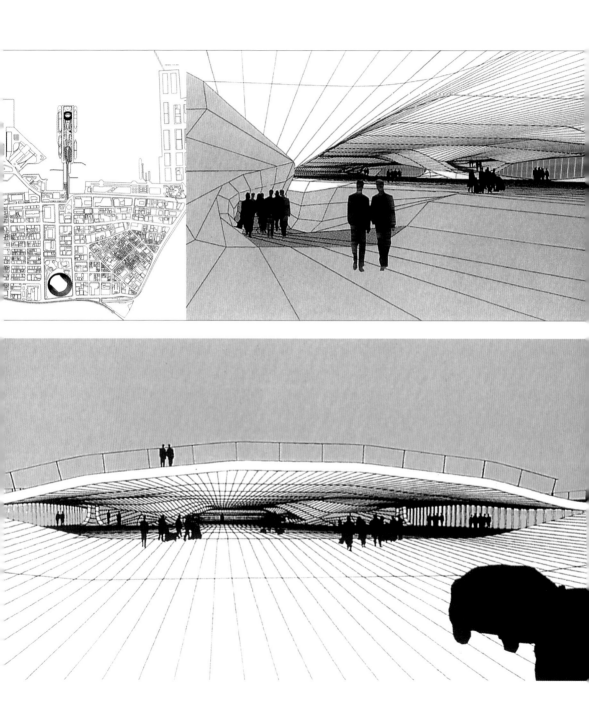

Yokohama International Port Terminal, Yokohama, Japan

The concept of ni-wa-minato, *suggesting a mediation between garden and harbour, was the starting-point of the project, which comprises a cruise passenger terminal and public spaces and facilities to be built on the Osanbashi pier. The artefact will operate as a mediating device between the two large social machines that make up the new institution: the system of public spaces of Yokohama and the cruise passenger flow, reacting against the rigid segmentation usually found in mechanisms dedicated to maintaining borders. The proposed structure will blur the borders between states, articulating differentially the various segments of the programme throughout a continuously varied form: from local citizen to foreign visitor, from* flâneur *to business traveller, from voyeur to exhibitionist, from performer to spectator.*

Using the deformed and bifurcated ground surface to create a complementary public space to Yamashita Park, this proposal will result in the first perpendicular penetration of the urban space within Yokohama Bay.

The future YIPT allows for the boundaries between domestic and international to be shifted to cater for the traffic fluctuations. This demand for flexibility is not translated into a homogeneous space, but into a highly differentiated structure, a seamless milieu which allows for the broadest variety of scenarios: an ideal battlefield where the strategic position of a small number of elements will substantially affect the definition of the frontier, allowing the terminal to be occupied by locals or invaded by foreigners. The position of the urban leisure facilities at the end of the pier, combined with the organisation of the circulation as set of interlaced loops, turns the dead end of the pier into a public space.

The surface of the ground folds onto itself, forming creases that provide structural strength, like an origami construction. The classical segmentation between building-envelope and load-bearing structure disappears. The use of segmented elements such as columns, walls or floors has been avoided in favour of a move towards a materiality where the differentiation of structural stresses is not determined by coded elements but by singularities within a material continuum, more efficient against earthquake stresses.

Foreign Office Architects, 'Yokohama International Port Terminal', *Architecture on the Horizon*, *AD* Profile 122, *AD* 66, July–August 1996, pp 76–7; Giuseppa Di Cristina (ed), *AD: Architecture and Science*, Wiley-Academy (Chichester), 2001, pp 88–94. Different versions of this text and pictures were published in *AD* 65, May–June 1995, pp xvii–xix, *Architecture After Geometry*, Peter Davidson and Donald L Bates (guest-editors), *AD* Profile 127, *AD* 67, May–June 1997, pp 70–3 and elsewhere. © 2012 John Wiley & Sons Ltd.

FOA, Yokohama International Port Terminal, Japan, 1994–95. Port of Yokohama site plan (top left). Entry to cruise terminal: bifurcation cruise terminal-apron, perspective rendering (top right). View of building from pier, perspective rendering (bottom). © Alejandro Zaera-Polo.

Field Conditions (1997)

Stan Allen

To this day a staple of design discourse, Stan Allen's 'field conditions' describe the state of perceptual but often invisible tension created by a system of physical spatial markers within the area where they are sited – or at times, well beyond. Surveying instances drawn from the history of art and architecture, as well as from contemporary science and technology, Allen argues that while traditional perceptions of space were based upon fixed and frozen patterns and geometries, or static visual images, today's technology and culture can better grasp the complexity of fluid, drifting and self-organising spatial systems, as they exist in nature, such as flocks, swarms or herds; or as defined by social sciences, such as crowds or mobs.

In architecture, Allen's 'field conditions' are also meant to favour a mode of composition that transcends the long-standing rift between classical and modern theories of form. With arguments similar to those invoked, in proximate contexts, by Lynn (see pages 28–47) and FOA (see pages 57–61) Allen suggests that a new, dialectic logic of 'flows' and 'vectors', sustained by new technologies of algorithmic notations, can bypass the oppositional patterns of Deconstructivist theory in architecture. The same strategy can help mediate between urban contextualism and abstraction, planning and laissez-faire, order and indeterminacy, and prompt designers to engage with the unpredictability of site and events, and with the 'messiness' of actual or 'low' practice. Allen's essay does not argue for any direct correspondence between the analysis of fluid fields and the design of fluid lines, either at the architectural scale or at the scale of urban design. For a different stance, see Lynn, 'An Advanced Form of Movement', also in *AD* 67 (pages 54–7; not included here).

From Object to Field *AD* May–June 1997

The term 'field conditions' is at once a reassertion of architecture's contextual assignment and at the same time a proposal to comply with such obligations.[1] Field conditions moves from the one toward the many: from individuals to collectives, from objects to fields. The term itself plays on a double meaning. Architects work not only in the office or studio (in the laboratory) but in the field: on site, in contact with the fabric of architecture. 'Field survey', 'field office', 'verify in field': 'field conditions' here implies acceptance of the real in all its messiness and unpredictability. It opens architecture to material improvisation on site. Field conditions treats constraints as opportunity and moves away from a Modernist ethic – and aesthetics – of transgression. Working with and not against the site, something new is produced by registering the complexity of the given.

A distinct but related set of meanings begins with an intuition of a shift from object to *field* in recent theoretical and visual practices (Figs 1 and 2). In its most complex manifestation, this concept refers to mathematical field theory, to nonlinear dynamics and computer simulations of evolutionary change. It parallels a shift in recent technologies from analogue object to digital field (Fig 3). It pays close attention to precedents in visual art, from the abstract painting of Piet Mondrian in the 1920s to Minimalist and Post-Minimalist sculpture of the '60s. Post-war composers, as they moved away from the strictures of Serialism, employed concepts such as the 'clouds' of sound, or in the case of Iannis Xenakis, 'statistical' music where complex acoustical events cannot be broken down into their constituent elements.[2] The infrastructural elements of the modern city, by their nature linked together in open-ended networks, offer another example of field conditions in the urban context. Finally, a complete examination of the implications of field conditions in architecture would necessarily reflect the complex and dynamic behaviours of architecture's users and speculate on new methodologies to model programme and space.

To generalise from these examples, we might suggest that a field condition would be any formal or spatial matrix capable of unifying diverse elements while respecting the identity of each. Field configurations are loosely bounded aggregates characterised by porosity and local interconnectivity. The internal regulations of the parts are decisive; overall shape and extent are highly fluid. Field conditions are bottom-up phenomena: defined not by overarching geometrical schemas but by intricate local connections. Form matters, but not so much the forms of things as the forms between things.

Field conditions cannot claim (nor does it intend to claim) to produce a systematic theory of architectural form or composition. The theoretical model proposed here anticipates its own irrelevance in the face of the realities of practice. These are working concepts, derived from experimentation in contact with the real. Field conditions intentionally mixes high theory with low practices. The assumption here is that architectural theory does not arise in a vacuum, but always in a complex dialogue with practical work.

The article is structured like a catalogue, with one thing after another. Part 1 is broadly concerned with issues of construction – the definition of the field, piece by piece – while Part 2 will treat questions of composition and the urban context.

Fig 1: Mondrian.

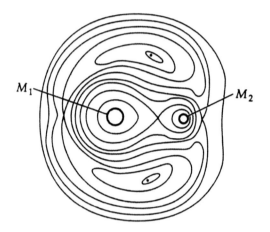

Fig 2: Evolutionary change.

Fig 3: Digital field.

Part 1 – Field Conditions: Architecture and Urbanism

Geometric Versus Algebraic Combination

The diverse elements of classical architecture are organised into coherent wholes by means of geometric systems of proportion. Although ratios can be expressed numerically, the relationships intended are fundamentally geometric. Alberti's well-known axiom that 'Beauty is the consonance of the parts such that nothing can be added or taken away' expresses an ideal of organic geometric unity. The conventions of classical architecture dictate not only the proportions of individual elements but also the relationship between individual elements. Parts form ensembles which in turn form larger wholes. Precise rules of axiality, symmetry or formal sequence govern the organisation of the whole. Classical architecture displays a wide variation on these rules, but the principle of hierarchical distribution of parts to whole is constant. Individual elements are maintained in hierarchical order by *extensive*[3] geometric relationships to preserve overall unity.

The mosque at Cordoba, Spain, under construction over a span of nearly eight centuries, offers an instructive counter example.[4] The type-form of the mosque had been clearly established: an enclosed forecourt flanked by the minaret tower, opening on to a covered space for worship (perhaps derived from market structures, or adapted from the Roman basilica). The enclosure is loosely oriented toward the *qibla*, a continuous prayer wall marked by a small niche (*mihrab*). In the first stage of the Cordoba Mosque (*c*785 to *c*800) the typological precedent was well respected, resulting in a simple structure of 10 parallel walls perpendicular to the *qibla*, supported on columns and pierced by arches, defining a covered space of equal dimension to the open court. The directionality of the arched walls operates in counterpoint to the framed vistas across the grain of the space. The columns are located at the intersection of these two vectors, forming an undifferentiated but highly charged field. Complex parallax effects are generated as the viewer moves throughout the field. The entire west wall is open to the courtyard so that once within the precinct of the mosque, there is no single entrance. The axial, processional space of the Christian church gives way to a non-directional space, a serial order of 'one thing after another'.[5]

The mosque was subsequently enlarged in four stages (Fig 4). Significantly, with each addition, the fabric of the original remained substantially intact. The typological structure was reiterated on a large scale, while the local relationships remained fixed. By comparison with Western classical architecture, it is possible to identify contrasting principles of combination: one algebraic, working with numerical units combined one after another, and the other geometric, working with figures (lines, planes, solids) organised in space to form larger wholes.[6] In Cordoba, for example, independent elements are combined additively to form an indeterminate whole. The relations of part to part are identical in the first and last versions constructed. The local syntax is fixed, but there is no overarching geometric scaffolding. Parts are not fragments of wholes, but simply parts. Unlike the idea of closed unity enforced in Western classical architecture, the structure can be added to without substantial morphological transformation. Field configurations are inherently expandable; the possibility of incremental growth is anticipated in the mathematical relations of the parts.

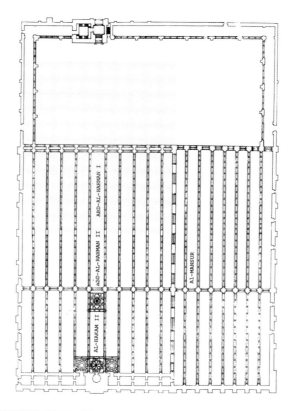

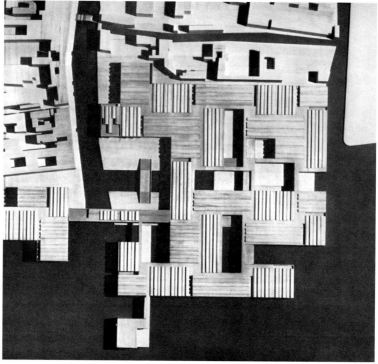

It could be argued that there are numerous examples of Western classical buildings that have grown incrementally and have been transformed over time. St Peter's in Rome, for example, has an equally long history of construction and rebuilding. But there is a significant difference. At St Peter's, additions are morphological transformations, elaborating and extending a basic geometric schema. This contrasts with the mosque at Cordoba where each stage replicates and preserves the previous stage of construction by the addition of repeated parts. And at Cordoba, even in later stages where the mosque was consecrated as a Christian church, and a Gothic cathedral was inserted into the continuous and undifferentiated fabric of the mosque, the existing spatial order resists recentring. As Rafael Moneo has observed: 'I do not believe that the Cordoba Mosque has been destroyed by all these modifications. Rather, I think that the fact that the mosque continues to be itself in face of all these interventions is a tribute to its own integrity.'[7]

To extend briefly the argument to a more recent example, Le Corbusier's Venice Hospital (Fig 5) employs a plan syntax of repeated parts, establishing multiple links at its periphery with the city fabric. The project develops horizontally, through a logic of accumulation. The basic block, the 'care unit' formed of 28 beds, is repeated throughout. Consulting rooms occupy open circulation spaces in the covered space between. The rotating placement of blocks establishes connections and pathways from ward to ward, while the displacement of the blocks opens up voids within the horizontal field of the hospital. There is no single focus, no unifying geometric schema. As at Cordoba, the overall form is an elaboration of conditions established locally.

Walking out of Cubism

Barnett Newman, it has been said, used a sequence of plane/line/plane to 'walk out of the imperatives of Cubist space and close the door behind him'.[8] The story of post-war American painting and sculpture is in large part a story of this effort to move beyond the limits of Cubist compositional syntax. Sculptors in particular, working in the shadow of the achievements of Abstract Expressionist painting, felt that a complex language of faceted planes and figural fragments inherited from pre-war European artists was inadequate to their ambitions. It was out of this sense of the exhaustion of available compositional norms that Minimalism emerged in the mid-'60s. Robert Morris' refusal of composition in favour of process, or Donald Judd's critique of composition by parts, evidenced this effort to produce a new model for working, a model that might have some of the inevitability that characterised the painting of the previous few decades.

Fig 4: Cordoba Mosque. Courtesy Stan Allen, drawing Gabriel Ruiz Cabrero.

Fig 5: Le Corbusier, Venice Hospital Project, 1964–65. © FLC/ADAGP, Paris and DACS, London 2012.

Minimalist work of the '60s and '70s sought to empty the work of art of its figurative or decorative character in order to foreground its architectural condition. The construction of meaning was displaced from the object itself to the spatial field between the viewer and the object: a fluid zone of perceptual interference, populated by moving bodies. Such artists as Carl Andre, Dan Flavin, Robert Morris or Donald Judd sought to go beyond formal or compositional variation, to engage the space of the gallery and the body of the viewer. In written statements, both Judd and Morris express their scepticism toward European (that is, Cubist) compositional norms and place their work instead in the context of recent American examples: 'European art since Cubism has been a history of permutating relationships around the general premise that relationships should remain critical. American art has developed by uncovering successive premises for making itself.'[9] Both single out Jackson Pollock for his decisive contribution. Judd notes that 'Most sculpture is made part by part, by addition, composed …' For Judd, what is required is consolidation: 'In the new work the shape, the image, color and surface are single and not partial and scattered. There aren't any neutral or moderate areas or parts, any connections or transitional areas.'[10] The aspirations of Minimalist work are therefore toward unitary forms, direct use of industrial materials and simple combinations: a 'pre-executive' clarity of intellectual and material terms. Minimalism's decisive tectonic shift activated the viewing space and reasserted the work of art's condition as 'specific object'.

Yet if Minimalism represents a significant advance over pre-war compositional principles, it remains indebted to certain essentialising models in its reductive formal language and use of materials. Its objects are clearly delimited and solidly constructed. (Donald Judd's later architectural constructions confirm this essential tectonic conservatism.) Minimalism develops in sequences, but rarely in fields. It is for this reason that the work of artists usually designated as 'Post-Minimal' is of particular interest here.[11] In contrast to Andre or Judd, the work of such artists as Bruce Nauman, Linda Benglis, Keith Sonnier, Alan Saret, Eva Hesse or Barry Le Va is materially diverse and improper. Words, movement, technology, fluid and perishable materials, representations of the body – all of these 'extrinsic' contents that Minimalism had repressed – return in modified form. Post-Minimalism is marked by hesitation and ontological doubt where the Minimalists are definitive; it is painterly and informal where the Minimalists are restrained; it remains committed to tangible things and visibility where the Minimalists are concerned with underlying structures and ideas. These works, from the wire constructions of Alan Saret, to the pourings of Linda Benglis, to the 'non-sites' of Robert Smithson introduce chance and contingency into the work of art. They shift even more radically the perception of the work, from discrete object to a record of the process of its making, in the field.

The artist who moves most decisively in the direction of what I am calling field conditions is Barry Le Va. Partly trained as an architect, Le Va is acutely aware of the spatial field implicated by the sculptural work. Beginning in the mid-'60s, he began making pieces, some planned in advance, others incorporating random process, that thoroughly dissolve the idea of 'sculpture' as a delimited entity, an object distinct from the field it occupies. He called these works distributions: '… whether "random" or "orderly" a "distribution" is defined as "relationships of points and configurations to each other" or concomitantly, "sequences of events".[12] As with the other examples described above, local relationships are more important than overall form. The generation of form through 'sequences of events' is somewhat related to the generative rules for flock behaviour or algebraic combination. Le Va signals a key compositional principle emerging out of Post-Minimalism, one that is linked to previous examples: the displacement of control to a series of intricate local rules for combination, or as 'sequences of events' and not as an overall formal configuration. And in the case of Post-Minimalism, this is often related to material choices. When working with materials such as wire mesh (Alan Saret), poured latex (Linda Benglis) or blown flour (Le Va), the artist simply cannot exercise a precise formal control over the material. Instead, the artist establishes the conditions within which the material will be deployed, and then proceeds to direct its flows. In the case of Le Va's felt pieces, it is a matter of relating fold to fold, line to line. In later works from the '60s, the materials themselves become so ephemeral as to function as a delicate registration of process and change.

Field Constructions

The common element in these two examples – one from within the culture of architecture, and one from outside – is a shift in emphasis: from abstract formal description towards a close attention to the operations of making. Questions of meaning are secondary. In the case of the Cordoba Mosque, the architects gave only rudimentary consideration to the exterior form (dictated by and large by the constraints of the site), but paid close attention to the measure and interval of the individual elements. Similarly, a contemporary architect such as Renzo Piano works from the individual joint outwards. For Piano, the joint is not an occasion to articulate the intersection of two materials (as is the case, for example, with Carlo Scarpa), but is instead a locus of an intensive design energy that proceeds outwards to condition the form of the whole.

What is proposed here is not simply a return to the mystification of construction and the phenomenology of materials. Rather, it is an attempt to go beyond the conventional opposition of construction and form-making. By looking for a precise and repeatable link between the operations of construction and the overall form produced by the aggregation of those parts, it becomes possible to begin to bridge the gap between building and form-making.

In *Studies in Tectonic Culture*, Kenneth Frampton has pointed to the split between the 'representational scene and the ontological construct', expressing a clear preference for the latter.[13] What is proposed here follows Frampton in its refusal of representation. The field is a material condition, not a discursive practice. But I also want to suggest that a return to the ontology of construction – solidly grounded in conventional tectonics – is not the only alternative to a scenographic or semiotic architecture. By remaining attentive to the detailed conditions that determine the connection of one part to another, by understanding construction as a 'sequence of events', it becomes possible to imagine an architecture that can respond fluidly and sensitively to local difference while maintaining overall stability.

Part 2 – Distributions and Combinations: Towards a Logistics of Context

Distributions

'Field conditions' is opposed to conventional Modernist modes of composition as much as it is to classical rules of composition. My thesis here is that in Modernist composition by fragments – montage strategies that work to make connections between separate elements brought together at the site of composition – the classical assumption that composition is concerned with the arrangement of, and connections among, those parts persists. As Robert Morris has put it, 'European art since Cubism has been a history of permutating relations around the general premise that *relationships should remain critical*.'[14] While painting and sculpture have gone beyond Cubism, architecture, I would argue, is by and large still operating with compositional principles borrowed from Cubism. The organisational principles proposed here suggest the new definition of 'parts', and alternative ways of conceiving the question of relationships among those parts. What is required is a rethinking of some of the most familiar elements of architectural composition. Field conditions is not a claim for novelty, but rather an argument for the recuperation of an existing territory.

Fig 6: Field diagrams: from top, left to right: patchwork, patchwork 2, axial symmetry, peripheral composition, striated, felt, block composition, mosaic, loose grid, striated 2, collision, linked assemblies. All images © Stan Allen.

The American City: Open Field

The rectilinear grid is one of architecture's oldest and most persistent organising devices. From the outset, the grid supports a double valence: at once a simple and pragmatic means to partition territory or standardise elements and at the same time an emblem of universal geometries, with potential metaphysical or cosmological overtones. Hence the Jeffersonian grid, projected unconditionally over the open territories of the western United States is at once a symbol of democratic equality and an expedient means to manage vast quantities of territory; an attempt to impose measure on the immeasurable. But as Colin Rowe has remarked in a different context, In America, the pragmatic tends to win out over the universal. Paraphrasing Rowe, we note that in this context, the grid is 'convincing as fact rather than as idea'.[15]

The earliest examples of gridded planning in the New World were Jesuit colonies, defensive enclaves organised hierarchically around the cathedral square in imitation of Spanish models. In sharp contrast to these self-enclosed units, and equally distant from the figural concepts of 18th-century town planning in Europe, the American cities of the Midwest and the West are local intrications and perturbations to the extended Jeffersonian grid. The town is an elaboration of the order applied to the farmland surrounding it. The grid is given as a convenient starting point, not as an overarching ideal. Over time, the accumulation of small variations establishes a counter principle to the universal geometry of the grid. In these American cities, pragmatics unpacks the ideality of the grid, in the same way as the unthinkable extent of the grid itself nullifies its status as an ideal object.

These cities are prototypical field conditions. Local variations of topography or history are smoothly accommodated within the overall order; borders are loosely defined and porous. They are connected with one another in larger networks. Organisation and structure display almost infinite variety within patterns that are publicly legible and institutionally manageable. Variation and repetition – individual and collective – are held in delicate balance.

Thick Surfaces: Moirés, Mats

All grids are fields, but not all fields are grids. One of the potentials of the field is to redefine the relation between figure and field. Legal and social theorist Roberto Mangabeira Unger has identified the traditional attributes of religious expression in the architecture of iconoclastic societies (that is to say, where explicit figuration is prohibited): 'The basic architectural devices of this expression were and are: blankness, vastness and pointing – pointing to a world outside this world …'[16] The conjunction, within this short catalogue, of concepts which might recall Modernist values of abstraction ('blankness') and even suggest a universal, undifferentiated grid ('vastness') with the more figural concept of 'pointing', implies something more complex than a simple opposition between the figurative and the abstract, between field and figure.

However, if we think of the figure not as a demarcated object but as an effect emerging from the field itself – as moments of intensity, as peaks or valleys within a continuous field – then it might be possible to imagine these two concepts as allied. While recognising a certain dependence on radical Modernist compositional models (Mondrian, for example), it seems important to differentiate this proposition from conventional Modernist compositional strategies. What is intended here is close attention to the production of difference at the local scale, even while maintaining a relative indifference to the form of the whole. Authentic and productive social differences, it is suggested, thrive at the local level, and not in the form of large-scale semiotic messages. Hence the study of these field combinations would be a study of models that work in the zone between figure and abstraction, models that refigure the conventional opposition between figure and abstraction, or systems of organisation capable of producing vortexes, peaks and protuberances out of individual elements that are themselves regular or repetitive.

A moiré is a figural effect produced by the superposition of two regular fields (Fig 7). Unexpected effects, exhibiting complex and apparently irregular behaviours result from the combination of elements that are in and of themselves repetitive and regular. But moiré effects are not random. They shift abruptly in scale, and repeat according to complex mathematical rules. Moiré effects are often used to measure hidden stresses in continuous fields, or to map complex figural forms. In either case there is an uncanny coexistence of a regular field and emergent figure.

In the architectural or urban context, the example of moiré effects begs the question of the surface. The field is a horizontal phenomenon – even a graphic one – and all of the examples described so far function in the plan dimension. Instead of refusing this characteristic, I would suggest examining it more closely. Although certain post-modern cities (Tokyo for example) might be characterised as fully three-dimensional fields, the prototypical cities of the late 20th century are characterised by horizontal extension. What these field combinations seem to promise in this context is a thickening and intensification of experience at specified moments within the extended field of the city. The monuments of the past, including the skyscraper – a Modernist monument to efficient production – stood out from the fabric of the city as a privileged vertical moment. The new institutions of the city will perhaps occur at moments of intensity, linked to the wider network of the urban field, and marked not by demarcating lines but by thickened surfaces.

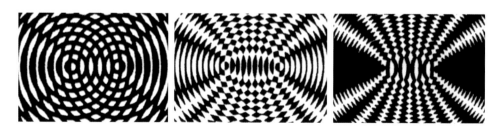

Fig 7: Moiré patterns.

Digital Fields

Analogue technologies of reproduction work through imprints, traces or transfers. The image may shift in scale or value (as in a negative), but its iconic form is maintained throughout. Internal hierarchies are preserved. A significant shift occurs when an image is converted to digital information. A notational schema intervenes. 'Digital electronic technology atomizes and *abstractly schematizes* the analogic quality of the photographic and cinematic into discrete *pixels* and *bits* of information that are transmitted *serially*, each bit discontinuous, discontiguous, and absolute – each bit "being in itself" even as it is part of a system.'[17] A field of immaterial ciphers is substituted for the material traces of the object. Hierarchies are distributed; 'value' is evened out. These ciphers differ one from the other only as place-holders in a code. At the beginning of this century, Viktor Shklovskly anticipated the radical levelling effect of the notational sign: 'Playful or tragic, universal or particular works of art, the oppositions of one world to another or of a cat to a stone are all equal among themselves.'[18]

This evening out of value has implications for the traditional concept of figure/ field. In the digital image, 'background' information must be as densely coded as the foreground image. Blank space is not empty space; there is empty space throughout the field. If classical composition sought to maintain clear relations of *figure on ground*, which modern composition perturbed by the introduction of a complicated play of *figure against figure*, with digital technologies we now have to come to terms with the implications of a *field-to-field* relation. A shift of scale is involved and a necessary revision of compositional parameters implied.

It might be noted that the universal Turing machine – the conceptual basis of the modern digital computer – performs complicated relational functions by means of serially repeated operations of *addition*. Paradoxically, it is only when the individual operations are simplified as far as possible that the incredible speed of the modern computer is achieved.

Flocks, Schools, Swarms, Crowds

In the late 1980s, artificial life theorist Craig Reynolds created a computer program to simulate the flocking behaviour of birds. As described by M Mitchell Waldrop in *Complexity: The Emerging Science at the Edge of Order and Chaos*, Reynolds placed a large number of autonomous, birdlike agents, which he called 'boids', into an on-screen environment. The boids were programmed to follow three simple rules of behaviour: first, to maintain a minimum distance from other objects in the environment (other boids, as well as obstacles); second, to match velocities with other boids in the neighbourhood; third, to move toward the perceived centre of mass of boids in its neighbourhoods. As Waldrop notes: 'What is striking about these rules is that none of them said "Form a flock" the rules were entirely local, referring only to what an individual boid could do and see in its own vicinity. If a flock was going to form at all, it would have to do from the bottom up, as an emergent phenomenon. And yet flocks did form, every time.'[19]

The flock is clearly a field phenomenon, defined by precise and simple local conditions, and relatively indifferent to overall form and extent (Fig 8).[20] Because the rules are

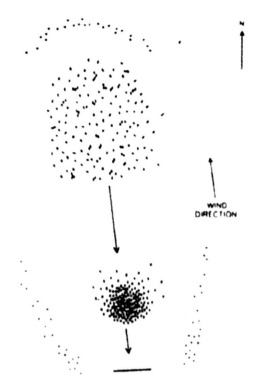

Fig 8: Order and chaos: flocks.

defined locally, obstructions are not catastrophic to the whole. Variations and obstacles in the environment are accommodated by fluid adjustment. A small flock and a large flock display fundamentally the same structure. Over many iterations, patterns emerge. Without repeating exactly, flock behaviour tends toward roughly similar configurations, not as a fixed type, but as the cumulative result of localised behaviour patterns.

Crowds present a different dynamic, motivated by more complex desires, interacting in less predictable patterns (Fig 9). Elias Canetti in *Crowds and Power* has proposed a broader taxonomy: open and closed crowds; rhythmic and stagnating crowds; the slow crowd and the quick crowd. He examines the varieties of the crowd, from the religious throng formed by pilgrims to the mass of participants in spectacle, even extending his thoughts to the flowing of rivers, the piling up of crops and the density of the forest. According to Canetti, the crowd has four primary attributes: the crowd always wants to grow; within a crowd there is equality; the crowd loves density; the crowd needs a direction.[21] The relation to Reynolds' rules outlined above is oblique, but visible. Canetti, however, is not interested in prediction or verification. His sources are literary, historical and personal. Moreover, he is always aware that the crowd can be liberating as well as confining, angry and destructive as well as joyous.

Composer Iannis Xenakis conceived his early work *Metastasis* as the acoustical equivalent to the phenomenon of the crowd. Specifically, he was looking for a compositional technique adequate to powerful personal memories:

Fig 9: Order and chaos: crowds.

Athens – an anti-Nazi demonstration – hundreds of thousands of people chanting a slogan which reproduces itself like a gigantic rhythm. Then combat with the enemy. The rhythm bursts into an enormous chaos of sharp sounds; the whistling of bullets; the crackling of machine-guns. The sounds begin to disperse. Slowly silence falls back on the town, taken uniquely from an aural point of view and detached from any other aspect these sound events made out of a large number of individual sounds are not separately perceivable, but reunite them again and a new sound is formed which may be perceived in its entirety. It is the same case with the song of the cicadas or the sound of the hail or rain, the crashing of waves on the cliffs, the hiss of waves on the shingle.[22]

In attempting to reproduce these 'global acoustical events', Xenakis drew upon his own considerable graphic imagination, and his training in descriptive geometry to invert conventional procedures of composition. That is to say, he began with a graphic notion describing the desired effect of 'fields' or 'clouds' of sound, and only later reduced these graphics to conventional musical notation. Working as he was with material that was beyond the order of magnitude of the available compositional techniques, he had to invent new procedures in order to choreograph the 'characteristic distribution of vast numbers of events'.[23]

Fig 10: Field diagrams: from top, left to right: cluster, open cluster, field vectors, striated 3, field vectors, twigs. All images © Stan Allen.

Crowds and swarms operate at the edge of control. Aside from the suggestive formal possibilities, I wish to suggest with these two examples that architecture could profitably shift its attention from its traditional top-down forms of control and begin to investigate the possibilities of a more fluid, bottom-up approach. Field conditions offers a tentative opening in architecture to address the dynamics of use, behaviour of crowds and the complex geometries of masses in motion.

A Logistics of Context

One of modern architecture's most evident failings has been its inability to address adequately the complexities of urban context. Recent debates have alternated between an effort to cover the difference between old and new (the contextualism of Leon Krier or the so-called 'New Urbanists'), and a forceful rejection of context (deconstruction, and related stylistic manifestations). The potential of a well-developed theory of field conditions is to find a way out of this polarised debate, acknowledging the distinct capabilities of new construction, and at the same time recognising a valid desire for diversity and coherence in the city.

How to engage all the complexity and indeterminacy of the city through the methodologies of a discipline so committed to control, separation and unitary thinking? This is the dilemma of the architect working in the city today. Architecture and planning, historically aligned with technical rationality and committed to the production of legible functional relationships, have had tremendous difficulty thinking their roles apart from the exercise of control. This is all the more true today when the real power of architecture has been eroded everywhere by a swollen bureaucratic apparatus. Architecture and planning, in a desperate attempt to survive, have simply opposed their idea of order to chaos: planning versus uncontrolled growth. But this is a kind of zero-sum thinking, in which architecture can only be diminished in the measure to which it relinquishes control over the uncontrollable. We thrive in cities precisely because they are places of the unexpected, products of a complex order emerging over time.

Logistics of context suggests the need to recognise the limits of architecture's ability to order the city, and at the same time, to learn from the complex self-regulating orders already present in the city. Attention is shifted to systems of service and supply, a logic of flow and vectors. This implies close attention to existing conditions, carefully defined rules for intensive linkages at the local scale, and a relatively indifferent attitude toward the overall configuration. Logistics of context is a loosely defined working framework. It suggests a network of relations capable of accommodating difference, yet robust enough to incorporate change without destroying its internal coherence. Permeable boundaries, flexible internal relationships, multiple pathways and fluid hierarchies are the formal properties of such systems.

Above all it is necessary to recognise the complex interplay of indeterminacy and order at work in the city. 'This place, on its surface, seems to be a collage. In reality, its depth is ubiquitous. A piling up of heterogeneous places,' writes Michel de Certeau. These 'heterologies' are not arbitrary and uncontrolled, but rather 'managed by subtle and compensatory equilibria that silently guarantee complementarities'.[24] Even a very simple model of urban growth, ignoring large-scale accidents of history or geography, but incorporating fine-grained difference in the form of multiple variables and nonlinear feedback, demonstrates how the interplay between laws and chance produces complex, but roughly predictable configurations of a non-hierarchical nature.[25] Field conditions and logistics of context reassert the potential of the whole, not bounded and complete (hierarchically ordered and closed), but capable of permutation: open to time and only provisionally stable. They recognise that the whole of the city is not given all at once. Consisting of multiplicities and collectivities, its parts and pieces are remnants of lost orders or fragments of never-realised totalities. Architecture needs to learn to manage this complexity, which, paradoxically, it can only do by giving up some measure of control. Logistics of context proposes a provisional and experimental approach to this task.

Notes
1   I first introduced the term 'field conditions', and a version of the conceptual structure outlined here, in the context of a studio taught at Columbia University in spring 1995. As the articles collected here demonstrate, I am not alone in my interest in the techniques and phenomena associated with the field. Jeff Kipnis and Sanford Kwinter should be mentioned. Here is Kwinter, for example, writing in 1986: 'This notion of "the field" expresses the complete immanence of forces and events while supplanting the old concept of space identified with the Cartesian substratum and ether theory … The field describes a space of propagation, of effects. It contains no matter or material points, rather functions, vectors and speeds. It describes local relations of difference within fields of celerity, transmission or of careering points, in a word, what Minkowski called the world' ('La Città Nuova: Modernity and Continuity', *Zone* 1/2 (1986), pp 88–9).
2   Xenakis, who has already an intimate connection to architecture, uses language and concepts very close to those utilised here, as described by Nouritza Matossian in her biography of Xenakis: 'A concept from physics served as a useful cognitive scheme for characterising the experience; the notion of the field, a region of space subject to electric, magnetic or gravitational forces. Just as the magnetic forces create patterns in a field of iron filings, so fields of sound might be created by varying the qualities and directions of the forces, ie dynamics, frequency, duration.' Nouritza Matossian, *Xenakis*, Kahn and Averill (London), p 59.
3   'One of the essential characteristics of the realm of multiplicity is that each element ceaselessly varies and alters its distance in relation to the others … These variable distances are not extensive quantities divisible by each other; rather each is indivisible, or "relatively indivisible", in other words, they are not divisible above or below a certain threshold, they cannot increase or diminish without changing their nature [my emphasis].' Gilles Deleuze and Felix Guattari, *A Thousand Plateaus*, University of Minnesota Press (Minneapolis, MN), 1988, pp 30–1.
4   The following discussion is adapted from Rafael Moneo, 'La vida de los edificios', *Arquitecture* 256 (September–October 1985), pp 27–36.
5   This well-known phrase is taken from Donald Judd's discussion of the paintings of Frank Stella. The order is not rationalistic and underlying but is simply order, like that of continuity, one thing after another. ('Specific Objects', *Arts Yearbook*, 1968, republished in Donald Judd, *Complete Writings, 1959–1975*, Nova Scotia College of Art and Design (Halifax, NS), 1975, p 184.
6   The term 'algebra' derives from the Arabic *al-jebr* ('the reunion of broken parts'), and is defined as 'the branch of mathematics that uses the positive and negative numbers, letters, and other systematised symbols to express and analyse the relationship between concepts of quantity in terms of formulas, equations etc; generalised arithmetic.' 'Geometry' on the other hand is a word of Greek origin and is defined as the branch of mathematics that deals with points, lines and solids and examines their properties, measurements and mutual relations in space. Word origins and definitions taken from *Webster's New World Dictionary*, World Publishing (Cleveland, OH), 1966.
7   Moneo, 'La vida de los edificios', p 35.
8   Cited by Rosalind Krauss in 'Richard Serra: Sculpture Redrawn', *Artforum* (May 1972).

9   Robert Morris, 'Anti Form', *Artforum* (April 1968), p 34.

10 Judd, *Complete Writings*, p 183.

11 In fact much of the work developed at nearly the same time. Post here implies a certain degree of dependence and opposition rather than chronological sequence. Note, for example, the absence of women in the ranks of the Minimalists; Post-Minimalism would be unthinkable without the contributions of Benglis or Hesse. A certain fluidity in these categories is required; Robert Morris, for example, is often grouped with the Post-Minimalists. See Robert Pincus-Witten, 'Introduction to Post-Minimalism' (1977) in *Postminimalism into Maximalism: American Art, 1966–1986*, University of Michigan Research Press (Ann Arbor, MI), 1987.

12 Jane Livingston, 'Barry Le Va: Distributional Sculpture', *Artforum* (November 1968).

13 Kenneth Frampton, *Studies in Tectonic Culture*, MIT Press (Cambridge, MA), 1995.

14 Morris, 'Anti-Form', p 34.

15 Colin Rowe, 'Chicago Frame', in *The Mathematics of the Ideal Villa and Other Essays*, MIT Press (Cambridge, MA), 1976, p 99.

16 Roberto Mangabeira Unger, 'The Better Futures of Architecture', *Anyone*, 1991, p 36. It is, of course, Jeff Kipnis who first called attention to the suggestiveness of Unger's formulation; see 'Towards a New Architecture', Greg Lynn (guest-editor), *Folding in Architecture*, *AD* Profile 102, *AD* 63, March–April 1993, pp 41–9.

17 Vivian Sobchak, 'The Scene of the Screen: Towards a Phenomenology of Cinematic and Electronic Presence', *Post-Script* 10 (1990), p 56.

18 Cited by Manfredo Tafuri in 'The Dialectics of the Avant-Garde: Piranesi and Eisenstein', *Oppositions* 11 (Winter 1977), p 79.

19 M Mitchell Waldrop, *Complexity: The Emerging Science at the Edge of Order and Chaos*, Simon and Schuster (New York), 1992, pp 240–41.

20 Linda Roy has studied swarm behaviour and its architectural implications in greater depth. See her upcoming article in *ANY*.

21 Elias Canetti, *Crowds and Power*, Farrar, Straus and Giroux (New York), 1984, p 29.

22 Matossian, Xenakis, cited from an interview, p 58.

23 Ibid, pp 58–9.

24 Michel de Certeau, 'Indeterminate', in *The Practice of Everyday Life*, University of California Press (Berkeley, CA), 1984, p 201.

25 This discussion of the Christaller model is taken from Ilya Prigogine and Isabelle Stengers, *Order out of Chaos: Man's New Dialogue with Nature*, Bantam Books (New York), 1984, p 197ff.

Stan Allen, 'From Object to Field', *Architecture After Geometry*, Peter Davidson and Donald L Bates (guest-editors), *AD* Profile 127, *AD* 67, May–June 1997, pp 24–31. Figures have been renumbered for this edition.

A revised version of this essay was published as 'Field Conditions' in Allen, *Points + Lines: Diagrams and Projects for the City*, Princeton Architectural Press (New York), 1999, pp 90–137; Allen, *Practice – Architecture, Technique and Representation*, second revised edition, Routledge (London), 2009; and Krista Sykes, *Constructing a New Agenda: Architectural Theory 1993–2009*, Princeton Architectural Press (New York), 2010, pp 118–33. See also: Allen, *Field Conditions Revisited*, published in conjunction with the exhibition 'Field Conditions Maribor', New York, October 2010. © 2012 John Wiley & Sons Ltd.

Nonlinear Architecture (1997)

Charles Jencks

Charles Jencks's introduction to *AD* Profile 129 sums up themes from his best-selling *Architecture of the Jumping Universe* (1995), relating aspects of systems theory ('the post-modern sciences of nonlinear dynamics') to developments in architectural design. The term 'nonlinear' is borrowed from the mathematic definition of nonlinear functions (functions where the output is not proportional to the input, or where the relation between two variables cannot be diagrammed as a straight line). As most complex but determinable functions can be transformed into series of linear ones, the term is generally intended to represent unpredictable or indeterminate systems, or systems where variables are not linked by stable relations of cause to effect. Contrary to the assumptions of modern, predictive science, the theory of self-organising systems posits that in some cases inert matter behaves as if endowed with some kind of free will, in patterns that never repeat themselves and, some argue, can never be predicted by external observers. This is said to be happening in particular when systems shift from one state to another through catastrophic jumps rather than gradual transformations (as in the case of a sand heap, which accrues gradually and predictably until the addition of a single, critical grain mutates the configuration of the pile in a sudden, destructive and chaotic way).

The unpredictability of nonlinear, self-organising natural systems is as much a matter of ideology and belief as it is a matter of fact, and the undecidability of some system developments can be interpreted metaphorically (as a contingency due to inadequacy of observation or to a shortage of data) or as an inevitable law of nature. Jencks is keen to remark that the apparently animated behaviour of matter is in such cases 'lifelike', ie, only an interpretive simile ('Landform Architecture', pages 92–5 (19–21 in original), and a similar metaphorical approach underpins his definition of 'nonlinear architecture': architecture characterised by complexity of form and continuous variations, visual qualities which are analogue to the dominant paradigms of today's nonlinear sciences. Jencks goes on to ask if this way of building is closer to our (anti-Galileian, post-Newtonian) understanding of nature, and of the cosmos.

In the second, longer essay Jencks reviews several 'nonlinear' buildings, recently built or still being built at the time, including Gehry's Guggenheim Bilbao and FOA's Yokohama Port Terminal, now considered icons of the digital age (but Jencks's first and most detailed review is devoted to Eisenman's Aronoff Center, a model of Deconstructivism). As Jencks emphasises, computers are indispensable to the making of all such buildings, as their geometric and constructive complexity could not be achieved without the assistance of digital tools. Jencks does not, however, interpret computers themselves as nonlinear machines (or machines following a nonlinear logic, in the terms mentioned above). The affinity between computers and complexity theory was, and still is, a powerful component of digital design theory, and it has often been related to anti-technological (organicist, naturalistic, romantic, or spiritual) interpretations of digital technologies – a creed that was widespread among architectural circles in the 1990s, and remains influential to this day.

Neil Denari, Beverly Hills House, 1996. Nonlinear Architecture made from a single bent surface, cut and spliced in parts for light and function. © NMDA 1997.

Nonlinear Architecture:
New Science = New Architecture? *AD* September–October 1997

Over the last 100 years many architects have proclaimed a new architecture based on emergent conditions of life. Ironically, under the Modernists, these proclamations became traditional as they resulted in yet one more version of the quite familiar: it was often not new, nor really architecture but rather building illustrating a novel idea. Hence the exasperation of Mies: 'one cannot have a new architecture every Monday morning'; hence the scepticism of the Old Modernists as they confronted the epoch of fashion, and a fast change that went nowhere.

However, another argument can be made – the premise of this issue of *AD* – which highlights a shift in philosophy and worldview. According to this, when there is a change in the basic framework of thought then there has to be a shift in architecture because this, like other forms of cultural expression, is embedded in the reigning mental paradigms. The question then becomes partly sociological: whether we really do have a new science, one different from the old modern linear sciences which grew from the Newtonian paradigm. Much has been claimed for the new sciences of complexity. These, the Santa Fe Institute predicts, will complement the reductivist sciences of the last 300 years. But, have the post-modern sciences of nonlinear dynamics sublimated the old ones? Are fractals and self-organising systems more general than Euclidean geometry and mechanistic systems? Are they more attuned to nature than linear mechanics? How far have scientists accepted complexity theories as primary explanations?

As Mae-Wan Ho and Peter Saunders suggest later, the mechanical, linear paradigm of science has been superseded: this does not mean that the scientific community, or a majority of scientists, now agree on the nonlinear paradigm; in fact, they may not even agree on positive formulations. The mechanistic worldview may have ended (nails in its coffin from quantum physics to chaos science over 80 years have seen to that), but there is no single heir such as organicism, complexity science, nonlinear dynamics, the new genetics, etc. They may be compatible but they command no single voice and theory. Yet, Mae-Wan Ho and Peter Saunders, in their explanations of the new science, and vigorous speculation, show very clearly what is at stake; a universe where, in Mae-Wan's words, there can be *reverse* information, back from RNA to DNA, where 'genes can jump horizontally', where 'intercommunication is instantaneous or nonlocal'. These, and many more wild facts which the new sciences are revealing, throw the mechanistic paradigm into doubt and lead us to assume that the universe is a lot more creative, free, self-organising and open than Newton, Darwin and others supposed.

Frank O Gehry, Guggenheim
Museum, Bilbao, Spain, 1993–97,
photograph of museum being
built. © Charles Jencks.

Benoit Mandelbrot, Random
Peano Curve. The following
generator, acting on the initiator
(0,1) yields a way of sweeping a
triangle: N=4, R=1/2, D=2.

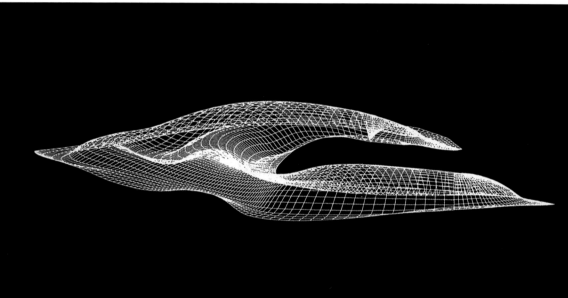

above: Shoei Yoh
Architects, Uchino
Community Centre,
1995: computer-
generated image of
roof framework.
© Shoei Yoh, Hamura.

left: Charles Jencks,
Fractal Table,
Scotland, 1995.
© Charles Jencks.

If we assume that there is a new science, and a *partial* consensus about its worth, the next question becomes: what are the recent exemplars of this new paradigm? Here, the answer includes the buildings presented in this issue, above all three of the seminal buildings of the '90s: Frank Gehry's Guggenheim Museum in Bilbao, Peter Eisenman's Aronoff Center in Cincinnati and Daniel Libeskind's Jewish Extension to the Berlin Museum. All three are nonlinear buildings and were partly generated by nonlinear methods including computer design and layout. Each one raises critical questions about the role of metaphor in architecture: that is, choosing and modifying a language of continuous variation and discovering new meanings inherent in its use. New Science = new language = new metaphors. Architecture not only reflects a different paradigm of thought but itself becomes a discipline of unfolding knowledge. The engineering inventions of Cecil Balmond, the aperiodic and fractal tiling of ARM, and other innovations extend architectural thought. As I will argue, it also may take responsibility for metaphorical invention.

Another issue is whether the paradigm is consciously pursued or not: are we seeing merely a parallel between science and architecture or something deeper? Is it only a question of using computers and designing curved buildings – a fashion – or a change in the mental landscape? Philip Johnson's recent conversion to the paradigm, evident in his Monsta House, suggests it is both. To be specific: how much do architects understand of fractals, emergence theory, folding, nonlinearity and self-organising systems? How much is this a formalist trend? Can they furnish a new iconography, a new style and set of meanings? Can one design a whole city fabric in their image?

The most profound question is: why does it matter? Is the new Nonlinear Architecture somehow superior, closer to nature and our understanding of the cosmos, than Old Modernism? Is it more sensuous, functional, liveable? Is it closer to aesthetic codes which are built into perception? Has it supplanted the traditions from which it has grown – Post-Modern and Deconstructivist architecture? The answer to these questions, which implicitly justify a change, might be 'yes', but it is too early to tell. There are other supporting arguments of a cultural and spiritual nature: architecture, to be true to the spirit of contemporary life and the life of forms in art, must explore new languages. Many will find this justification enough. A new urban language is evident in ARM's Storey Hall, one which could provide an order as understandable as the classical and modern, yet more variable and surprising.

Further innovations, or mutations in this emergent tradition, include the land-form building. The landscape as building has emerged as a new complex type and now there are quite a few built examples to judge: those by Eisenman, Miralles, Koolhaas, Gehry, Ben van Berkel and those about to be constructed by Foreign Office Architects and Morphosis. Partly motivated by maximum return on real-estate, a cynical realism, they are also intended to return architecture to a greater landscape tradition. There are several more motives at work in this runaway paradigm – its plural goals and styles are irreducible – so Nonlinear Architecture will prosper as a major movement into the millennium, fed by the new sciences of complexity. My particular hopes for its direction are outlined on page 15,* but wherever it goes this new approach will challenge both the Newtonian and traditional architecture that have gone before.

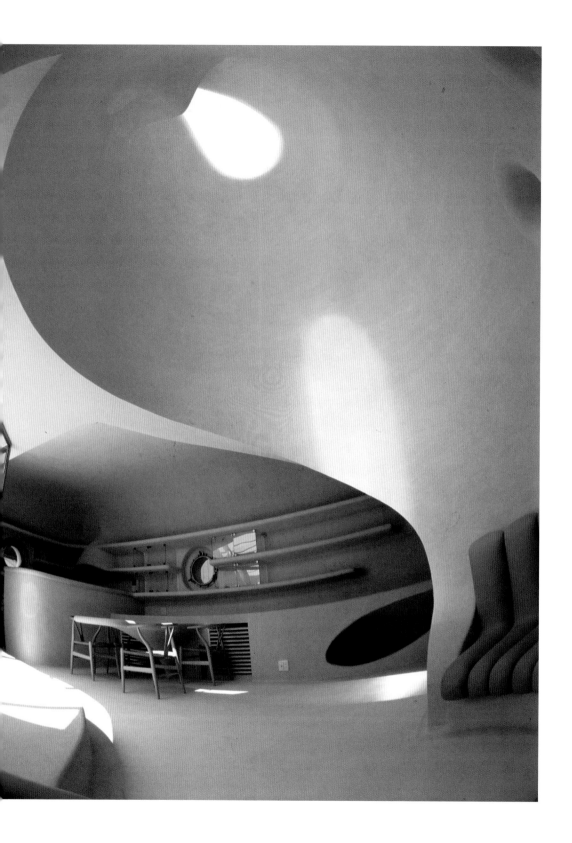

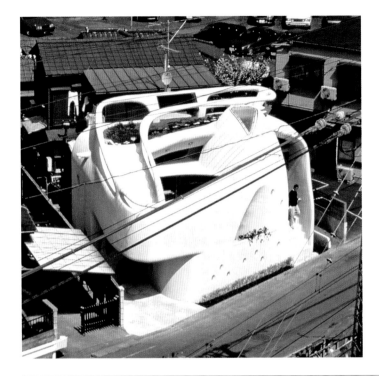

Ushida Findlay
Partnership,
Truss Wall House,
Tokyo, 1993:
interior (opposite);
exterior (left).
© Ushida Findlay.

Complexity Definition and Nature's Complexity

In the last few years there have been over 30 definitions of Complexity but none has achieved canonic status, so here is a compound definition:

> *Complexity is the theory of how emergent organisation may be achieved by interacting components pushed far from equilibrium (by increasing energy, matter or information) to the threshold between order and chaos. This important border or threshold is where the system often jumps, bifurcates or creatively interacts in a new nonlinear, unpredictable way (the Eureka moment) and where the new organisation may be sustained through feedback and the continuous input of energy.*
>
> *In this process quality emerges spontaneously as self-organisation, meaning, value, openness, fractal patterns, attractor formations and (often) increasing complexity (a greater degree of freedom).*

The direction of the universe? Or its narrative?

---

*   The page number relates to the original opening page of the essay 'Landform Architecture', the next essay in the chapter.

Landform Architecture:
Emergent in the Nineties *AD September–October 1997*

The complexity paradigm in architecture, based loosely around the sciences of complexity, has reached maturity. Two traditions have developed in parallel: one in architecture, another in science. These overlap fortuitously and, in the case of architecture, consciously. Some of the architects I will discuss here consciously adopt the underlying ideas of nonlinear science and its many suggestive methods of production and design.

Three major buildings of the early 1990s are finished or nearly so – Peter Eisenman's Aronoff Center, Daniel Libeskind's Jewish Museum and Frank Gehry's Bilbao Museum – and work by lesser known architects such as Enric Miralles, Zvi Hecker, the groups ARM and Ushida Findlay has widened this growing tradition. While it does not dominate professional practice – thankfully no approach does – it is moving into a central position without losing vigour. This sustained, broadening creativity is one of its most promising aspects. Surprisingly, even quite a few High-Tech architects are flirting with the paradigm and one of the best of them, Nicholas Grimshaw, has complex structures nearing completion. Complexity Building, Cosmogenic Design, Nonlinear Architecture, call it what you will, is extending and deepening its roots and now has many practitioners.[1]

The work I will discuss here is part of this emergent tradition, the part concerned with an issue close to urban design and Earth Art: that is, how can one handle a large volume of city building without becoming too monumental, clichéd or oppressive in scale. One of the answers is the landform building: architecture as articulated landscape. There are opposite forces creating the landform structure, such as real estate pressure to cram as much activity into the tightest space possible (something that leads to the shed space) and the idea that environmental forces – wind, gravity, the flow of traffic – and the landscape as a site of tectonic activity, can inspire new thinking. Between cynicism and inspiration landform architecture is emerging as one of the most potent ideas today. Rather than merely illustrate the new paradigm with examples, I will discuss several buildings in depth, analysing their quality as architecture, since ultimately it is this quality that matters.

From Matter to *Mutter*

Peter Eisenman's addition to Cincinnati University is one of the first completed essays in the genre. It stacks up different activities and spaces on to a pre-existing building, just as one geological formation pushes sediment and rock on to another. The result is part collision – the earthquake of forms that everyone comments on – and part intermeshing of tectonic plates. A new kind of grammar results from these waves of compression: a staccato, clunky, somewhat awkward language which, nevertheless, has its own peculiar grace. Why is this? After having visited the building twice I have come to the conclusion that it is because the volumes are mid-scale, often about the size of a person and always subtly changing, thus constantly attracting our interest. They become a new form of ornament that roots the body in what would otherwise be a labyrinth of confusion.

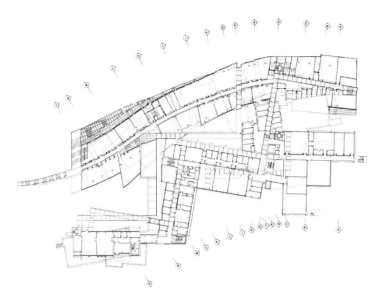

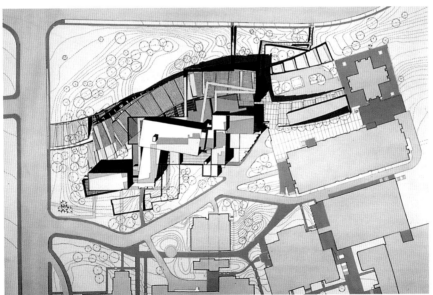

top: Eisenman Architects (with Lorenz and Williams), Aronoff
Center for Design and Art, University of Cincinnati, 1000 OC, plan
600 level. © Courtesy of Eisenman Architects.

above: Eisenman Architects (with Lorenz and Williams), Aronoff
Center for Design and Art, University of Cincinnati, 1989–96, site
plan. © Courtesy of Eisenman Architects.

top: Eisenman Architects (with Lorenz and Williams), Aronoff Center for Design and Art, University of Cincinnati, 1989–96, aerial view.

above: Eisenman Architects (with Lorenz and Williams), Aronoff Center for Design and Art, University of Cincinnati, 1989–96, drawing of atrium. All images © Courtesy of Eisenman Architects.

These mid-scale forms weave in and out of each other like tartan, or shake and tilt against each other like shards after an avalanche. The logic behind these stuttering cubes – and Eisenman, like Palladio, invites the user to become involved in the high game of architecture – is a colour code marking the design process. Light blues, flesh pinks and greens relate what chunk belongs to what design idea and why it is shifted or tilted or shimmering. The overall result is a new system which, in an unlikely comparison, reminds me of the Rococo, or the pastel delicacies of Robert Adam. Rococo also shimmers in fractured planes of light and Adamesque architecture has a similar colour-tone but the prettiness and conventionality of both could not have been further from Eisenman's intention.

He seeks to provoke and shock, to decentre perspective, deprivilege any one point of view, cross boundaries, blur categories (especially the boundary between the old stepped building and his new segmental attachment). 'There is no preferred place for the viewer to understand', Eisenman says, invoking the contradictory perspectival space of Piranesi.[2] To achieve these multiple-readings he has adopted several different methods which, characteristically, are diagrammed clearly, so that aficionados can follow the moves. Chevrons are tilted back and forth off the existing building; they set up one system against which a segmental line – mostly of studio space – is played. This line is 'torqued', 'overlapped', and 'stepped' both as a solid and void. Other moves are made, which I find impossible to understand (could 'phase shift' really be a 'tilt'?). But the result is a relatively new way of generating a sensual architecture.

Inevitably, such a complexity of different formal strategies could only be worked out on a computer and built by using laser technology and a special coordinate system of construction points. Since a team of engineers and contractors had to be trained to create this new architecture, it is a pity no film was made during production; so, if it is ever repeated in the future, the system will have to be reinvented. One of the most convincing parts of the interior is near the main entrance from the garage side. One comes through a hybrid grid of window/door/wall – into a symphony of staggered, staccato forms. Overhead, skylights and fluorescent tubes cut up chunks of space; below one's feet, cheap vinyl tile marks the interweaving systems, while the pastel cubes to either side dovetail and layer through each other. The 2,000 students who stream through to the art and architectural lessons will be kept tense and alert by these cut-up fragments. At the same time the forms make no semantic demand, have no figural message; they are completely abstract.

The lack of representational form (aside from the overall 'earthquake') can be considered a virtue for a modest, infill building, but there is one obvious problem with the whole scheme. Given its high degree of compression, its ceilings and walls pressing in everywhere, and given its very deep plan – a typical fact of life in the landform tradition – it cries out for release, for greenery, light from above, a view to the outside from the central atrium. This space, however, in spite of its inwardness, is another one of the small triumphs of the building. Atrium, plaza, square, piazza – the Spanish Steps? None of the prototypes of the public realm is invoked, but they are all implied by the way the broad stairway mounts in gentle steps to one side of the triangular 'piazza' below (with its restaurant). This is a convivial social space mixing several uses, a public realm which only lacks nature and a symbolic focus.

On a positive level, Eisenman has created a new fabric which is always changing subtly, one in which the architectural drama consists in traces of the design methods pushing through each other. Basically, a set of seesawing, blue chevrons marks the old grid while the pink and green segments mark the new formal methods; a tilt to one side, an earthquake to another and the trapezoidal crush of windows and floors between. It is a new visual language of staccato landforms and straight tangents. As a geological metaphor, it is more mica than flowing lava, more awkward chunky crystals than the flowing landforms which characterise most building in the genre. Whereas Greg Lynn and Shoei Yoh propose more supple, continuous forms, a single roof that slides over different areas and only inflects a bit to accommodate a function, Eisenman's grammar is more charged. As Sanford Kwinter has argued, structures that interest late 20th-century scientists are often concerned with 'matter in the throes of creation'; that is, matter pushed far from equilibrium so that it self-organises.[3] This kind of matter is not inert and dead. The noble scientist Ilya Prigogine, who has done more to interpret the issues at stake than others, speaks in metaphorical terms about the way that blind matter – pushed far from equilibrium – can suddenly see. Per Bak's 'self-organising criticality', the theory of how sandpiles self-organise when they reach a critical state, is one example. Each piece of sand, when the pile reaches the critical angle, is in touch with every other one, can 'see every other one', and this sudden holistic organisation brings the system to life; or, rather, to lifelike dynamic behaviour. The same is true of tectonic plates pushed to critical compression, or any material system pushed to the threshold between order and chaos.

Since all matter in this state transforms itself and becomes closer to the living organism I will christen it *mutter*, after the German for mother. Mother earth is an old metaphor of regeneration, but what I am implying is the potential for all dead matter to act, at the threshold of chaos, in a spontaneous, interactive way – as if it were free; as if it had a mind of its own, like a mother.

In a recent scheme for a museum and ferry terminal on Staten Island in New York, Eisenman has pushed the deep landform building in a more crystalline direction. White spirals of translucent glass and steel ratchet their way over a dense traffic intersection of boats, pedestrians and buses. The flow of traffic becomes one generator of the forms, while wind and water also play a role.

Diagrams of laminar flow used to test aeroplanes and boats create a swirling grammar and Eisenman is also inspired by the fractal shapes of the Stealth Fighter. But, as rendered on the computer, this grammar is again chunky and staccato. It rises and curves in tangents, like an ice-flow bent around a rock. Perhaps this metaphor reveals something about the design since the old terminal for the ferry – the rock – makes the new museum and circulation space, above it, twist and tilt. Here we are closer to Greg Lynn's ideal of a continuous structure deformed by circumstance, a flow-diagram punctuated by events. The shed-space and the super-skin, the real-estate realism and the cosmic gesture. Is it a Stealth Fighter, UFO, ice-flow, spiral of crystals, or layered laminar diagrams – or, simply, dense packing? In Britain, developers call repetitive close-packing 'rent-slab capitalism' and it has, deservedly, given Modern architecture a bad name.

above: Eisenman Architects, Staten Island Institute of Arts and Sciences, Staten Island, New York, 1997, computer rendering.

below left: Eisenman Architects, Staten Island Institute of Arts and Sciences, Staten Island, New York, 1997, horizontal section study, cut two-thirds of the way up on the building diagram.

below right: Eisenman Architects, Staten Island Institute of Arts and Sciences, Staten Island, New York, 1997, horizontal section study, cut a third of the way up. All images © Courtesy of Eisenman Architects.

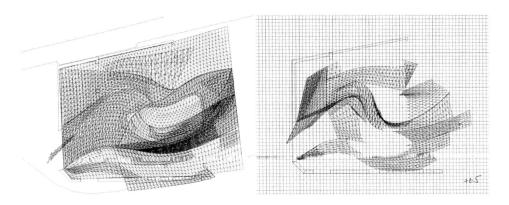

above: F-117A Stealth Fighter. © Aero Graphics, Inc./CORBIS.

below: Enric Miralles, Eurhythmics Centre, Alicante, Spain, 1993–94, earth movements under entry ramps. The rise and spread of waveforms from A to G and from H to P can be felt through this 'cinematic sectioning'. © Miralles Tagliabue EMBT Studio.

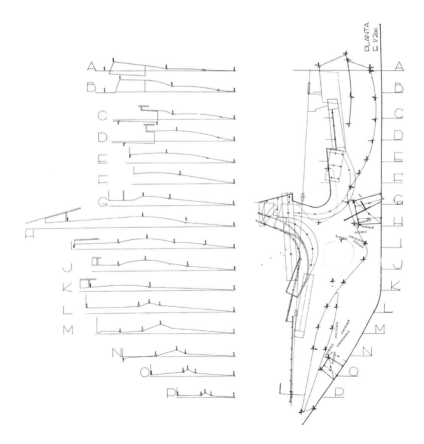

How does this horrible truth impinge on the landform tradition? At Cincinnati, Eisenman really has subtracted the deep plan of its pathos and meanness. The reality is cheap, the materials minimal and ordinary – fluorescent tubes and linoleum – but these necessities have been transformed into an exciting symphony of very rich complexity. In effect, Eisenman has turned dumb matter into syncopated *mutter*. The shift in the sign works; it looks like it will again on Staten Island.

The Cinematic Section
Enric Miralles, the Barcelona architect, has developed various notation systems for dealing with the landform building. He depicts the sprawling context of his buildings with a Hockneyesque method of photo-collage; that is, he splices together a continuous image of changing perspectives that wanders about in a higgledy-piggledy manner but still keeps a fractal identity, a self-similar quality. Secondly, he has devised what could be called 'cinematic sectioning': the analysis of a large land-mass by making many cuts through it. The resulting sections reveal a sequence of varying topography, as if one took cinema stills and flipped through them to animate movement across the land. Cinematic sectioning has been used to depict the complex site of the Eurhythmics Centre in Alicante, Spain. Through the notation one follows the rise and fall of land waves as they move under ramps, and the method also choreographs the movement of people on the ramps. From these and other large-scale movements the building is generated. Indeed, the overall undulation of the Centre is another fractal, this time one which mimics the surrounding mountains. So the landform building not only sprawls like a geological formation but is actually a microcosmic representation; an idea not far from the way in which a Chinese garden 'borrows the landscape'.

Cinematic sectioning is a method of controlling the design of very large structures and it was used by several groups who entered the Yokohama Port Terminal Competition in 1995, an important event for the new paradigm with Greg Lynn, Reiser + Umemoto and the winners, Foreign Office Architects (FOA), all producing interesting Nonlinear Architecture. The young team of FOA (Farshid Moussavi and Alejandro Zaera-Polo) worked previously for both Rem Koolhaas and Zaha Hadid and are connected to the Architectural Association in London, with all the apostolic succession this implies. It is no surprise that their entry pushes several ideas of Complexity Architecture – folding, superposition and bifurcation – a step beyond their teachers.

Their landscape-building for Japan is a long, low horizontal folded plate of steel that will undulate across the water. Its structural strength is provided by the self-similar folds and the gentle undulations of the plates – flowing forms which are obvious metaphors of the sea. Paradoxically, the hard surface resembles a dry desert. It could be a moonscape pockmarked by activities strewn about in a carefully careless way, chaotic compositional tactics that Koolhaas termed 'confetti' when he deployed them at the Parc de la Villette.

The multi-layered topography for Yokohoma achieves both diversity and unity, disjunction and continuity. The architects are looking for a seamless structure, an alternative to collage and radical eclecticism, with which to deal with difference; a system they describe as 'continuous but not uniform'. They achieve this, to a degree, by folding various functions into a continuous surface full of feedback loops of circulation. If built, the rich mixture of different uses may be hard to administer because the usual visual borders do not orient and divide different kinds of passengers. One can imagine international and local travellers arriving late for a ship and becoming mixed up together as they head for one of those eye-shaped folds that peer from one level to the next. These 'bifurcations', as the architects call them following the complexity paradigm, unite different levels. Importantly they do so with a smooth continuity, rather like the way origami folds unite a complex pattern into a single sheet of paper.

In contrast to Eisenman's staccato grammar, the grid, the fold and undulation are employed in a soft way that blurs distinctions. One floor warps a bit of itself into another, producing a characteristic 'floor/door/window' and a sloping 'floor/ramp', the latter idea developed by Koolhaas. A challenge for architects today is to see if this idea can work better than it does at Frank Lloyd Wright's Guggenheim Museum.

As the model and sections indicate, this ferry terminal is a very abstract system, a landscape of otherness, a surprising flatscape without the usual orientation points; it does not look like a building at all. The generic nature of the scheme, the architects claim, is well-suited to our stage of globalised late-capitalism and, like Mies van der Rohe, they turn a universal system into a kind of transcendental space: a sacred space without a religion. Artificial land, second nature, has reached an apotheosis.

The Fractal Landform

If FOA, this time like Eisenman, prefers an abstract system to a representational one, then the Israeli architect Zvi Hecker reverses the preconception with his Jewish school in Berlin. The Heinz-Galinski School creates an extended landform out of explicit metaphors. Snake corridors, mountain stairways, fish-shaped rooms are pulled together with an overall sunflower geometry. It sounds constricting, even Procrustean, but, on the contrary, the sunflower, with its spiral of movement towards a centre can generate a general order, especially, as here, when tied to two other geometries – the grid and concentric circles. The three systems, like Eisenman's tilts, make every room slightly different, or self-similar, and the sunflower spiral results in a very strong pull to the heart of the school (the architect, when he saw it from a helicopter, said it looked like 'a friendly meeting of whales'). Some will find this centrality too obvious, the imagery too readable and insistent, but again one is surprised by the generality and abstraction of the grammar.

The small institution for 420 pupils is the first Jewish school to be constructed in Germany for 60 years. Built in the leafy suburbs of Charlottenberg, it literally keeps a low profile – two to three storeys – and threads its sunflower geometry amid the existing trees. The most satisfying aspect is its urbanity. It creates tight curving streets, or walkways, which give a sense of mystery not unlike a historic town, where contingency has created the odd shapes and spaces. Here a restricted palette of grey concrete, silver corrugated metal and white stucco is interwoven with trees. Each of the three colours, as with Eisenman's pink, green and blue, corresponds with a different geometric system.

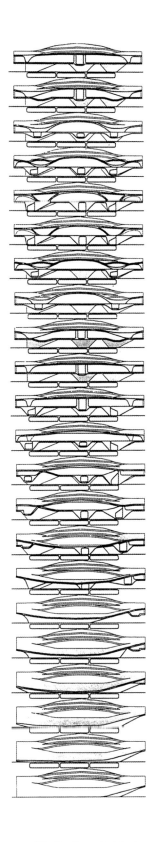

left: FOA, Yokohama International Port Terminal, competition winner, 1995. 'Cinematic sectioning' shows a folded plate in steel – a self-stiffening structure. © Alejandro Zaera-Polo.

below: Zvi Hecker, Heinz-Galinski School, Berlin, 1993–95. © Charles Jencks.

This allows contractors to understand and build a complex woven structure and also, of course, allows the complexity to be interpreted. The point is generally true of these landform structures. They depend on systematic logic, both for construction and orientation; not the simple logic of one grid, but three or four systems in tandem. Again, the contrast with Modern architecture is quite obviously that between complexity and simplicity, although it is not an absolute contrast. Here, for instance, simple materials, simple formulae and abstraction have generated the complexity.

Six of the sunflower petals curve counterclockwise around a circular green and one enters a void where the seventh might have been. This semi-public space, with its subtle mixture of cobbles and grass, metal and stucco, Jewish ruins and concrete, gives a strong sense of identity: the physical counterpart for the strong community life which goes on here. Part Torah school, part synagogue, part community facility with public meeting rooms, the Heinz-Galinski School has to play an ethnic role in Berlin which is not dissimilar to Libeskind's Jewish Extension to the Berlin Museum: it must fit in and yet be unmistakably other.

Several discreet signs, such as a Jewish star, are placed in the background and their presence is felt at the same level as the architectural symbolism; for instance, the plan of the six petals, which is also punched into the concrete. The latter becomes a decorative logo and explanatory map for new visitors. It also suggests the wider intentions of Hecker, which are to produce a cosmic order based on the omnipresent spiral form and, in particular, the solar dynamics of the sunflower. He has underlined the paradox of 'a wild project' that has 'very precise mathematical construction'. 'Above all', he notes 'is its cosmic relationship of spiral orbits, intersecting one another along precise mathematical trajectories.'[4] The mixture of an abstract system and a few discrete signs and images is finely balanced.

The group ARM (Ashton Raggatt McDougall), a Melbourne office, also reaches this balance in some of its post-modern buildings, and the opposition is usually a symbolic programme set against technical virtuosity. At Storey Hall in Melbourne, ARM has created one of the most exuberant expressions of the new paradigm. The building, on one of the main downtown streets of Melbourne, is part of the highly urbanised campus of RMIT. Its explosion of green and purple fractals (with yellow and silver highlights) sends up its neighbours to either side. At the same time, like Gaudí's Casa Batlló with which it is comparable, it also makes subtle acknowledgements to these neighbours with its cornice line, window scale and basic tripartition. Basically, however, like Eisenman's Cincinnati addition, it is proposing a new urbanism, a new system which is a discrete shift from those of the past. No longer the classical ordonnance, no longer the boredom of Miesian curtain wall! Here is a different way of ordering the landscape which is more organic and chaotic than both the classical and modern systems. Potentially, if it were generalised as a whole street system, it could be just as harmonious as those of the past. Why doesn't some architect try it on a whole street – create the new subtle order of urbanism? The system awaits its Alberti.

At street level, Storey Hall presents a large green and purple doorway – quite a shock. The green folded plates of concrete blur into purple folds ('blurring', again as with FOA, is a favourite term of the architects, here likened to smeared lipstick). As justification Howard

ARM, Storey
Hall, Melbourne,
Australia, 1993–96.
Fractal forms of
window, doorway,
bronze surface
and metal cornice
are based on the
aperiodic tiling
pattern derived
by Roger Penrose
– a new, always
changing order
for urbanism.
© Charles Jencks.

ARM, Storey
Hall, Melbourne,
Australia, 1993–96,
section. © ARM
Architecture.

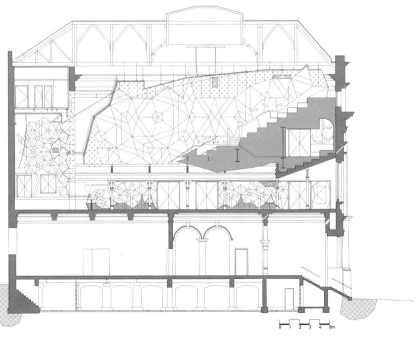

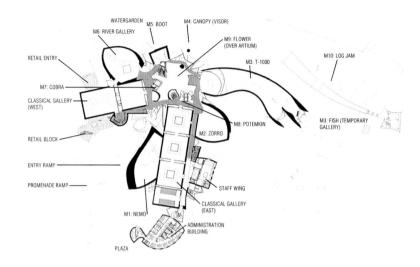

Frank O Gehry, Guggenheim Museum, Bilbao, Spain, 1993–97. Self-similar petals erupt in the centre and curl under the bridge, which ties the museum to contemporary technology and the urban landscape. All images © Charles Jencks.

Raggatt cites the fact that green and purple were the heraldic colours of the previous inhabitants, Irish and feminist groups. In this and other ways, the building takes its cues from history, the typical post-modern method of building in time and historical depth.

Most evident are the patterns of bronze fractals – lozenge shapes, both fat and thin – that dance over the concrete surface. These are versions of the famous Penrose tiling pattern, which I will explain shortly, and they are self-similar to the doorway and other forms in metal: so the variety of shapes is harmonic, related and fractal, but hardly ever self-same (as in a Modernist building).

The bronze panels of the facade are articulated further by a green, linear meander, and the surface-squiggles look as if they were folds in a rock, or skin. Finally, to the left and on the *piano nobile* (to use the classical term of the adjoining buildings) is a linear part of the Penrose pattern, punched violently through the surface. The architect, Howard Raggatt, ironically quoting one of the responses to the building, speaks of this jagged void as if 'Roger Rabbit went through the concrete wall'; but significantly he sees the point of appropriating the unusual image through metaphor and popular culture.[5] He lists the variety and overlap of metaphors – 'broken vegemite jar, kryptonite building, gates of hell, Ivy League creeper, green house for leprechauns, the true geometry of space, from Plato's to Einstein's cave' – suggestive, contrary images which provoke different readings.

Inside the building the variegated themes are elaborated. A high entrance space breaks through several levels, surmounted by a twisting stair and is compressed to one side by the cave entrance. The first floor foyer is further compacted by three surfaces: large, abstracted fractals of the facade, folded plates of a bigger dimension. Finally, one reaches the auditorium, where the concentration of themes is even more intense.

The auditorium ceiling erupts overhead with the Penrose pattern – now in acoustic tile – that is at once reptilian and cavelike. The metaphor of an undulating skin is maintained, but developed to accommodate lighting and the requirements of music, drama and lectures. Here, and on the walls and stage, the fractal grammar is rendered in different scales and in opposite tastes. If Eisenman's system at Cincinnati is abstract, cool but Rococo, ARM's system is representational, hot and Art Deco. At a general level, both architects have used the computer to generate a new grammar based on complexity theory, although because the structure of Storey Hall is old this cannot be elaborated in volume.

One of the most important contributions of the building is the development of the Penrose tiling pattern into an order that connects facade, floor, walls and ceiling into a single ornamental system. Roger Penrose, the Oxford mathematician, inventor and author, discovered a tiling pattern with five-fold symmetry that was previously thought to be impossible. Using a fat and thin rhombus, he created an aperiodic tiling system which, however far it is extended, never results in a cyclical pattern. This unusual, self-organising order was later in 1984 discovered to exist in nature. It was termed a quasicrystal, because it had an orientational but not translational order, whereas a crystal has both. Like a crystal it has a holistic order, but it also has a higher degree of complexity, since the pattern is everywhere slightly different. Quasicrystals, with a fractal self-similarity, are potentially more suited to architecture than the repetitive use of the square because they are not self-same – in a word, boring.

To recognise the Penrose enigma one has to break the pattern down into 10-sided decagons, which resemble faceted footballs. One begins to discover that each football overlaps with another on a thin rhombus. At Storey Hall a more emphatic supergraphics, a green linear pentagon, is laid over the decagons. The two rhythms then dance together in gentle syncopation, two distinct beats played off against each other. The result may be somewhat overbearing on the street, but in the foyer and auditorium it makes for appropriate, visual music.

Even if they have not answered it, the architects of Storey Hall have posed a very interesting question: what if a whole street were ordered this way, what if a new complexity grammar replaced the self-same rhythms of classicism and Modernism? What if the city grew like a quasicrystal, and an ever-changing order emerged which was never quite repeated?

The Japanese-based Ushida Findlay Partnership has not quite answered this question either, but also seeks a fractal urban order. This is based on continuous curves, such as the spiral. The Truss Wall House, Soft and Hairy House and House for the Millennium are more fluid and continuous than the other buildings illustrated here, because a monotone white surface unites all planes. It absorbs those elements – fixtures and windows which are usually separated in colour and form. Kathryn Findlay, who grew up on a Scottish farm, speaks of a fluid, rubbery architecture and, like Eisenman, she favours models such as the slime mould and metaphors taken from movement, because they represent flexibility, and activity close to the body.

Fluid Fractals

No architect has yet reached this state of organic flexibility. The Surrealists proposed it in the 1920s and Salvador Dali admired Gaudí's works because they were viscous or, as he called it, 'edible architecture'. Frank Gehry, at the new Guggenheim Museum in Bilbao, has been approaching this fluidity; he has pushed the grammar he first developed at the Vitra Museum in more supple directions. Smooth, continuous forms in steel and limestone flow towards a centre point to erupt in a flower of petals. Where before at Vitra the units were distorted boxes, they are now more linear, smooth and continuous. The grammar has an all-over, seamless continuity like Ushida Findlay's work.

The new museum has the presence of a robust, urban plant. It might be a hardy bulb or bush pushing its way opportunistically through holes in the pavement. Tough, riotous, savage – sprouting against the odds, for light and life, it is the image of Gaia overcoming the harsh city hardscape, maybe even a weed thriving on toxic waste. No, it is too graceful for that, but the burgeoning energy is unmistakably present, erupting from below, climbing over the rectilinear structures like a creeper which cannot be suppressed. Actually, many of the gallery spaces are rectilinear – an effective contrast to what happens above – and one of them stretches under the high-speed motorway and bridge to reach up on the other side. This petal serves as another entrance. It also becomes another landform that ties the building into large-scale technology and the sprawl of the city, urban realities that are accepted not denied by this inclusive work.

Frank O Gehry, Guggenheim Museum, Bilbao, Spain. © Charles Jencks.

Frank O Gehry, Guggenheim Museum, Bilbao,
Spain, 1993–97. Inside the Guggenheim Museum
curved glass walls compress into the space and
layer it with the pinched arris so that reflections
and transparencies are made even more
ambiguous. All images © Charles Jencks.

Does any other building command an urban setting with such presence, indeed capture the landscape with such power? Chartres? The Acropolis? Ronchamp? These three sacral structures come to mind because they, too, stand out from the context and at the same time give the landscape a direction, even supporting role. When one sees the new Guggenheim from the surrounding hills, it seems like a silver magnet drawing a grey city together. Overpowering, resplendent, exuberant – a cathedral caught like Laocoon in the embrace of a slippery snake, trying to squeeze out. Metaphorical excess? Inevitable, when confronted by these glowing, exploding curves – a supernova of museum as cathedral, looking for worshippers who love the new science.

Actually, on a more pedestrian level, Gehry has related the museum to three city scales: that of the bridge, captured by an entry tower that snakes under it; that of the existing roof tops, whose heights are acknowledged by the atrium and lower forms: and the Bilbao River, an important historical waterway, which is taken into the scheme, both literally through large windows and the viscous, silvery forms.

To connect the museum to the city, Gehry has used a limestone (from Granada) which relates to the sandstone of adjacent structures. He has also designed a very large city space, an atrium even more powerful than New York's original Guggenheim, which also has a large expanding space at its centre. The Bilbao atrium does not have a function beyond orientation and thus it could be conceived as both a pure aesthetic space and public town square, opening out to the river. Aware that this relative freedom allowed him to upstage Wright at his own game of spatial gymnastics, Gehry says, only partly ironically, that he intends to have a holographic portrait of that wilful architect looking down on visitors – jealously, disapprovingly. Formally, the new atrium takes the exterior grammar and turns it inside out, so that the petal shapes compress inwards, and bend upwards with curved glass.

The result is a new kind of ambiguous architecture, more folded on to itself than the glass box which introduced Modernist notions of transparency. Here are reflections of reflections and the self-similarity of crystals, the handling of glass facets and their intersections which causes a virtual image to splinter into many layered fragments. Views are partly veiled by walls of light that lead the eye up to the public ramps and roof terraces, which in turn give onto the urban landscape and river – making the museum a celebrant of the city.

While the Bilbao museum has a diversity of form and colour, what remains in the mind is the organising metaphor – the robust flower with its riotous petals blowing in the wind. There are approximately 26 self-similar petals, which reach out and come to a point which extends as a line. Just as light and shadow are sculpted by the flutes of a Doric column, so a shadow line is created by the pinched petals. The arris or fillet defines each volume in a much more supple way than at Vitra; perhaps this is a visual refinement, but it is also a clear example of the way that Gehry and the tradition he is in are learning step by step from their own work.

Like so many other buildings in the paradigm, this one has had the fat trimmed off by computer, using a program called 'Catia', developed by the French aeroplane manufacturer Dassault. The complex steel framing was kept to a minimum, as was the cutting of the masonry; necessary economising when dealing with curved buildings. There is always a lot of wastage when one carves from block, unless the offcuts can be used or kept to the minimum. Gehry, like Grimshaw and others, has spoken of the way in which new computer software, designed for other technologies such as aircraft, can be used to cut the cost of fabrication by a large percentage. Here the Catia system has worked out the volumes following a wood model and calculated exact dimensions as seen from any point, or any cut through a complex curve. These dimensions can be translated into the bent steel undersheets and then the pre-bent titanium cladding allowing all the tolerances to be worked out ahead of time in the factory. This cuts costs, but it results in the same size titanium panel throughout, a rigidity which I criticise elsewhere in this issue, because it is out of keeping with the general approach – that is, fractals, self-similarity, and varying the module to suit the curve and function.

Not Inform but Emergent Form

The new complexity paradigm in architecture is evolving simultaneously in different directions. Landform buildings are perhaps the most prominent of the species, but they do share qualities with the others. One area of overlap is the concern for organic metaphors of design: the petals of Zvi Hecker and Frank Gehry, and the geological formations of Elsenman and Miralles. Another is the attempt to get closer to nature and its fractal language, as ARM and Ushida Findlay are doing. To some extent they are all producing an artificial landscape; a construction in-between the reality of the city, a building and the landscape.

There is more than one way to see these buildings, and the Spanish architectural critic, Luis Fernandez-Galiano, has seen them within a tradition of art that stems from the writings of Georges Bataille.[6] This French philosopher attacks the notion of hieratic form in architecture and proposes, instead, a 'formlessness' which several artists have sought. Yves-Alain Bois and Rosalind Krauss, in an exhibition at the Centre Pompidou entitled 'Inform', showed the kind of work that approaches formlessness. The dust and broken shards of Robert Smithson; the rusted, rotted and collapsed forms of Lucio Fontana; the wasted forms of Robert Morris and Andy Warhol typify much of this work involved, as it is, with entropy. The problem of the art, aside from the fact that its predictability becomes boring, is that none of it is truly informal, formless or entropic. It is still very much 'patternmaking', even if of a minimal kind. It is hard to approach a condition of complete chaos, but computer programs can help our progress along this road if we want to travel it.

One of the few architects to use entropy in this way is Coop Himmelblau, who often composes buildings according to a method not far from throwing sticks into a random heap (as in the game of 'Pick-up-Sticks'). This, however, is not the method used by Eisenman, Libeskind, ARM or the others. Rather, they have used random means to allow an organisation to emerge: they have been very selective about the initial conditions – the fractal shape grammars – and the final stage of fine-tuning, that is, after a stage of random generation. In short, they do not pursue formlessness but emergent form, the *mutter* emerging from matter.

The intention may be the desire to get closer to the reality behind nature, the generative qualities behind both living and dead matter, that is, once again, the cosmogenic process which complexity theory has recently tried to explain. Representing emergence and creativity *per se* cannot be done, but it can be presented by an architecture that is as fresh and unlikely as one finds here.

Adapted from the last chapter of *The Architecture of the Jumping Universe*, Revised Edition, Academy Editions (London), 1997.

Notes

1   The leading practitioners of Cosmogenic Design or Nonlinear Architecture or the Architecture of Emergence are Eisenman, Gehry, occasionally Koolhaas and the Organic-Tech architects. Certain buildings by Daniel Libeskind and Kisho Kurokawa fall into this tradition but were unfinished at the time of writing and so not discussed here. Other examples of Nonlinear Architecture in progress are Nicholas Grimshaw's Stock Exchange, Berlin and Kisho Kurokawa's Fukui City Art Museum.

     Works that might have been illustrated in a longer discussion include Kijo Rokkaku's Budokan, Tokyo, 1990–93; Kathryn Gustafson's gardens in France; Günther Domenig's Stone House, Austria, 1985–95, and perhaps his Z-Bank; Nigel Coates' Penrose Institute, Tokyo, 1995; Philip Johnson's Monsta House, New Canaan, 1996; the roof structures of Japanese architects Coelacanth, Shoei Yoh, Hitoshi Abe and the sculptural projects of M Takasaki. In addition, there are the folded plate works of engineers Ted Happold and the Frei Otto group and the nonlinear structures of Cecil Balmond; the wooden structures of Herb Greene, Imre Makovecz and Bart Prince, and some of Reima Pietilä's work, especially the early Dipoli Centre and Kiillemoreeni.

     Important theorists and designers who are developing the paradigm include Jeff Kipnis, Greg Lynn, Bahram Shirdel and Ben van Berkel. A very early work to explore the form language of folding and curves is Frederick Kiesler's Endless House, 1959, developed from his Endless Theatre of 1926.

2   Peter Eisenman quoted in Joseph Giovannini. 'Campus Complexity', *Architecture*, AIA Journal (Washington), August 1996, pp 114–25.

3   Sanford Kwinter, 'The Genius of Matter: Eisenman's Cincinnati Project', in *Re:working Eisenman*, Academy Editions (London), 1993, pp 90–7.

4   Zvi Hecker, quoted in pamphlet *Heinz-Galinski-Schule*, Berlin, Aedes Galerie und Architekturforum, January 1993, p 14.

5   Howard Raggatt and ARM, 'New Patronage', from pamphlet *RMIT Storey Hall, Faculty of Environmental Design*, RMIT (Melbourne), 1996, pp 8–9.

6   Luis Fernandez-Galiano, 'Lo Informe', *Arquitectura Viva 50*, September–October 1996.

Charles Jencks, 'Nonlinear Architecture: New Science = New Architecture', Charles Jencks (guest-editor), *New Science = New Architecture*, *AD* Profile 129, *AD* 67 September–October 1997, pp 6–9. © 2012 John Wiley & Sons Ltd.

Charles Jencks, 'Landform Architecture: Emergent in the Nineties', Charles Jencks (guest-editor), *New Science = New Architecture*, *AD* Profile 129, *AD* 67 September–October 1997, pp 15–31; adapted from the last chapter of Jencks, *The Architecture of the Jumping Universe: A Polemic: How Complexity Science is Changing Architecture and Culture*, second revised edition, Academy (London), 1997. © 2012 John Wiley & Sons Ltd.

Hypersurfaces (1998)

Lars Spuybroek and Kas Oosterhuis

The twin Fresh Water and Salt Water Pavilions, built by the Dutch office NOX for the water theme park of Neeltje Jans, Holland, from 1994 to 1997, were presented, respectively, by Lars Spuybroek and Kas Oosterhuis in *AD* Profile 133, *Hypersurface Architecture*. The two buildings quickly rose to digital stardom in the late 1990s, and they exemplified many of the central topics of the first wave of digital design theory: complex curvilinear shapes, sinuous and elongated lines of movement in space, interactive and immersive environments augmented by digital multi-media technologies.

Spuybroek's essay turns to Marcos Novak's pioneering theory of 'liquid architecture' (from Michael Benedikt's *Cyberspace: First Steps*, 1993) to highlight the fusion of tectonic virtuosity and media technologies embedded in the building, where visual, acoustic and atmospheric devices react, driven by electronic sensors, to the movement of bodies inside the building but also to external environmental and meteorological data. The visitor, 'a body without distinction between feet and eyes', is exposed to waves of unusual sensations which affect all senses, including the sense of movement (or proprioception), and induce an impression of imbalance, dizziness and vertigo.

In an almost coeval essay, also published in *AD*, and which in turn points to the work of Spuybroek, Brian Massumi describes the digital sensorium as a heightened state of perceptual experience, similar to that invoked by architectural phenomenologists but multiplied by the power of digital tools, to achieve almost hallucinatory bodily experiences (Brian Massumi, 'Strange Horizon: Buildings, Biograms and the Body Topologic', *Hypersurface Architecture II*, *AD* Profile 141, *AD* 69, September–October 1999, pp 12–19; not republished here). Alongside this ultra-sensorial registry of affects, Spuybroek's and Oosterhuis's essays also comment on the digital and analogue geometries of splines, and offer an early description of parametric design as a tool aimed at the informational integration of design and construction, anticipating the design methodologies of today's (2012) Building Information Modelling.

LARS SPUYBROEK **Motor Geometry** *AD* May–June 1998

'There's this *thing*, this ghost-foot,' said one of Oliver Sacks' patients. 'Sometimes it hurts like hell. This is worst at night, or with the prosthesis off, or when I'm not doing anything. It goes away when I strap the prosthesis on and walk. I still feel the leg then, vividly, but it's a *good* phantom, different – it animates the prosthesis, and allows me to walk.'[1]

What is it that animates a mere mechanical extension? How is it that the body is so good at incorporating this lifeless component into its motor system that it recovers its former fluency and grace? The body does not care if the leg is made of flesh or of wood, as long as it fits; that is to say, it fits into the unconscious body model created by the different possible movements. Proprioception, the neurologists term it: the body's power of unconscious self-perception. Our legs are a 'comfortable fit' by their very nature, but only because the leg coincides exactly with the ghostly image invoked by the automatism of walking.

Once a leg is frozen immobility, however, it very soon no longer 'fits'. Sacks reports one such instance: 'When, after a few weeks, the leg was freed from its prison of plaster, it had lost the power to make all kinds of movements that were formerly automatic and which now had to be learned all over again. She felt that her comprehension of these movements had gone. [...] If you stop making complex movements, if you don't practise them internally, they will be forgotten within a few weeks and become impossible.'[2] With practice and training, the movements of the prosthesis can become second nature, regardless of whether it is of flesh, of wood or – a little more complex – of metal, as in the case of a car. That is the secret of the animation principle: the body's inner phantom has an irrepressible tendency to expand, to integrate every sufficiently responsive prosthesis into its motor system, its repertoire of movements, and make it run smoothly. That is why a car is not an instrument or piece of equipment that you simply sit in, but something you merge with. Anyone who drives a lot will recognise the dreamlike sensation of gliding along the motorway or through traffic, barely conscious of one's actions. This does not mean that our cars turn us into mechanical Frankensteins but that the human body is capable of inspiriting the car and making its bodywork become the skin of the driver; this must be true, otherwise we would bump into everything. If we did not merge with the car, if we did not change our body into something 4 x 1.5 metres (13 x 5 feet), it would not be possible to park the car, take a curve, or overtake others. Movements can only be fluent if the skin extends as far as possible over the prosthesis and into the surrounding space, so that every action takes place from within the body, which no longer does things consciously but relies totally on 'feeling'.

When this haptic sense of extension is taken seriously it means that everything starts inside the body, and from there on it just never stops. The body has no outer reference to direct its actions to, neither a horizon to relate to, nor any depth of vision to create a space for itself. It relates only to itself. There is no outside; there is no world in which my actions take place, the body forms itself by action, constantly organising and reorganising itself motorically and cognitively to keep 'in form'. According to Maturana and Varela: 'there is no structured information on the outside, it becomes information only by forming itself through my body, by transforming my body, which is called action ...'[3]

'Hey, we are lost!' Michael said to his guide. The guide gave him a withering glance and answered: 'We are not lost, the camp is lost!' In a flash Michael realized a very important aspect of what separated his vision of the world from that of his guide: for Michael, space was fixed, in which a free agent moved around like an actor on a stage, a vast space in which you could lose your way. The guide however saw space as something within, rather than outside the body, a fluid and changing medium in which one could never lose one's way when the only fixed point in the universe consisted of himself, and although he might be putting one foot in front of the other he never actually moved.[4]

This, of course, is the nomad's view of the world; the view of somebody on the move, because only by the prosthetic act of walking does the whole space become one's own skin. The tent nomads carry with them is part of that walking; it never interrupts space, as a house does. So every prosthesis is in the nature of a vehicle, something that adds movement to the body, that adds a new repertoire of action. Of course, the car changes the skin into an interface, able to change the exterior into the interior of the body itself. The openness of the world would make no sense if it were not absorbed by my body-car. The body simply creates a haptic field completely centred upon itself, in which every outer event becomes related to this bodily network of virtual movements, becoming actualised in form and action.

Where there is close vision, space is not visual, or rather the eye itself has a haptic, non-optical function: no line separates earth from sky, which are of the same substance, there is neither horizon nor background, nor perspective nor limit nor outline of form nor centre; there is no intermediary distance, or all distance is intermediary.[5]

In Tamás Waliczky's short film *The Garden* (1992), made with video manipulation and computer animation, we see a little girl running around a garden, extending her hands towards a dragonfly, sitting down under a big tree, climbing up the ladder of a slide, and then sliding down. We see all this and at the same time nothing like it. In fact, during the whole movie the little girl does not move at all, or rather, she moves her hands and feet, but her head never leaves the centre of the screen. We see the tree folding under her legs, we see the rungs of the ladder shrink and bulge under her feet, we see the slide deform under her body. Nothing moves, but everything changes shape. As the girl reaches her hand out to the dragonfly, we see the insect grow disproportionately large then shrink and disappear the moment she shifts her attention.

The girl does not move around in a perspective world where things are between the eye and the horizon; rather, through her actions she is in perfect balance and stays fixed on the vertical axis: she has become the vertiginous horizon of things, the vanishing point of the world. Things become part of her body by topological deformation, not by perspective distortion. She has become the gravitational centre of a field, or better, a sphere of action – a motor field – her own planet ... This is not perception but proprioception. Everything immediately becomes networked within the body, where the seen is the touched and the felt, where no distinction can be made between the near and the far, between the hand of manipulation and the sphere of the global.

An eye acts as if it were a hand; not as a receptive but as an active organ, and what is at hand is always nearby and close, without any sense of depth or perspective, and without background or horizon. So every action becomes prosthetic because it extends the feeling reach of the skin, and, vice versa, every prosthesis, and I mean every technological device, becomes an action, a vector-object, a twirl in the environmental geometry. Every change of a muscle tone in the motor system has its topological effect, because outside and body are networked into one object with its own particular coherence, where seeing and walking and acting are interconnected in one (proprioceptive) feeling skin, without top or bottom but with an all around orientation; without the orthogonality of the vertical and gravitational axis of the body's posture in relation to frontal and horizontal perspective, but a three-dimensionality where images and actions relate to one and the same geometry, without any X, or without any Y, or without any Z.[6]

FreshH$_2$O eXPO, Zeeland, The Netherlands, 1994–97
Liquid architecture is not the mimesis of natural fluids in architecture.[7] First and foremost it is a liquidising of everything that has traditionally been crystalline and solid in architecture. It is the contamination of media. The liquid in architecture has earlier been associated with the easing back of architecture for human needs, of real time fulfilment. This soft and smart technology of desire can only end up with the body as a residue, where its first steps in cyberspace will probably be its last steps ever. But the desire for technology seems far greater and a far more destabilising force, since our need for the accidental exceeds our need for comfort.

FreshH$_2$O eXPO (as our design office NOX named the project), generally known as the Fresh Water Pavilion, has been seized by the concept of the liquid. Not only its shape and use of materials but the interior environment tries to effect a prototypical merging of hardware, software and wetware. The design of this interactive installation was based on the metastable aggregation of architecture and information. The form is shaped by the fluid deformation of 14 ellipses spaced out over a length of more than 65 metres (213 feet).

Imagine the curves connecting all the ellipses being torn apart, bent and twisted again by outside forces – the wind, dunes, ground water, the Well – while internal forces try to maintain the ellipses; that is, attempt to stay smooth. The basis of the geometry is the vector-based changing of splines linking the ellipses. In this way, line and force become connected. The spline with its control points and tangential handles in 3-D modelling software derives from naval architecture where a curve was created by a wooden spline bent by the positioning of several weights at the 'control points'. Line is not separated from point, but every vertex is the basis of a vector. If one changes the position or direction of the vector, the others change in accordance with their mutual dependency. In this case, the line becomes an action, and not the trace of an action. H$_2$O eXPO is a bundle, a braid of splines. It derives its coherence from movement. In its soft network no distinction is made between form and deformation.

From the beginning, we wondered if we could design something that was completely in line with the law governing wheelchair accessibility (eg, the steepness of ramps) while at the same time devise a prosthetic geometry, a geometry of wheels, a geometry of speed and imbalance? Not one part of the building is horizontal, no one slope stays within the same

gradient. Conceptually, the building has not so much been 'placed on' the ground as 'dug out' of the ground. The essential instability is achieved through the concept of the ground as being 'all around'. The floor becomes hyperdimensional and tries to become a volume.

When dealing with a haptic, three-dimensional body – a body without the distinction between feet and eyes – the difference between floor and ceiling becomes irrelevant. With this kind of topological perception action is no longer ground-based, with your eyes transported blindly. Buildings are generally guided by this dichotomy of transport and vision, where the programmatic is on the floor and the formal is in the elevation. In this building, the information on the floor is blended with the deformation of the volume, to paraphrase Jeffrey Kipnis.

In H$_2$O eXPO there is no horizon, no window looking out. There is no horizontality, no floor underlining the basis of perspective. This is, of course, the moment of dizziness, because walking and falling become confused; or, as the manual for 3D Studio MAX observes in the chapter on animation: walking and running are special cases of falling … This imbalance is the very basis of this building, and also the basis of every action, because not one position is without a vector. This building is not only for wheelchairs and skateboards, it is also for the wrong foot, the leg one happens to stand on … That is why, instead of a window, there is a well. The Well is another kind of horizon, more like a window to the centre of the earth: a hidden horizon, not horizontal, but vertical, on the axis of vertigo, of falling.

Where, then, is the point of action. Where is the source of the Well? Here, just like a surfer, the body is placed on a vector and obliged to react to that outer force, although it can change its direction or goal any time. The architecture charges the body because its geometry is such that points become vectors. The source of the action in architecture that has become transported and moved – its geometry has become a prosthetic vehicle by contamination – is exactly in-between body and environment. This is not subject versus object, but an interactive blend. Part of the action is in the object and when this is animated, the body is too.

The interactivity is not only in the geometry: the action moves through the material – not a form with a certain speed or on the move, but action in the form.[8] The design does not distinguish architecture and information as separate entities, nor as separate disciplines. The project is not restricted to materials such as concrete and steel, which were considered to be liquid, but utilises cloth and rubber, ice and mist, fluid water (taking over the action and wetting not only the building, but also the visitor), in addition to electronic media, interactive sound, light and projections. The material is not separated from the so-called immaterial. There is only substance and action.

The continuous surface of the interior is covered with different sensing devices. Imagine walking or running up the central slope towards a wire-frame projection on the

NOX/Lars Spuybroek, FreshH$_2$O eXPO (Fresh Water Pavilion), Neeltje Jans, The Netherlands, 1994–97, exterior views. All images © Lars Spuybroek.

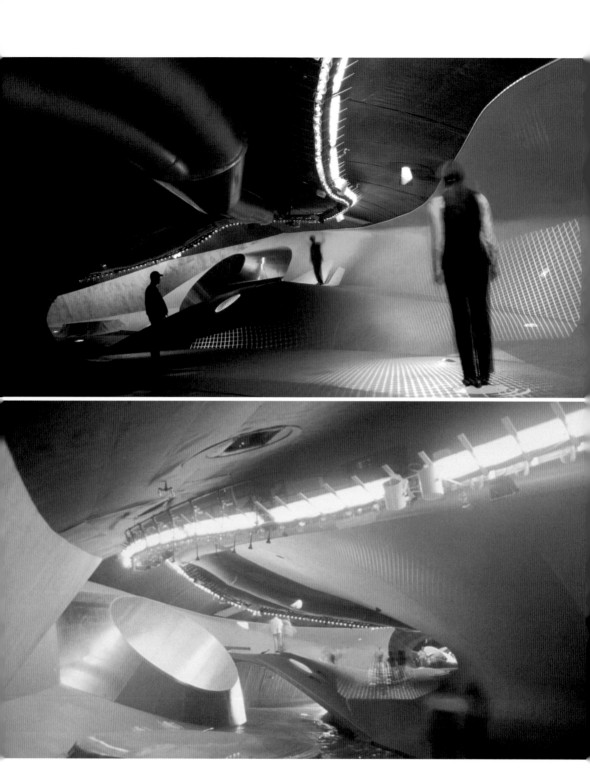

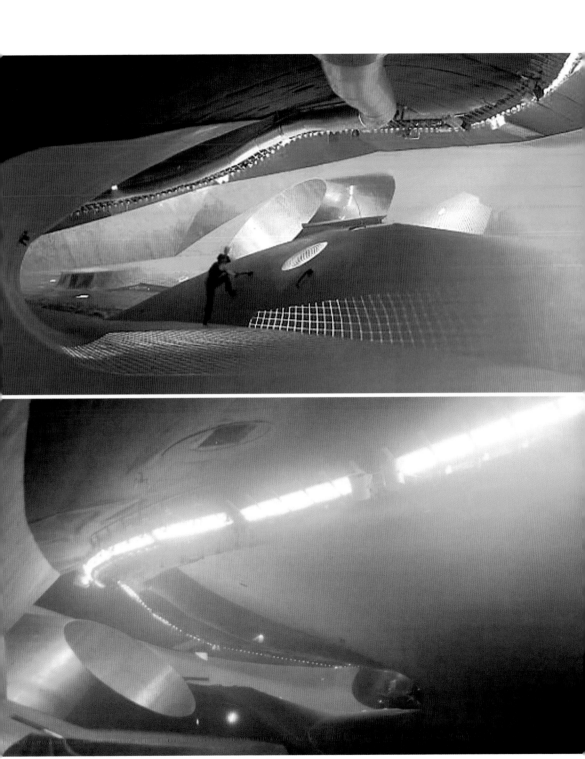

NOX/Lars Spuybroek, FreshH$_2$O eXPO (Fresh Water Pavilion), interior views. All images © Lars Spuybroek.

floor. In the course of this you activate a series of light sensors and step right into the projection, where you are covered in a grid of light. The waves begin to run through the mesh. Now you start to run with the waves, activating more sensors and creating more waves … The vertigo of the motor system is inextricably linked to sensory hallucination.

At the same time, the pulse of light going through the sp(L)ine – a line of numerous blue lamps – is speeded up by the crowd activating the light sensors. When you dare to step on a touch sensor, ripples suddenly shoot out from your feet: circular decaying waves in the wire-frame projection. Somebody else jumps on to the second sensor, a few metres away from you. Ripples then shoot out from their feet too, interfering with your ripples halfway. As you both begin to jump up and down you are pushing away the sound and activating the light running along the sp(L)ine: suddenly a high level of blue light splits in two and slowly fades away. Further on, a sphere is projected in wire-frame on a steep slope between handles that are gently operated by four people. The action causes the sphere to deform in as many directions, while at the same time 'pulls the sound' from the Well. With their hardest pulling action, the light on the sp(L)ine is frozen in its last position.

Why still speak of the real and the virtual, the material and the immaterial? Here, these categories are not in opposition or in some metaphysical disagreement, but more in an electroliquid aggregation, enforcing each other, as in a two-part adhesive; constantly exposing its metastability to induce animation. Where is the sun in all this? Excluded and reflected by the outer skin of stainless steel, it is left behind in a museum.[9] The building is lit from the inside out, by the endogenous sun of the computer. This must be why the light is so blue: making hundreds of thousands of real-time calculations, shining on everybody, and rendering the action; the motor systems of the shadowless, spectral bodies coinciding exactly with the reality engine of the computers.

Notes

1   Oliver Sacks, *The Man Who Mistook His Wife for a Hat*, Picador (New York), 1986, p 66.
2   Oliver Sacks, *A Leg to Stand On*, Picador (New York), 1991, Afterword, note 2.
3   H Maturana and F Varela, *The Tree of Knowledge*, Shambhala Publications (Boston), 1984, chapter 7.
4   Derrick de Kerckhove, *The Skin of Culture*, Somerville House Publishing (Toronto), 1995, p 29.
5   Gilles Deleuze and Félix Guattari, *A Thousand Plateaus*, Athlone Press (London), 1988, p 492.
6   Maurice Nio and Lars Spuybroek, 'X and Y and Z – A Manual', *ARCHIS* 11, 1995.
7   Marcos Novak, 'Liquid Architecture', in Michael Benedikt (ed), *Cyberspace, First Steps*, MIT Press (Cambridge, MA), 1993, p 225.
8   Maurice Nio and Lars Spuybroek, 'De Strategie van de Vorm', *De Architect*, 57, November 1994.
9   Paul Virilio, 'The Museum of the Sun', *TechnoMorphica*, V2_Organisation (Rotterdam), 1997, also *The Art of the Motor*, University of Minnesota (Minneapolis), 1995; *The Function of the Oblique*, AA Publications (London), 1996 and *ARCH+* 124/125, p 46.

Lars Spuybroek, 'Motor Geometry', *Hypersurface Architecture*, Stephen Perrella (guest-editor), *AD* Profile 133, *AD* 68 May–June 1998, pp 49–55. Other versions: *ARCH+* 138, October 1997, pp 67–75 (as 'Motorische Geometrie'); Joke Brouwer and Carla Hoekendijk (eds), *TechnoMorphica*, V2_Publishing (Rotterdam) 1997, pp 143–66; *2A+P 0* (as 'Geometria Motoria'), 1997, pp 58–63; *SPACE* 2, 1999, pp 110–14; Lars Spuybroek, *The Architecture of Continuity*, V2_Publishing (Rotterdam), 2008, pp 32–45.

KAS OOSTERHUIS Salt Water Live: Behaviour of the Salt Water Pavilion *AD* May–June 1998

Real Water

The Salt Water Pavilion is entered under a giant wave about 6 metres (20 feet) long which floods the lower floor of the pavilion: the WetLab. As you flow with the water down to the WetLab you enter an underwater world. Water drips from the walls and flows over the floor; as the wave fills the WetLab you experience the tidal movements of the sea. You are pushed back by the rising water level and have to wait for low tide before you can cross over to the other side. In the middle of the floor the water is drawn away. The changing colours of the dimmed lights reflect on the wet surfaces of the floor, walls and ceiling, creating an immersive underwater experience.

In this wet atmosphere the glowing Hydra is like giant seaweed. Sound travels through the Hydra, which is constantly changing colour. The sound is like a foreign language: you can follow the verbal flow but it remains incomprehensible. The Hydra is a continuous object: its multiple lines travel through the entire pavilion following the visitor; sometimes as construction, sometimes as interface but always transmitting information by ways of light and sound. Within the Hydra there are multi-coloured fibre-optic cables and, every 2 metres (6.5 feet), an active speaker system. All fibres and speakers are controlled by a central computer and react to visitors, changing weather conditions or pre-programmed algorithms.

Real Worlds

After climbing out of the WetLab you approach a panoramic view of the surrounding landscape. At first, only a strip of sky is seen outside, then the horizon of the flat, Dutch delta landscape. Finally, you look down on and hover over the Oosterschelde sea. The panoramic window is the only place inside the pavilion which offers a view of the surroundings. The view is controlled by the airbag: an inflatable object that fits exactly in the opening of the window. When inflated it fills the entire space, closing the view. The closing and opening of the airbag is also controlled by the central computer – part of the overall programme of the pavilion.

Virtual Water

After surveying the landscape you turn and walk on to the wave-floor and into the Sensorium. The wave-floor is the gigantic torsion-volume that divides the entire building body into two parts: the WetLab and the Sensorium.

In the Sensorium you are surrounded by all kinds of virtual representations of water. The five curved lines that stretch from one pole to the other correspond with the outer lines of the building body. Multi-coloured fibre-optic cable in these lines illuminate the Sensorium from behind the polycarbonate skin

In both poles there is a set of red lights that is controlled by an interface in the Hydra. Pressing the interface causes the poles to be activated – to glow in bright red colours. The colour and dimming of the fibres is controlled by a series of sensorial parameters. The colour sequence is generated from bitmaps of all kinds of weather types taken from

Kas Oosterhuis/ONL, Salt Water Pavilion, Neeltje
Jans, The Netherlands, 1994–97, interior view:
environment of the Sensorium. © ONL bv.

the Internet. The dimming of the fibres is controlled by the biorhythm of the building, which changes according to an algorithm that has the weather conditions and water level outside the building as its input.

In addition to the colour-scape there is a sound-scape in the Sensorium. Behind the polycarbonate skin there is an array of speakers which makes it possible for the sound to move dynamically through the space of the Sensorium.

The same interface that controls the lights in the polar regions allows the sound to be influenced. Sound samples can be added to the sound-scape by pressing the interface or pushing the sound towards a certain region in the Sensorium.

Virtual Worlds

On both the surface of the wave-floor and the polycarbonate skin of the Sensorium can be seen immersive projections of a series of virtual worlds. These all depict different perceptions of water or fluidity.

They are generated by two SGI O2 computers and their input comes from an interface that is integrated in the Hydra. With six high-resolution data projectors the worlds are projected on to the surface of the Sensorium. The six worlds are as follows: 1. *Ice* – the navigator moves through slowly pulsating ice masses; 2. *H₂O* – swarms of H_2O molecules flow through space. The navigator can travel with the swarm and try to catch a molecule; 3. *Life* – multiple intelligent creatures float in virtual space. The navigator attracts some of them while others are very shy; 4. *Blob* – a fluid mass is constantly deforming while the navigator floats around or through it; 5. *Flow* – the navigator is captured in a flow; 6. *Morph* – the navigator floats between two morphing sky-scapes. Due to the extreme wide-angle view, the clouds rush by.

With these virtual worlds the building is extended into virtual space. The physical space continues seamless in virtual space. The navigator determines its own path and by doing so contributes to the sound- and colour-scape of the Sensorium.

The Making: Parametric Design

To construct a design like the Salt Water Pavilion we had to develop a method that would maintain both absolute control and absolute flexibility during the construction period. We developed the concept of parametric design. Every inch of the building is different because of its fluid geometry. With this particular design method we describe the fluidly varying lines of the building volume in terms of parameters.

Kas Oosterhuis/ONL, Salt Water Pavilion,
interior views. All images © ONL bv.

Kas Oosterhuis/ONL, Salt Water Pavilion, exterior views. All images © ONL bv.

To stay in control both economically and aesthetically, we constructed a three-dimensional database that was linked to the three-dimensional model. From this database was generated the data for every specific participant in the building process. The builder received only a few principal details together with various tables concerning the parametric values. This data was used sometimes directly as input for CNC machines and at other times used on the building site.

Parametric design enabled us to stay in control of the building concept that we developed for the Salt Water Pavilion. Instead of fixing the building in two-dimensional drawings it was able to remain liquid within its three-dimensional database

Kas Oosterhuis, 'Salt Water Live, Behaviour of the Salt Water Pavilion',
Stephen Perrella (guest-editor), *Hypersurface Architecture*, *AD* Profile 133,
AD 68, May–June 1998, pp 56–61. © 2012 John Wiley & Sons Ltd.

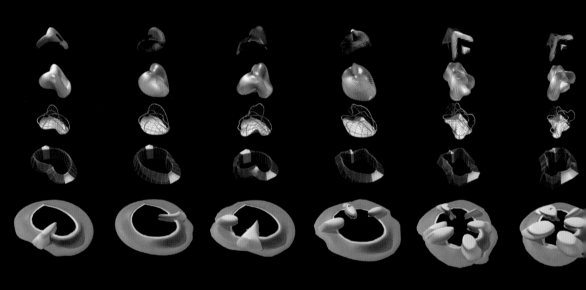

Embryologic Houses© (2000)

Greg Lynn

Greg Lynn's Embryologic Houses© epitomise the spirit and achievements of digital mass-customisation and computational morphogenetics at the turn of the millennium, on the eve of the dotcom crash which would dampen the technological optimism of the 1990s. Almost coeval to the author's celebrated Coffee and Tea Piazza, a non-standard series of 99 teapots for the Italian silverware manufacturer Alessi, the Embryologic Houses© project explores the logic of digitally designed and produced variations at the scale of building, as each of the Embryologic Houses© is a two-floor residential unit set in a landscaped environment, with a floor space ranging between 167 and 300 square metres (1,800 and 3,200 square feet); the series itself is parametrically determined and open-ended.

Given the size limits of digital production, which are set by the dimensions of what can be fabricated in a single piece, larger objects, such as houses, must be built by the assembly of smaller pieces, individually fabricated using non-standard technologies (CNC milling, stereolithography, etc) then assembled on site. To this end, the project envisages a system of nine steel frames and 72 aluminium struts, meant to support up to 2,048 digitally fabricated panels, each endlessly variable within parametric limits; using technologies borrowed from the automobile, naval and aeronautic industries, a change in every individual component can be 'transmitted throughout every other element in the system'. But the implementation of this apparently banal technical requirement would soon appear as a major impediment to digitally based construction: the 'scalability' of the blob, ie, the transfer of non-standard technologies from the small scale of fabrication (a teapot) to the large scale of construction (a building) became a major design issue early in the 21st century.

Greg Lynn FORM, Embryologic
Houses©, 2000. Exploded axonometric
view of six House system components.
© Greg Lynn FORM.

Embryologic Houses© *AD* May–June 2000

The Embryologic Houses© can be described as a strategy for the invention of domestic space that engages contemporary issues of brand identity and variation, customisation and continuity, flexible manufacturing and assembly and, most importantly, an unapologetic investment in the contemporary beauty and voluptuous aesthetics of undulating surfaces rendered vividly in iridescent and opalescent colours. The Embryologic Houses© employ a rigorous system of geometrical limits that liberate models of endless variations. This provides a generic sensibility common to all Embryologic Houses©, but no two buildings are ever identical. The technique engages the need for any globally marketed product to have brand identity and variation within the same graphic and spatial system, allowing both the possibility for recognition and novelty. In addition to design innovation and experimentation, many of the variations in the Embryologic Houses© come from an adaptation to contingencies of lifestyle, site, climate, construction methods, materials, spatial effects, functional needs and special aesthetic effects. For the prototyping stage, six houses were developed, exhibiting a unique range of domestic, spatial, functional, aesthetic and lifestyle constraints.

There are no ideal or original Embryologic Houses©: every one is perfect in its mutations. The formal perfection does not lie in the unspecified, banal and generic primitive but in a combination of the unique, intricate variations of each instance and the continuous similarity of its relatives. The variations in specific house designs are sponsored by the subsistence of a generic envelope of potential shape, alignment, adjacency and size between a fixed collection of elements. This marks a shift from a modernist, mechanical technique to a more vital, evolving, biological model of embryological design and construction.

Traditionally, modern architecture, and especially domestic space, has been conceived as an assembly of independent parts, or a kit. The advent of industrialised factory-line fabrication and the marketing, distribution and assembly of these components conspired to support the generic kit-of-parts house. Likewise, the atmosphere of a limited advertising and media culture engendered a broad interest in simple generic structures of identity. The banal modernist notion of generic housing involved the invention of a mass-produced minimum structure to which customisations, additions, modifications and alterations could be performed by the addition of components. This kit-of-parts identity was an appropriate technique for this cultural and industrial moment. With the progressive saturation of our imaginations by an advanced advertising media culture – which becomes more and more creative, artistic and cunning in its techniques of creating desire for formal variation and uniqueness while maintaining brand identification – a more advanced generic identity is not only possible, but necessary for contemporary domestic space.

---

top: Greg Lynn FORM, Embryologic Houses©.
Matrix of structural frames.

bottom: Greg Lynn FORM, Embryologic
Houses©. Glass Base matrix plan and elevation.
All images © Greg Lynn FORM.

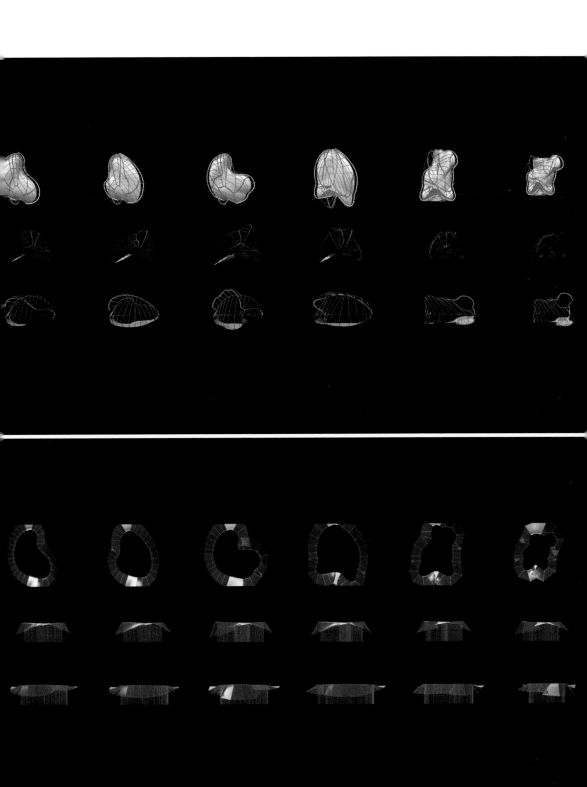

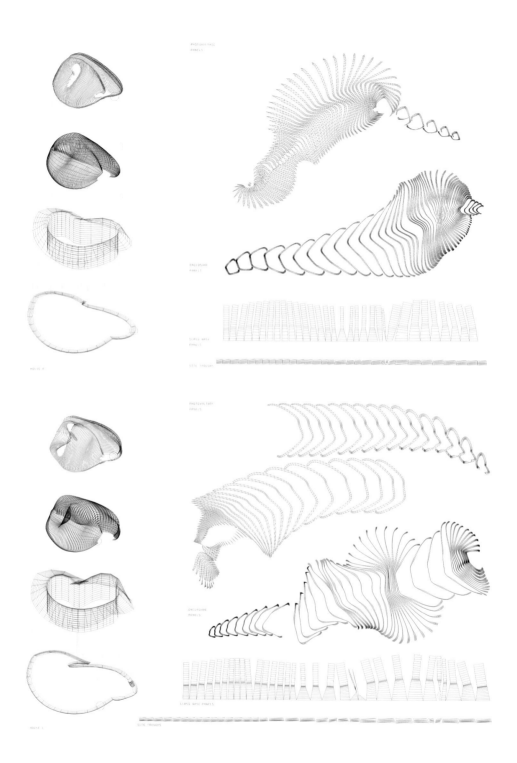

The domestic envelope of every Embryologic Houses© [sic] is composed of 2,048 panels, nine steel frames and 72 aluminium struts, networked together to form a monocoque shell. Using design techniques of flexible manufacturing borrowed from the automotive, naval and aeronautical design industries, every house in the line is of a unique shape and size while conforming to a fixed number of components and fabrication operations. The form and space of the houses are modified within the predefined limits of the components. In addition, a change in any individual panel or strut is transmitted throughout every other element in the whole. A set of controlling points is organised across this surface so that groups of these generic panels can bud into more specific forms or 'nodules'. In every instance, there is always a constant number of panels with a consistent relationship to their neighbours. In this way, no element is ever added or subtracted. In addition, every element is inevitably mutated so that no two panels are ever the same in any single or multiple configuration and no area of the interior is ever identical to any area on the surface. Those panels, with their limits and tolerances of mutation, have been linked to fabrication techniques involving computer-controlled robotic processes. These include ball-hammered aluminium, high-pressure water-jet cutting, stereolithography resin prototyping through computer-controlled lasers, and three-axis CNC milling of wood-composite board.

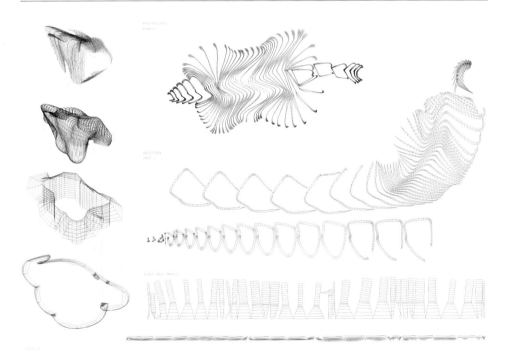

opposite and above: Greg Lynn FORM, Embryologic Houses©. The form and space of the houses is modified within the predefined limits of the components. In addition, a change in any individual panel or strut is transmitted throughout every other element in the whole. Here the structural elements are shown flattened. All images © Greg Lynn FORM.

Greg Lynn FORM, Embryologic Houses©. Prototype model view. © Greg Lynn FORM.

Embryologic Houses© are designed as a flexible, curvilinear surface rather than as a fixed set at rigid points. Each encloses two floors. The upper floor of 55 to 110 square metres (600 to 1,200 square feet) is a gently sloped dish with custom-designed furniture, appliances and entertainment equipment. The lower floor is a single level of 110 to 185 square metres (1,200 to 2,000 square feet). The voluptuous fenestration, apertures, openings and orientation to light, air, human and mechanical penetration occur through a technique of curvilinear shreds, louvres and pores that derives from the topology of the surfaces. Rather than being cut into the surface, these apertures are achieved via an alternative strategy of tears, shreds and offsets in their soft geometry. Any dent or concavity of surface provides an opportunity for domestic occupation and the integration of apertures.

The surface envelopes are connected to the ground so that any alteration in the object is transmitted outward into the landscape. For instance, a dent or concavity in the envelope generates a lift or plateau in the ground. In this way, a deformation in the object has a corresponding effect on the field around it, facilitating openings, views and circulation on a potential site.

The landscape is pulled upwards at the two poles of the house, generating a mound garden that rings the house. The houses are adaptable to a full range of sites and climates. The minimum requirement for any site is a 30 metre (100 foot) diameter clear area with less than a 30 degree slope. A sea of mounds planted with alternating strips of decorative grasses surrounds each house. Nestled within these wave mounds, an undulating berm of earth receives the house. The berm slopes from the lower level to the upper level of the house in order to meet the front and back entries. The house appears to be buried in the ground from some orientations, while appearing to float above it from others. Wherever the exterior form of the house is indented, a corresponding garden pod is formed, off which a formal garden flows. These microclimate pods with their corresponding gardens are ringed by a perimeter of drift gardens that feather into the wave landscape of grasses.

Greg Lynn, 'Embryologic Houses', Ali Rahim (guest-editor), *Contemporary Processes in Architecture*, *AD* Profile 145, *AD* 70, May–June 2000, pp 26–35.
© 2012 John Wiley & Sons Ltd.

Versioning (2002)

SHoP/Sharples Holden Pasquarelli

Taking a stand against the 'stylistically driven' excesses of digital design in the years leading up to the 'dotcom crash', in September 2002 the New York office SHoP, guest-editing *AD* Profile 159, *Versioning*, argued for a renewed interest in the actual practices of building, advocating a more hands-on approach to the production process. While a rejection of the formal exuberance of the 1990s was widespread in the new, post-2001 socio-cultural environment, the shift from form to process in design was also due to technical issues: free-form objects were proving difficult and expensive to construct at full scale, warranting SHoP's call for a new 'intelligence of fabrication', based on the search for a 'common language between design and execution'.

The contributing authors, reviewed in the introduction, interpreted 'versioning' in somewhat diverse ways (the architectural definition of the term is to this day unclear), but the editors' essay, illustrating works of their own practice, pertinently illustrates various attempts to 'erode the barriers' between design and construction. The featured buildings often look angular, not curvilinear, and follow simplified geometries; the final recommendation to use digital tools to facilitate the early involvement of and collaboration between participants in the design and construction process anticipates the agenda of Building Information Modelling software, which was in development at the time.

Introduction to *Versioning: Evolutionary Techniques in Architecture* AD September–October 2002

> Everything that's worth understanding about a complex system can be understood in terms of how it processes information.
>
> *Dr Seth Lloyd, Professor of Mechanical Engineering, MIT*

'Versioning' is an operative term meant to describe a recent, significant shift in the way architects and designers are using technology to expand, in time as well as in territory, the potential effects of design on our world. A 'second generation' of digital architects and theorists are emerging who have placed an emphasis on open models of practice where the application of technology promotes technique rather than image. The content within this issue of *AD* is meant to be direct and straightforward, although versioning is an open, gestural idea and the range of contributions should signal the pluralistic nature of the concept. Versioning can be seen as an attitude rather than an ideology. It allows architects to think or practise across multiple disciplines, freely borrowing tactics from film, food, finance, fashion, economics and politics for use in design, or reversing the model and using architectural theory to participate in other problem-solving fields. Versioning is important to architects because it attempts to remove architecture from a stylistically driven cycle of consumption.

The computer has enabled architects to rethink the design process in terms of procedure and outcome in ways that common practice, the construction industry and conventional design methodologies cannot conceive of. This, in turn, has had an equally profound impact on legal practices, insurance liabilities and design/production partnerships, thereby initiating a restructuring of the traditional relations of power, responsibility and accountability in design. Versioning implies the shifting of design away from a system of horizontal integration (designers as simply the generators of representational form) towards a system of vertical integration (designers driving how space is conceived and constructed and what its effects are culturally).

Versioning relies on the use of recombinant geometries that allow external influences to affect a system without losing the precision of numerical control or the ability to translate these geometries using available construction technology. It advocates the use of vector-based information over pixel-based simulation and representation:

representation : modelling :: modelling : versioning

While simulation remains a useful formal estimate of future organisational strategies, versioning of vector-based information allows immediate results to be transformed and refined as the previous tests feed additional data through the framework of intentionality. Both the desired design objectives and methodology thereby become simultaneously accelerated and adaptive.

Traditionally, the term implies the copying of a type or original. Yet, in this context, versioning should not be understood as originating from a singular identifiable model, prototype or master form in which all variations or evolutions can be measured by, or traced to, one specific source. In fact, versioning no longer relies on the necessity of the archetype to be manipulated and changed over time with the end goal of producing a master type for eventual mass production. Instead, versioning can be characterised by a set of conditions organised into a menu or nomenclature capable of being configured to address particular design criteria. The primary source is constructed from a set of detail types comprising a menu, and organised around a collection of specific detailed actions capable of evolving parametrically to produce specific effects or behaviours.

For example, the nomenclature of automobile highways offers a model to help illustrate this point. There is no original source highway or correct proportional system based on the image of road or speed. Most highways are made up of components such as 'loops', 'spurs', 'plains', 'bifurcations' and 'crossovers'. These highway menu-types change their position relative to desired traffic behaviour in order to optimise movement efficiencies across changing terrains. No base prototype exists, nor is there an image-based set of relationships underlying the design. Instead, design decisions are based on an organisational strategy capable of responding to the effects of speed, turning radius, gradients, congestion and the landscape, to create a fluid behaviour of variable movement. The highway can be regenerated continuously to adapt to changing manufacturing techniques, yet maintains its clarity as an object-space-time construction.

The question of what is original or a copy is no longer of any relevance. By not relying on a formal apparatus or protoform, the practice of versioning is capable of responding in a nonlinear manner to multiple influences. By developing an elemental vocabulary of conditions in the planning stages for each project or project type, the practice of architecture becomes less about a search for a specific overriding form and more about a specific formal means of production to address variable conditions.

In the work of Office dA, we can see their use of the brick as a building component to test the notion of aggregation and seriality of construction much in this way. In their Tongxian Arts Centre project, the potential of the exception to the singular element creates possibilities for new resolutions of surface, edge, corner, circulation and tectonics. The geometry of the structure moves past the simulation of folding and pliancy in image and towards a method of design and execution. Ingeborg Rocker places the argument of originality, difference and emerging technologies within the context of the corporate identity machine to question versioning's role in the production of form. She questions the desire, or plausibility, of design's relationship to representation when new models of practice are allowing architecture to become an informed result of differentiated effects. Another key element of versioning is its ability to question time and its relationship to other cultural processes. In his essay, Ed Keller firmly positions recent technological advances in fields as disparate as biotechnology and DJ remixing, and links them to a discussion of 'new forms of time' which emphasise the potential effects versioning can have on the city/machine and the speed at which a self-regulating mechanism for temporal/cultural control emerges. In this way, Keller argues that versioning advances the 'genetic substance' of architectural design.

Versioning also extends to methods of practice where nontraditional use of architectural theory is appropriated by other disciplines. Anna Dyson discusses the advances in the field of industrial ecology, where methods for disassembly and reuse can be built into the design process through techniques of versioning. She continues with a projection of emerging advances in biotechnology that shift the economic paradigm for the development and gestation of materials. Panelite's materials-research work exposes the process of making new building products from a singular technique while allowing for difference at multiple scales. Its products seamlessly integrate both theory and technique to create an aesthetic that is not image based. Similarly, the work of inventor David Levy suggests how design solutions are discovered by using the external actions which will act upon the device while allowing for continuous feedback from both the manufacturing and organisational requirements. The ability to see the device, understand it without using directions and fabricate it quickly, drives a resultant aesthetic that is highly specific yet more inclusive.

If versioning operates at different scales within a design, it should also operate at different scales of practice. Helen Castle's interview with three partners of Buro Happold Consulting Engineers begins to examine how a 700-person design consulting firm uses new technologies and theories of versioning to operate on multiple continents and on projects ranging in size from 185 to 18,500,000 square metres (2,000 to 200 million square feet). At the same time, Vishaan Chakrabarti writes an essay on the political manifestations surrounding the notion of the sole practitioner and the corporate practice in this new climate. How can these new techniques allow smaller firms to take on larger projects, and what types of alliances are the result of these shifts of scale and responsibility? And, if versioning allows small firms to perform large, can the corporate behemoth suddenly act lithe and tactical?

Rick Joy, William Massie and SYSTEMarchitects present some of their recent work, projects in which they are heavily involved in the building of their structures, allowing them to control all aspects of the work. Versioning here is instrumental in allowing the practice of architecture and design to return to a vertical organisational structure similar to the master builder of the Renaissance. Their invention of new forms of digital drawing and manufacturing is closer to Brunelleschi's systems of variable brick models than it is to the image-generating machines of the architects of the 'dot-blob bust'. When building the Duomo in Florence, Brunelleschi modelled multiple brick shapes and sizes using wooden moulds constructed from versioned templates to respond to specific loading conditions when assembled in different combinations. No singular or master brick form is used to address the overall static behaviour throughout the structure. The work of the architects profiled in this issue can be local or international, but the designers use the technology to create a true integration of the process of construction no matter what space/time conditions exist. They are using innovating building materials and construction techniques to expand the possibilities of design and effect, and to keep all aspects of construction under their control. In contrast, when the blob is left in its rendered state it leaves us flat, no matter how sophisticated are the continuous recalculations of the

NURBS geometries. The form may use every data-crunching animation technique to process multiple variables, but the result is too often all image. The texture maps cloaking them are similar to the banal skins of consumption architecture. Without making the intentional connection between the digital geometries on the screen and the execution of a technique to produce that geometry at building scale, the work seems limited.

Can versioning alter the distinction between the 'aesthetic object' and the 'theoretical text' and collapse this distinction where the object and the text are one and the same with the technique of manufacturing? Can the forces that make the object, both in the generation of the broad strokes and specific resolutions, combine with an intelligence of fabrication to become a 'process product'? Here the form, the forces that shape it, and the assemblage of materials in which we execute the ideology are part of the same gesture. This is not a call to replace the human act of design with algorithms, but a critical search for a common language between design and execution. The resulting control of these processes empowers the architect to take on the role of the translator of unforeseen relationships simultaneously in imagined and real space. The techniques and processes are not far off in the future, but available right now. Are you ready?

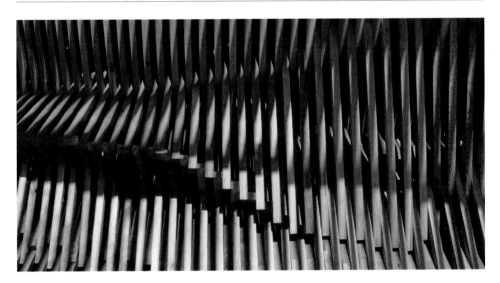

SHoP, Dunescape, New York City, 2000.
Surface translation of SHoP's MoMA/P.S.1
Contemporary Art Center for Warm Up
2000 installation. Here the architecture
of surface, structure and programme
collapse into one. © David Joseph.

Eroding the Barriers *AD* September–October 2002

As technology collapses traditional hierarchies, and promotes the transgression of disciplines, the barriers between architect and builder are being eroded. SHoP's work attempts to explore and improve the effectiveness with which new techniques can be exported to the built realm.

Driven by programme and technique, as opposed to formal or stylistic considerations, Dunescape (an 'urban beach' installation in the courtyard of the P.S.1 Contemporary Art Center), was deployed and configured as a landscape in which surface, structure and programme were collapsed into a singular entity, articulated through a triangulated frame that accommodated programme shifts by varying the position of each frame relative to the next. Changes in surface and loading conditions were met by altering the angle, depth and locus of triangulation within each frame. Rather than the traditional set of descriptive drawings, the construction documents were full-scale colour-coded templates for manufacture and assembly of the frames. The simplicity of the system, comprising only two components (50mm x 50mm (2 x 2 inch) cedar sticks and 75mm (3-inch) wood screws), fostered an accelerated learning curve, and construction was 'fast tracked' with templates and materials for each day's work arriving on site as the installation progressed.

below: SHoP, Rector Street Pedestrian Bridge, connecting Lower Manhattan with Battery Park City and the World Financial Center, New York, 2002, sectional model. Photograph Seong Kwon. © SHoP.

bottom: SHoP, Rector Street Pedestrian Bridge, view looking north on West Street. Photograph Seong Kwon. © SHoP.

As with P.S.1, the Rector Street Pedestrian Bridge (connecting Lower Manhattan with Battery Park City and the World Financial Center, and replacing connections lost on 11 September), had its inception in process, not form. Of paramount concern, in addition to the conceptual importance of the bridge in its site context, were construction sequencing, traffic flow on West Street, respect for the priorities and processes of the various agencies on site and response to community concerns over placement of the bridge and its access points. Initial design activity focused on communicating these issues in a comprehensive and inclusive manner to all the many parties involved.

Schedule was critical, as the crossing was needed to restore function to the area, and use of a prefabricated box-truss system already approved by the New York City Department of Transportation allowed the main structure to be erected immediately once the bridge's location had been agreed upon. The enclosure is supported by steel ribs mounted to the box-trusses, and the animated pattern of the facade is composed of only two panel sizes, with position and spacing varied to optimise conditions of natural light, air circulation, weather protection and view. The apertures were sized to allow views towards Ground Zero, but to discourage sightseeing. The panels were keyed to shop-welded mounting brackets on the ribs, and the drawings included lay-down and sequencing diagrams for all parts, speeding up assembly on the site.

above, left and opposite top: SHoP, carousel for Mitchell Park, Greenport, New York, completed June 2001 (Bolt tooling photographs Karen Ludlam). All images courtesy SHoP.

below. SHoP, carousel for Mitchell Park, carousel house with shade arbours beyond. Photograph Karen Ludlam. Courtesy SHoP.

Working within the arena of public authority, control of the process becomes an exceedingly relevant issue. Mitchell Park, in Greenport, New York, offered SHoP an early opportunity to test and develop its approach, and to challenge notions regarding vitality of design and control of the architect over work in the public realm.

The elevation of the park's carousel house was derived by modelling the Doppler effect of the ride's motion and music, and extrapolating from the model a glazing pattern made economical by limiting the number of glass shapes used in a repeating but non-uniform wave. The carousel house's structure was modelled on a steel and timber flitch-beam system, but rather than the timber bolts normally used in combination with oversized washers for load distribution, SHoP custom-designed and had fabricated stainless-steel sex bolts with oversized heads for an updated interpretation. Working with criteria provided by the project's structural engineers, the bolts were modelled in 3-D and milled directly from digital files.

A camera obscura building, planned for a second phase of construction in Mitchell Park, will expand this degree of control and involvement. Designed and fabricated entirely within a 3-D digital environment, the construction of the camera is communicated as a kit of custom parts accompanied by a set of instructions much like those included with a model aeroplane kit. Primary aluminium and steel components will be laser-cut using digital files directly extracted from the computer model, with crucial information etched into the components for ease of fabrication. Much of the fabrication will take place off site; prefabricated panels will bolt into the concrete foundation and to each other, ensuring the required level of precision for the rest of the camera's structure and elements to attach to.

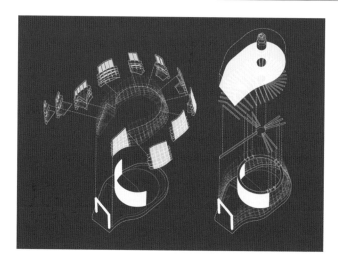

SHoP, camera obscura, assembly sequence. © SHoP.

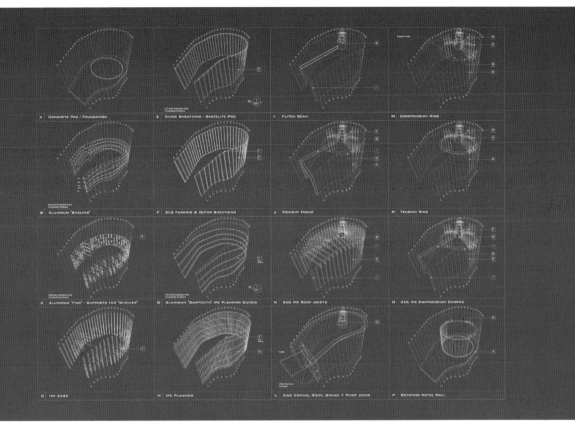

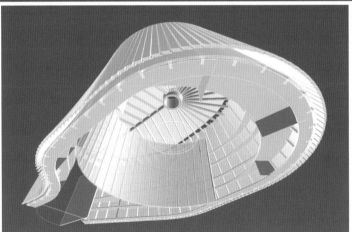

top: SHoP, camera obscura, planned for a second phase of construction in Mitchell Park, Greenport, New York, component index.

above: SHoP, camera obscura, worm's-eye view. All images © SHoP.

below: SHoP, camera obscura, fin schedule and sawtooth schedule.

bottom: SHoP, camera obscura, sectional composite. All images © SHoP.

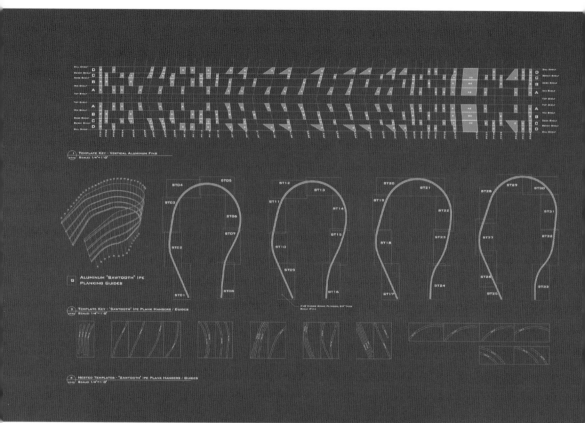

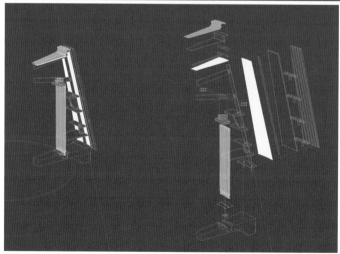

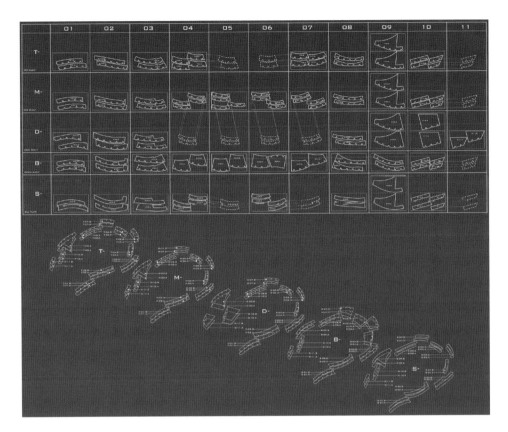

SHoP, camera obscura, shelf schedule. © SHoP.

An early test of the use of computer-aided manufacture in an architectural application was A-Wall, an exhibition trade show booth commissioned by *Architecture* magazine. Conception and execution of the booth utilised a spectrum of techniques from digital design and fabrication of the titanium cladding (laser-cut directly from 3-D files), to 'glue and screw' production of the structural modules. Both normative and nonstandardised approaches to building systems, utilised in this manner, give way to heterogeneous manufacturing and assembly techniques. The optimisation of an assembly-based technique requires revised drawing procedures that better facilitate the fabrication and construction processes.

These techniques are now being translated to construction on a larger scale. A new 25,000 square metre (265,000 square foot) School of the Arts for Columbia University is currently in the planning stages, and will for the first time house all of the school's five divisions under one roof. Expanding the traditional role of the design architect, SHoP has been involved since the project's outset, performing feasibility studies that include programme and zoning analysis, as well as developing a responsive structural system to accommodate the complexity of the horizontal programme on a vertical site.

SHoP, residential condominium project, 366
West 15th Street, New York, rendering. © SHoP.

SHoP, study for the School of the Arts, Columbia University,
New York, 2002, model and structural elevation. © SHoP.

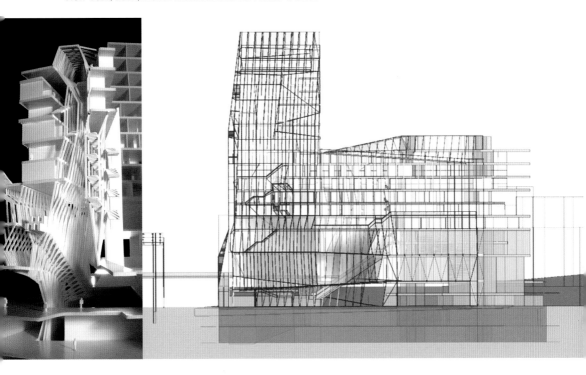

Expanding the role of the architect in another arena, SHoP is currently working in partnership with Jeffrey M Brown Associates to develop a residential condominium project in Manhattan's meatpacking district. The facade of the new addition utilises techniques similar to that employed on previous projects, with a 'kit of parts' panel system modelled in 3-D and laser-cut from digital files. This type of partnership not only validates the architect's position as an integral member of the project team, but also utilises the in-house knowledge base of a developer-contractor and the input of the trades to the design process. Early involvement of all parties allows experimental design to become a collaborative process, one that allows a higher level of design to exist without increasing the cost of construction.

SHoP/Sharples, Holden, Pasquarelli, 'Introduction', SHoP (guest-editors), *Versioning: Evolutionary Techniques in Architecture*, *AD* Profile 159, *AD* 72, September–October 2002, pp 7–9. © 2012 John Wiley & Sons Ltd.

SHoP/Sharples, Holden, Pasquarelli, 'Eroding the Barriers', SHoP (guest-editors), *Versioning: Evolutionary Techniques in Architecture*, *AD* Profile 159, *AD* 72, September–October 2002, pp 90–100. © 2012 John Wiley & Sons Ltd.

Topological Architecture (1998–2003)

Stephen Perrella and Bernard Cache

Bernard Cache and Gilles Deleuze's theory of the Objectile, or generic object – for Deleuze and Cache, the new technical object of the digital age – was a catalyst for the digital turn in architecture, and remains to this day a powerful source of inspiration for digital design. The theory is set forth in Deleuze's book *The Fold: Leibniz and the Baroque* (first published in French in 1988; translated into English in 1993), and Objectile later became the name of Bernard Cache's architectural office. The first essay presented here, by Stephen Perrella, is a précis of end-of-millennium design theory: the Objectile is an open-ended notation which allows for infinite parametric variations; these can be directly fabricated using file-to-factory technologies, thus enabling the serial reproduction of non-identical parts, where ranges of limited variations can be mass-produced at no extra cost. Stephen Perrella introduced Cache's emphasis on fabrication as a tectonic alternative to the image-based environment otherwise prevalent in the 1998 *AD* Profile on 'hypersurfaces', which he guest-edited and from which the essay is excerpted.

Perrella also noted that Cache's model of openness and indeterminacy in digital design notation could theoretically put design (or some design choices) in the hands of the end-user, thus threatening the traditional notion of architectural authorship. Both Perrella and Cache then saw this as an ideological stance against modern capitalist standardisation (whereas the same notion, as well as the marketing strategies of mass-customisation from which it derives, is often seen today as an expression of post-modern consumerism). The coda to Perrella's essay refers to Cache's investigation of textile tectonics and topological geometries, which, following Gottfried Semper and Felix Klein, Cache interpreted as the most ancient and ancestral way of making – as well as the most recent and technologically advanced (see Cache's essay 'Digital Semper', in *Anymore*, C Davidson (ed), Anyone Corporation (New York), 2000, pp 190–97).

Five years later, Cache's essay on Objectile's Philibert De L'Orme Pavilion tackles the thorny issue of scalability in the fabrication of complex geometrical objects (see pages 124–30 and 131–45). In the case of Objectile's Pavilion the assembly of 45 non-standard panels on a frame of 13 structural elements requires the design of 180 connecting pieces which must be redesigned by hand for each variation in the geometry of the panels. As this eliminates the cost benefits of nonstandard production, Cache's solution is to borrow the technology of associative design and manufacturing from engineering and mechanical fabrication. Associative software can automatically assess changes in one component of the system and redesign all connecting pieces and related parts as necessary. Cache concludes that this vindicates his firm's investment in software design, aiming at the development of automation in file-to-factory technologies.

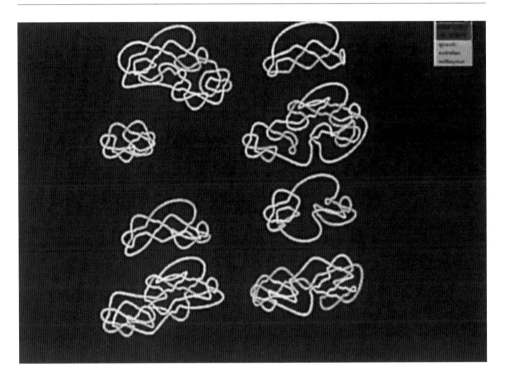

Bernard Cache/Objectile,
algorithmic knots.
© Bernard Cache.

STEPHEN PERRELLA Bernard Cache/Objectile: Topological Architecture and the Ambiguous Sign *AD May–June 1998*

The work of Objectile (Bernard Cache, Patrick Beaucé and Taoufik Hammoudi) utilises design strategies situated within contemporary modes of production as a means to effect critical practices. Cache's development of the implicit relevance that materiality and fabrication have for architecture is significant, derived from the thought of Gilles Deleuze: particularly with respect to topology, the fold and planes of immanence. In *The Fold*, Deleuze refers specifically to Bernard Cache, a theorist in his own right: the closest evidence perhaps of Deleuze's proximity to architecture.[1]

Cache's theories are a rigorous source of what may be called the 'topologising' of architecture: a trajectory that is disseminating within the architectural field, not only as a result of the increasing presence of computer technology but due to the increasing complexity of contemporary life. It is ironic, yet interesting, that Cache's applications and implementations put the issue of authorship in architecture at risk.

Drawing upon a variety of scales and design problems, Cache's theories have reworked the classical tenets of architecture, stemming from Vitruvian theory with its basis in Platonic form. Translating Deleuze's rereading of Leibniz and the Baroque, Cache reworks the fundamental geometry of architecture: substituting the square, circle and triangle, with the frame, vector and inflection, which have tremendous import through their generative dynamics, in contradistinction to the combinatory logic of Platonic forms.

Cache's fundamental argument that all form consists of either convex or concave curvature, stems from his analysis of inflection – what Leibniz calls an 'ambiguous sign'. For Cache, an inflection has the characteristics of a geometric undecidable, which works outwardly from its centre. This is defined as an 'intrinsic singularity'.[2] The inflection works in a generative way, disseminating a geologic of openness and responsiveness to the potentials of an encounter.

Cache translates the fundamental dynamics of curvature, situated between the earth and the sky, describing topological relationships between geography and architecture, inside and landscape: filtered through a complex double frame. This is reflected most clearly in his furniture designs which are predominantly of wood, exploiting the inherent contours of the material.

Much of the work of Bernard Cache and Objectile is achieved through computer milling. Computer programming is just one of the many sites of inquiry of this philosopher, mathematician and businessman, whose theories are also insinuated in information technology. Cache has evaluated three computer-modelling paradigms that affect the discipline of architecture: one of which, he insists, architects have not, as yet, considered. While well-known to architectural practice, the dominant softwares are specifically avoided for being too inflexible.

Bernard Cache/Objectile, artificial landscape (top left); acoustic wood panel (top right); non-standard bistro table (bottom left); decorative wood panel (bottom right). © Bernard Cache.

At the other end of the spectrum is the higher-end, animation software. Although this is easily capable of creating fluid forms based upon animation and radical deformation, it is not geared towards full-scale fabrication. Instead, Cache chooses to rework software which is more familiar to industrial designers, who create precise components for mass production. It is the 'exact-modelling' software environment, Cache argues, that has the greatest potential for architectural variegation. This represents an interesting alternative to much of the content in this volume on hypersurface theory, whereby radical image-forms generated by high-end computers translate algorithmic data into complex configurations, exemplified by the work of Marcos Novak.

The overall objective of hypersurface theory is to allow for Other forces – cultural forces or subtle, sub-dominant forces – to influence, determine and destabilise the pure authority of the author/architect. The exact modelling of Cache's work is an interesting foray into an already dominant mode of production (manufacturing industries), where the generation of materialised form is determined by profit-motivated, consumer-driven corporations. The mainstream corporation is what Cache, in his most Marxist moment, seeks to displace. Therefore Cache's work is, indeed, a strategy that calls into question the dominant powers, but by working within these powers seeks to challenge them, as close to the heart of the tradition as is possible (hence his close reading of Vitruvius).[3] This raises the issue of how other practices interpret the complexities of the contemporary world and how one may work within that complexity to further its chaosmotic potential.[4]

The ability of Cache's middle-range, modified software to produce the necessary tolerance for industrial design production is significant: taking what used to be the parameters of the Industrial Revolution and mass production and reworking the systemic to accommodate infinite variation. This procedure has the potential to reconfigure a determinant that has a considerable impact on our built environment. Even though this places Cache's modus operandi on a middle scale, in terms of architecture (furniture, body, ornament and so forth), it is here that he establishes an important connection between Deleuze and Guattari's theories of indeterminacy and the very forces of capitalism; and here that he locates a critical schema within an inhabitable plane of immanence.

Cache is intent upon forging a direct connection between the multiplicity of consumer desire and the dominant modes of production that drive capitalism. He wants the mode of production to be placed in the hands of the consumer, a tactic that presents a significant challenge to the corporations of sameness that shape cultural identity. His interest here is in liberating the consumer from the repressive forces of consumer culture, seeking instead to celebrate alterability that can become an inherent feature within aggregate production.

Cache wishes to maximise the flexibility and variability available within the mode of production; an ability that goes much further than mere self-determination. If infinite variegation is a fact of production, then identity as such is rendered in a far more complex way, leading us back to Cache's theories of Subjectiles and Objectiles. The scope of these theories is extensive, offering a substantial contribution to a theory of hypersurfaces.[5] His most recent project for a Textile Museum is outlined as follows.

Textile Museum

This project investigates knot and string theory, questioning how a knot can be obtained when the inflexion loops onto itself, or how to escape from organicism when the open surface closes itself to form a solid. The question arises from the structure of the mathematical functions we use when we design 'objectiles' as opposed to 'subjectiles'.

In a Semperian mode, structure is subordinated to cladding. Thus textile technology comes prior to tectonics, ceramics and stereotomy.

The key element of textile is the knot. Our software development of knot generation provides very different results starting with traditional patterns, I.e. Arabic, Celtic, and so forth, and then developing them further with Penrose spatial structures, and then finally becoming the building itself.

Knot models are being used in various human sciences. For Gottfried Semper the knot was much more than just a technical element; it deals with a basic sense of corporeity, hence our detailed images. However, these images also allow us to study architectural detailing, like the lines of intersection between the several interlacing elements. The knot also works on the architectural pattern of the patio, which until now we considered as a horizontal torus. With the use of an interlace the different patios are perceived as overlapping one another.

Such architecture can only be built with the support of good non-standard technologies. The interesting problem of establishing a horizontal floor within this building may be considered.

Finally, this knot architecture plan seems particularly well suited to a museum with different sections. These can become circuits which are bifurcated at the crossings.

Notes

1   Gilles Deleuze, *The Fold: Leibniz and the Baroque*, Tom Conley (trans), University of Minnesota Press (Minneapolis), 1993, p 14.
2   Bernard Cache, *Earth Moves: The Furnishing of Territories*, Michael Speaks (ed), Anne Boyman (trans), MIT Press (Cambridge, MA), 1995, p 34.
3   Bernard Cache presented a lecture at Columbia University during the autumn of 1997, where he unfolded a specific attachment to and interrogation of Vitruvian theory. A transcript of that lecture is to appear in the forthcoming *Columbia Documents of Architecture and Theory*, vol 7.
4   Felix Guattari, *Chaosmosis: An Ethico-Aesthetic Paradigm*, Paul Bains and Julian Pefanis (trans), University of Indiana Press (Bloomington), 1995.
5   Ibid, p 92; in particular, his discussion of half-object, half-subject.

Stephen Perrella, 'Bernard Cache/Objectile, Topological Architecture and the Ambiguous Sign', Stephen Perrella (guest-editor), *Hypersurface Architecture*, *AD* Profile 133, *AD* 68, May–June 1998, pp 66–9; Giuseppa Di Cristina, *AD: Architecture and Science*, Wiley-Academy (Chichester), 2001, pp 128–31. © 2012 John Wiley & Sons Ltd.

Bernard Cache/Objectile, Philibert De L'Orme Pavilion, presented
at Batimat 2001, series of connecting pieces. © Bernard Cache.

BERNARD CACHE Philibert De L'Orme Pavilion: Towards an Associative Architecture AD March–April 2003

Objectile's aim is to develop procedures, both software and hardware, that will make digital architecture a reality at an affordable cost for small architectural practices and the average consumer. After an initial series of experiments at the scale of objects, furniture and sculpture, Objectile developed a series of timber decorative panels that are basic building components. The firm now focuses on small-scale architecture where current state-of-the-art software is just starting to make it possible to contemplate a fully digital architecture.

The Semper Pavilion presented at Archilab (1999) in Orléans, France, was the first piece of digital architecture where everything from design procedures to manufacturing process was generated on the same software platform. Complex interlacings and undulating surfaces were algorithmically generated and then manufactured on a numerical command router right to the very last detail: for example the control of the tool path that creates texture on the surfaces. But such a small piece of architecture required two months' work for the office. Furthermore, were we to change the pavilion design, most of the operations would have to be repeated without significant time-saving.

Hence we have made the move towards fully associative design and manufacture, which for us appears to be the key issue for digital architecture. In an associative architecture, design procedures rely on a limited number of geometrical and numerical parents that can be easily modified and then regenerate the whole design of the building as well as its manufacturing programmes. In a small-scale architecture like the Philibert de L'Orme Pavilion (presented at Batimat 2001, in Paris), associativity means establishing a seamless set of relations between a few control points and the 765 machining programmes needed for manufacture on a numerical command router.

Due to the double-curvature cladding of a nonorthogonal structure, every single piece is different: the 12 structural elements, the 45 curved panels machined on both sides, and the 180 connecting pieces. Further, the need for automatic naming of the pieces became an issue. The following examines what were the state-of-the-art processes at the time of manufacture of this second pavilion, and explains why Objectile continues to focus on software development.

Projective Architectural Skeleton

The general architecture of the Philibert de L'Orme Pavilion is a projective cube, the three sets of ridges of which are arranged to converge in finite space. By moving these three vanishing points, the whole of the pavilion can be reconfigured down to the very last technical detail. In a similar manner to the way Philibert de L'Orme conceived his famous 'trompes' as a general system of two intersecting conical shapes,[1] this pavilion was designed as a homage to the inventor of stereotomy, which would eventually be systematised by another French architect, Girard Desargues.

It is very important to remember that projective geometry has implications much deeper than Brunelleschian representation, and that its fundamental concepts still remain to be integrated within computer-aided design (CAD) systems. As a result, we suggest the next generation of CAD software lies somewhere between 1550 and 1872.

Curvature

Just as a set of parallels is to be considered as a cone, the vertex of which is a vanishing point, so each wall of the pavilion was considered as a plane to be deformed into an ellipsoid tangent to the corresponding plane of the projective cube defined by its two vanishing points and centred on the third vanishing point. Because of the lack of projective geometry in current CAD software, such a procedure still needs to be implemented. When we designed the pavilion we drew an intuitive curve, but now we are close to a mathematical solution based on the principal sections of the ellipsoid. This involves intermediary constructions based on intersecting circles. For example, two circles might not always intersect as a figure in the real plane, but always have two intersection points in complex space. Unfortunately, current CAD software does not enable us to take advantage of Poncelet's Principle of Continuity;[2] otherwise we would easily deform a standard cube with planar faces into a projective cube with curved faces. This is just one example of what we can expect from future projective CAD software.

Bernard Cache/Objectile,
Philibert De L'Orme
Pavilion, front view.
© Bernard Cache.

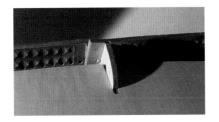

Bernard Cache/
Objectile, Philibert
De L'Orme Pavilion,
connecting piece.
© Bernard Cache.

Panelling

Each curved wall is divided by a 3 x 3 metre (10 x 10 foot) grid into nine panels using our software, which can deal with any type of dividing line. In this pavilion, they were curves resulting from the intersection of the curved surface of the walls with the four structural planes. Given the dividing lines and a series of 23 parameters, such as the width of the joints between panels or the diameter of the ball-nose tool, the abstract surface of the wall with no thickness is converted into the series of nine panels, each filed in a directory with a proper name and automatically oriented to the way it has to be positioned on the machine table.

One strong hypothesis of the Philibert de L'Orme Pavilion was that each wall was referred to the plane given by the corresponding face of the projective cube. This plane was to make things easier by providing a common reference to the machine table, the MDF boards, the assembly of the rough shape and its two counter shapes, the corner supports connecting the nine panels to the structure, and last but not least the orthogonal plane to the vertical tool of a three-axis router.

However, our software applications now enable us to do without this reference plane. Of course everything becomes more complex, but we are now able to automatically determine, for each of the panels, the plane that minimises the initial enclosing block of matter from which we start the machining operation. Not only do we minimise the matter needed, but we simplify all the manual operations required to prepare the rough shape. This is the way we conceive of digital architecture: we concentrate all the complexity in the software and the machining operations in order to make the manual operations fewer and more intuitive. Note that the two options of a common reference plane or a specific plane that minimises the enclosing block correspond to the two traditional techniques of stereotomy: 'la taille par équarissement' and 'la taille par panneaux'.

Interlacings

Another strong De L'Ormian feature of the pavilion is the interlacings carved into the panels on three of the walls and the roof. One need only pay a visit to the church Saint-Etienne du Mont, 100 metres (330 feet) behind the Pantheon in Paris, to be convinced that Philibert de L'Orme actually built there the most Semperian piece of architecture. Knots and interlacings have been a constant leitmotiv of this French Renaissance architect. Furthermore, if we consider the vocabulary of Desargues's Brouillon Project (1638), we can observe continuity between the French order of Philibert de L'Orme – a ringed tree trunk with knots and cut branches – and the basic concepts of the author of the mathematical treatise: trunks, knots, branches and foldings. Everything appears as if one of the most contemporary domains of topology (knots) were coiled into the very origin of projective geometry, anticipating the architectural geometry that would be presented by Felix Klein in his Erlanger Programm (1872).

A general knot theory is still lacking that would evidence the mathematical entity left invariant throughout the various configurations assumed by the same knot submitted to deformations. Nevertheless there exists a palette of techniques to generate knots on the basis of graphs. Objectile's application transforms these mathematical techniques into design tools which, for instance, enable us to vary the thread thickness. We are aware of the fact that interlacing screens introduce an intermediary state between transparency and opacity and create the shallow-depth spaces experimented within much traditional architecture, such as Islamic, and which continue to be examined by contemporary artists such as Brice Marden. If we accept the historians' position that the Modern Movement takes root in Laugier's writings, we could date the birth of modern architecture by a gesture of demolition: the destruction of the rood screen within the whitewashed cathedral of Amiens, a recommendation by none other than Laugier himself. Transparency is an old and essential myth of modern society that has taken new forms only with developments in information technology.

Panel-Machining Programs

Objectile's software applications are written in order to cope with surfaces with any type of curvature and without any process of standardisation, be these surfaces spheric, toric, swept or ruled, never mind triangulation. As a result, every single panel is to be machined with specific programs through a series of eight operations: contouring elements in boards; drilling the elements in order to establish a precise positioning of one element on top of the other with dowels; engraving them to prevent any mistake in assembly; surfacing the inner face of the panel; contouring the support at each corner of the panel; surfacing the outer face of the panel after turning it upside down; contouring the panel; and contouring the interlacings.

Manufacturing programs (G-code) must be absolutely error-free because they go directly from our computers in the office to the machine without any third-party control. Therefore they must be automatically generated. We are currently in the process of rewriting this software (to make the design and generate the B-code for objects that always vary), in order to refer each panel to the plane that will minimise the enclosing block. The series of operations will then be more complex because undercutting situations will have to be taken into account.

Structure and Connecting Pieces

Because the curvature of the panels is a general architectural problem that leads to a complex manufacturing process, we were aware that there was no other way to solve this than by writing our own software. Meanwhile, we largely underestimated the time needed to draw and generate the programs for the 12 structural elements and the 180 parts needed to connect the panels together and to the structure. Because of the projective geometry of the pavilion, each of these connecting pieces is different, and their geometry, although planar, has to be built between planes that make varying angles.

Once each of the pieces was drawn, they were held within an associative network of relations that made them dependent on the position of the three vanishing points. Moving any one of the three points would affect the whole geometry of the pavilion down to the very last elements, and their machining programs. We then made some progress in regard to the Semper Pavilion, achieving a first-level associativity. Once the project was finished we could then change it and produce a series of varying pavilions.

But it took us two months to design all 192 pieces, and the whole drawing process remained what we call 'a manual process' because we had to keep moving our mouse with our hand. Two months of detailing for an experimental pavilion is no big deal, but think of a real building. The design process in itself has to be automatised, and we cannot have a piece of software written for each type of design problem.

The solution consists in the logic of assembly and components, which creates a second level of associativity. Instead of drawing each single piece, we built up a component model which, again, lies upon a limited number of geometrical and numerical elements that we call 'pilots'. Once this model is worked out, we can create a component in the project by clicking its corresponding geometric pilots and fine-tuning its numerical parameters. But the component is not an isolated geometry; it can be said to be 'intelligent' because it carries with it a series of tools and processes that allows the component to interact with the surrounding parts and to generate their machining process.

Digital Architecture

What is digital architecture? Regarding the shape of buildings themselves, our answer is that we don't know. We have no clue about the future look for architecture and we very much question contemporary free forms when they become a cliché and sacrifice the past to the advantage of an absolute present. Marketing strategies are the new form of tyranny, and information technology can appear only as a *deus ex machina* if these strategies succeed in making us forget our own history. However, we hope that our explanations here will go some way towards the argument that digital technologies really put at stake the architecture of information lying behind the buildings, and that this architecture with digits also has to be designed. This is the task on which Objectile is currently focusing.

Notes
1   Philippe Potié, *Philibert De L'Orme: Figures du Projet*, Parenthèses (Marseilles), 1996.
2   Jean Victor Poncelet, *Traité des propriétés projectives des figures* (Paris), 1822.

Bernard Cache, 'Philibert De L'Orme Pavilion: Towards an Associative Architecture', Mark Taylor (guest-editor), *Surface Consciousness*, *AD* Profile 162, *AD* 73, March–April 2003, pp 21–5; Neil Leach, David Turnbull and Chris Williams (eds), *Digital Tectonics*, Wiley-Academy (Chichester), 2004, pp 103–09. © 2012 John Wiley & Sons Ltd.

Morphogenesis and Emergence (2004–2006)

Michael Hensel, Achim Menges and Michael Weinstock

Morphogenesis and the theory of evolution have long provided a source of inspiration and an apt simile for computer-based design, with parametric script in lieu of genetic code, and the instantiation of script into different material events in lieu of the variations of phenotypes exposed to external (environmental) forces. The term 'emergence' derives from system theory, where it defines properties of a system which cannot be derived from the sum of its parts – a notion often associated with complexity theory, to the study of nonlinear behaviours and to self-organising systems. In the history of digital design theory such arguments have sometimes warranted romantic, spiritualistic or anti-technological interpretations of digitality, and have spurred similarly minded design strategies, but the 2004 *Emergence* issue of *AD*, followed by other *AD* Profiles guest-edited by the Emergence and Design Group in 2006 and 2008, signals a step in a different direction.

As they apply the principles of self-organisation to buildings seen as systems, or even eco-systems, both in their tectonic and thermodynamic aspects, Michael Hensel, Achim Menges and Michael Weinstock are keen to point out the difference between 'emergent' properties in life and in computation, and the gap between nature and machinic production. The introduction to the 2004 Profile refers in particular to the teaching and research undertaken by the team, and other associates, at the Architectural Association in London. The second essay, by Achim Menges (2006) applies the theories of self-organising systems to structural design, form finding and research on physical materials. The term often used by Menges in this context, 'performative', an apparent conflation of 'form' and 'performance', has been largely adopted by the design community and is still in use.

In Menges's theory, performativeness is the quality of material systems that perform through deformation, or which visibly deform to self-organise and resist new external forces (loads, for example). All materials deform under stress, and such deformations can and often must be carefully calculated, but in classic engineering the new visual configuration of structures after an elastic (reversible) deformation is seldom taken into account for design purposes. Conversely, Menges applies the logic of self-organising systems to structural systems of which the deformation under stress is the salient quality – figural as well as structural. This pertains to unusual or irregular materials such as soap bubbles and catenary ropes, but also to textiles, perforated membranes, post-tensioned timber tiles, paper strips or honeycombs (see the examples featured in the essay). The structural behaviour of such inelastic, anisotropic or nonhomogeneous materials or composite structures was until recently impossible to calculate, and could only be approximated using physical models – often at real size, due to the non-scalability of structural tests. This is where digital modelling is now changing the game, as the behaviour of non-conventional ('nonlinear') materials, and even of irregular, natural materials, such as timber or stone, can now to some extent be calculated, and structures made with such materials can be designed and fabricated by digitally controlled machines – machines which can theoretically emulate the skills, adaptivity and alert manipulation of expert artisan makers.

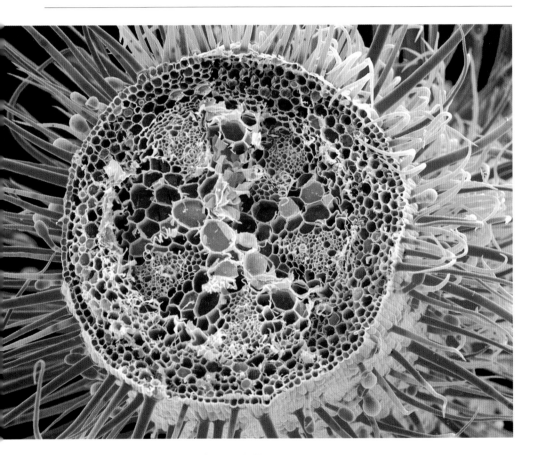

Coloured scanning electron micrograph (SEM) of a section through the stem of a geranium plant. With the close-packed bundles of differentiated vessels and specialised cells, it is the perfect example of integration and differentiation in a plant stem. The geometrical arrangement and close-packed integration produces a complex structure, strong but flexible, and capable of differential movement. Photograph © Steve Gschmeissner/Science Photo Library.

MICHAEL HENSEL, ACHIM MENGES AND MICHAEL WEINSTOCK
Introduction to *Emergence: Morphogenetic Design Strategies* *AD* May–June 2004

Emergence and Morphogenesis

It makes little sense to characterise emergence as either solely abstract or purely a means of production; in emergence the two are inextricably intertwined. As used in the sciences, the term refers to the 'emergence' of forms and behaviour from the complex systems of the natural world. A substantial body of knowledge falls under this term, occurring in the overlapping domains of developmental biology, physical chemistry and mathematics.

The techniques and processes of emergence are intensely mathematical and have spread to other domains where the analysis and production of complex forms or behaviour are fundamental. In 'Morphogenesis and the Mathematics of Emergence', Michael Weinstock traces the origins of the concepts and provides an account of the mathematical basis of processes that produce emergent forms and behaviours, in nature and in computational environments. The mathematical models can be used for generating designs, evolving forms and structures in morphogenetic processes within our computational environments.

Morphogenetic strategies for design are not truly evolutionary unless they incorporate iterations of physical modelling, nor can we develop systems that utilise emergence without the inclusion of the self-organising material effects of form finding and the industrial logic of production. Emergence requires the recognition of buildings not as singular and fixed bodies, but as complex energy and material systems that have a life span, and exist as part of the environment of other buildings, and as an iteration of a long series that proceeds by evolutionary development towards an intelligent ecosystem.

Physical form-finding experiments in architecture are thought to have begun with Gaudí. Frei Otto's pioneering work on form finding is well documented and in 'Frei Otto in Conversation with the Emergence and Design Group' he discusses his development of modelling through form-finding techniques in the context of his interest in natural systems, the relation of experimental models to geometry, iterative mathematics and irregularity.

New form-finding methods are needed for the forms capable of change for the adaptation that emergence demands. In 'Finding Exotic Form' Michael Hensel, of OCEAN NORTH, presents the case for a digital and dynamic form-finding technique that suggests a material means of form adaptation in situ. His argument is developed through a design for the World Center for Human Concerns, an architectural study of a 'parasite building' in which structural and circulatory independence from the host is achieved through the skin of the draped volume.

Data, Genes and Speciation

The Emergence and Design Group, founded by Michael Weinstock, Achim Menges and Michael Hensel, present their case for a morphogenetic strategy in the design study of a high-rise building, placed in the context of their argument for integrating structural criteria and behaviour into material systems of vertical urbanism. In 'Fit Fabric' they propose high-rise buildings as surface structures, explore flexure and stiffness, and present models taken from natural structures for geometry, pattern, form and behaviour. Their evolutionary process has produced a design for high-rise structures in which a helical structural system and an intelligent skin are integrated into a versatile material system. The evolutionary technique here is the development of a population of forms from which the fittest is evolved.

The relation of an individual to a population and to a species is a matter of fierce debate, and within developmental biology the argument between Dawkins and Gould has extended for decades. In 'Types, Style and Phylogenesis' Farshid Moussavi and Alejandro Zaera-Polo of Foreign Office Architects discuss the systematisation of their work into a phylogram of species, and the implications of this new organisational paradigm regarding the methods and techniques that they have refined during their 10 years in practice. They discuss phylogenesis in the context of reflections on the architectural ideologies of 'type' and 'style', and explain their changing design approach in recent work.

'Emergent Technologies and Design' is a new Master of Architecture programme at the Architectural Association Graduate School, and is the first of its kind in the world. It was developed, and is directed, by Michael Weinstock and Michael Hensel. Achim Menges is the studio master. Professor Chris Wise, director of expedition engineering and chair of civil engineering design at Imperial College, London, is an eminent design engineer, and as external examiner to the masters programme evaluates the work of the graduating students. In 'Drunk in an Orgy of Technology' he reflects on their intoxication with technology, mathematics and computers, and their pioneering engagement with emergence. A short account of two MA dissertation projects is presented. 'Data-Graphics and Continuous Datasets', by Lina Martinson, explores the digital imaging, mapping and modelling of complex material systems. The increasing currency of complex morphological articulation in contemporary architecture requires the introduction of imaging technologies from medicine and science. 'HybGrid' by Sylvia Felipe and Jordi Truco, is an adaptable structure developed through a design strategy that combined digital and material processes. The structure has a multiplicity of stable states that link changing spatial requirements to a corresponding formal and structural articulation. The structure makes use of redundancy and elastic behaviour, which are further explored in the context of the article in 'Adaptable Equilibrium' by Wolf Mangelsdorf of Buro Happold, who also teaches in the Emergent Technologies and Design masters programme. He presents an argument, developed from the study of natural structures, for inbuilt redundancy and multiple load paths as primary requirements for the materialisation of the new concepts of adaptability and controlled dynamics.

Complex forms and systems emerge in nature from evolutionary processes, and their properties are developed incrementally through the processes that work upon successive versions of the genome and the phenome. In 'Evolutionary Computation and Artificial Life in Architecture', Dr Una-May O'Reilly of the Computer Science and Artificial Intelligence Lab at MIT, Martin Hemberg and Achim Menges explore the potential of genetic algorithms as design tools for architecture. The development of 'genetic engines' that model evolutionary and growth processes are demonstrated in the context of two morphogenetic design experiments. The argument for the combination of evolutionary computation with advanced digital modelling and the constraints of manufacturing techniques is developed.

Complex forms in architecture demand new tools and new approaches to design. In 'Engineering Design: Working with Advanced Geometries', Charles Walker, leader of the Advanced Geometry Unit (AGU) at Arup & Partners, in conversation with the Emergence and Design Group, discusses AGU's search for a new paradigm, for new organisational principles and the integration of physical and digital modelling in its processes. The collaboration with architects and artists includes Toyo Ito for the Serpentine Gallery Summer Pavilions in 2002, Anish Kapoor for the Marsyas sculpture in the Unilever series at Tate Modern, and David Adjaye for the British Pavilion at the Venice Biennale 2003. Each of these structures required an exploration into the phenomena of the 3-D bracing of interlocking planes, the algorithm as a generative tool, the buckling stability of flat plates, and the manipulation of stressed skins to achieve sculptural form.

Behaviour, Material and Environment

The emphasis on increasing density in mature urban conglomerates is a notable feature in the future strategies of many metropolitan and regional authorities. When very large numbers of people are concentrated in one place, the resources needed to maintain the environmental quality of public and private spaces increase exponentially. Social interaction is more complex and more intense, and this has to be ameliorated by spatial and infrastructural design that maximises qualitative as well as quantitative factors. Emergence provides models for life cycles, and the way in which different life cycles interact with each other in an ecosystem. This is the key to understanding the ecology of densely occupied environments in which topological, structural and programmatic integration facilitates human activities. In 'Morpho-Ecologies' Achim Menges presents two of his architectural research projects that explore the dynamic relations and behaviour of occupation patterns, environmental modulations and material systems.

In natural systems most sensing, decision-making and reactions are entirely local, and global behaviour is the product of local actions, with a high degree of functionality in the material itself. All natural material systems involve movement, often without muscles, to achieve adaptation and responsiveness. In 'Biodynamics' Professor George Jeronimidis examines natural dynamic systems, the material behaviour that enables adaptation, and presents the case for implementation of these models in architecture and engineering.

In natural morphogenesis the information or data of the genome and the physical materials drawn from the environment for the phenome are inextricably intertwined, one acting on the other, and each in turn producing the other. The logic of natural production studied in the sciences of emergence offers a model of seamless integration to replace the conventional separation of design and material production. The search for manufacturing and construction solutions for the complex geometry of contemporary architecture necessitates the development of new methods and tools, and this in turn demands the seamless integration of digital modelling and computer-aided manufacturing. Waagner

Biro is the manufacturing contractor best known for complex geometry constructions. In 'Manufacturing Complexity', Johann Sischka, in conversation with the Emergence and Design Group, discusses the construction strategies and methods of complex geometry structures, such as the dome of the German Reichstag and the roof of the Sony Center in Berlin, and the roof of the Great Court of the British Museum in London.

This issue could be divided into three sections which delineate the strategy for this initial exploration of emergence in architecture. In the first section, 'Emergence and Morphogenesis', the mathematical techniques for modelling the emergence of forms and behaviour from the complex systems of the natural world are juxtaposed with form-finding techniques for stable and dynamic material forms. In the second section, 'Data, Genes and Speciation', the focus is on geometry, pattern and behaviour, and the computational and material evolution of 'populations' and 'species' of architectural forms with complex behaviour. The third section, 'Behaviour, Material and Environment', is concentrated on the adaptive behaviour of natural and architectural material systems and the industrial potential for a seamless integration of their design and production.

Section of complex nest structure built by Apicotermes termites. 20 centimetres (8 inches) across, the structure is made from soil and woody material, with external holes to ventilate the horizontal layered passages, which are vertically connected by an internal spiral staircase. The complex form emerges from the collective behaviour of a large number of termites following very simple rules. Photograph © Pascal Goetgheluck/Science Photo Library.

Emergence Defined
A Mini-Bibliography

1 John Holland, *Emergence: from Chaos to Order*, Oxford University Press (Oxford), 1998

'We are everywhere confronted with emergence in complex adaptive systems – ant colonies, networks of neurons, the immune system, the Internet, and the global economy, to name a few – where the behaviour of the whole is much more complex than the behaviour of the parts.'

'... it is unlikely that a topic as complicated as emergence will submit meekly to a concise definition, and I have no such definition to offer. I can, however, provide some markers that stake out the territory, along with some requirements for studying the terrain ...'

Both quotes are from the opening chapter of *Emergence: from Chaos to Order*, 'Before We Proceed'. Holland's concentration on well-defined technical concepts as a foundation for a framework for studying emergence is excellent. He explores three kinds of concepts – purely mathematical concepts, systems and games concepts, and general informal concepts. Modelling is central to the book and to his discussion.

2 Steven Johnson, *Emergence, the Connected Lives of Ants, Brains, Cities and Software*, Scribner (New York), 2001; Allen Lane/Penguin Press (London), 2001

In discussion of complex, adaptive systems:

'The movement from low-level rules to higher-level sophistication is what we call emergence', and '... a higher-level pattern arising out of parallel complex interactions between local agents'.

This is a good general read, covering many fields. In particular the second section, covering what Johnson identifies as the four principles of emergence – local interaction of neighbours, pattern recognition, feedback and indirect control – are a good, if general, introduction. The book also offers a short history of the intellectual development of what Johnson calls 'the bottom-up mindset'.

3 'Self-Organisation, Emergence and the Architecture of Complexity', Francis Heylighen in *Proceedings of the 1st European Conference on System Science*, Paris

'Emergence is a classical concept in systems theory, where it denotes the principle that the global properties defining higher order systems or "wholes" (e.g. boundaries, organization, control ...) can in general not be reduced to the properties of the lower order subsystems or "parts". Such irreducible properties are called emergent.'

'The spontaneous creation of an "organised whole" out of a "disordered" collection of interacting parts, as witnessed in self-organising systems in physics, chemistry, biology, sociology ... is a basic part of dynamical emergence.'

This interesting paper concentrates on the dynamics and evolution of emergent properties.

Michael Hensel, Achim Menges, Michael Weinstock, 'Introduction', *Emergence: Morphogenetic Design Strategies*, Michael Hensel, Achim Menges and Michael Weinstock (guest-editors), *AD* Profile 169, *AD* 74, May–June 2004, pp 6–9. © 2012 John Wiley & Sons Ltd.

ACHIM MENGES **Polymorphism** *AD* March–April 2006

Natural morphogenesis, the process of evolutionary development and growth, generates polymorphic systems that obtain their complex organisation and shape from the interaction of system-intrinsic material capacities and external environmental influences and forces. The resulting, continuously changing, complex structures are hierarchical arrangements of relatively simple material components organised through successive series of propagated and differentiated subassemblies from which the system's performative abilities emerge.

A striking aspect of natural morphogenesis is that formation and materialisation processes are always inherently and inseparably related. In stark contrast to these integral development processes of material form, architecture as a material practice is mainly based on design approaches that are characterised by a hierarchical relationship that prioritises the generation of form over its subsequent materialisation. Equipped with representational tools intended for explicit, scalar geometric descriptions, the architect creates a scheme through a range of design criteria that leave the inherent morphological and performative capacities of the employed material systems largely unconsidered. Ways of materialisation, production and construction are strategised and devised as top-down engineered, material solutions only after defining the shape of the building and the location of tectonic elements.

An alternative morphogenetic approach to architectural design entails unfolding morphological complexity and performative capacity from material constituents without differentiating between formation and materialisation processes. Over the last five years I have pursued related design research through projects and also in educational collaboration with various colleagues at the Architectural Association (AA) and other schools. Based on concepts of developmental biology and biomimetic engineering, the core of such a morphogenetic approach is an understanding of material systems not as derivatives of standardised building systems and elements facilitating the construction of pre-established design schemes, but rather as generative drivers in the design process.

Extending the concept of a material system by embedding its material characteristics, geometric behaviour, manufacturing constraints and assembly logics allows for deriving and elaborating a design through the system's intrinsic performative capacities. This promotes an understanding of form, materials and structure not as separate elements, but rather as complex interrelations in polymorphic systems resulting from the response to varied input and environmental influences and derived through the logics and constraints of advanced manufacturing processes. This demands new modes of integrating design techniques, production technologies and system performance, a cross-section of which will be discussed here. Through a series of five morphogenetic design experiments ranging from homologous systems[1] to polytypic species,[2] the characteristics of integral form-generation processes enabled through parametric association, differential actuation, dynamic relaxation, algorithmic definition and digital growth will be examined. Discussing the organisational potentialities and spatial opportunities that arise from such a design approach would go beyond the scope of this article.[3] The focus is therefore placed on presenting relevant tools and methods for such an integral approach to design.

Form-Finding and Dynamic Relaxation: Membrane Morphologies

The disconnection of form generation and subsequent materialisation emblematic for current design approaches manifests itself in the 'hard control' that the architect needs to exert on the constructs he or she designs. Before any material realisation can take place, the designer must define the precise location and exact shape of all elements, geometrically controlling the maximum amount of points needed to describe the system to be constructed. However, such a design method fails to notice the potential of using the capacity for self-organisation inherent to material systems. This suggests a design process based on the strategic 'soft control' of minimal definition that instrumentalises the behaviour of a material system in the formation process. Integrating the logics of form, material and structure was investigated in a series of membrane structures[4] developed by Michael Hensel and myself as exhibition installations for different locations. Membrane structures are of particular interest for such an exploration, as any resultant morphology is intrinsically related to the material characteristics and the formation process of pretensioning. Thus a viable design method cannot be based on geometric hard control over a maximum number of points of the system, but should be based on the local exertion of force on strategic points.

Form-finding, as pioneered by Frei Otto,[5] is a design technique that utilises the self-organisation of material systems under the influence of extrinsic forces. In membrane structures, the displacement of particular boundary points and the consequent pretensioning force are correlated with the material and form, in that the form of the structure can be found as the state of equilibrium of internal resistances and external forces. Form-finding processes for membranes can be physically modelled and simulated through digital dynamic relaxation. The latter involves a digital mesh that settles into an equilibrium state through iterative calculations based on the specific elasticity and material make-up of the membrane – isotropic in case of foils, anisotropic in case of fabrics – combined with the designation of boundary points and related forces. The same software applications can usually also generate the associated cutting patterns if the membrane is to be constructed from relatively nonelastic material.

In the project presented here, the material consists of nylon fabric with different elasticity in the warp and weft direction. An additional design aspect was the introduction of holes cut into the fabric that considerably alter the behaviour of the membrane. These holes were critical as they expanded the performance range of the system. While traditional form-finding methods focus on structural behaviour of material form resulting in monoparametric assessment criteria, the aim of this project was the exploration of a multiparametric approach. Thus the additional capacity of the perforated membrane system to modulate visual permeability as a differentiated exhibition screen was understood as being intrinsically related to the structural form. In order to instrumentalise this relation, two operations were of critical importance for the design process: first, the parametric specification and subsequent confection of each membrane patch defined by boundary points and cutting lines expressed within the object coordinate space of the patch and, second, the pretensioning action defined through the relocation of the object boundary

Michael Hensel and Achim Menges, Diploma Unit 4 - Architectural Association, form-finding and dynamic relaxation. Initial form-finding experiment of 'minimal hole' configuration. 'Membrane Morphologies 02' installed at the Architectural Association, London. Photograph © Achim Menges.

points towards anchor points described in the coordinate space of the exhibition room. Feeding back information between examining different values of local parametric variables and testing altering positions for the anchor-point coordinates creates multiple membrane morphologies that all remain coherent with the construction logics of the system. A specific configuration can be developed through corroborating and negotiating different behavioural characteristics and specific performance requirements. The resulting membrane morphology settles into a stable state of unity between form and force. At the same time the correlated complex curvature of the membrane and the opening of the holes provide for different degrees of visual permeability resulting in the varied exposure of the exhibits.

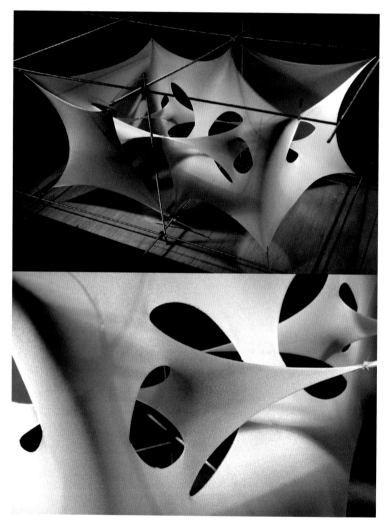

Michael Hensel and Achim Menges, form-finding and dynamic relaxation. Close-up view of 'minimal hole' configuration. 'Membrane Morphologies 02' installed at the Architectural Association, London. Photographs © Michael Hensel.

Differential Surface Actuation: Metapatch Project

In most form-finding processes, operations focus on the exertion of force on strategic system-points, which leads to a 'global' manipulation of the overall system. In this context, 'global' refers to the entirety of a system, while 'local' describes a sublocation. It is important to realise that the self-organising capacity of material systems is not limited to 'global' form-finding processes such as the one mentioned above. It can also be deployed in a 'local' manner. One such exploration is the project developed by Joseph Kellner and David Newton[6] in the context of the Generative Proto-Architectures studio led by Michael Hensel and myself at Rice School of Architecture. This experiment was driven by the hypothesis that the material capacity of a system consisting of uniform elements can be employed to achieve variable yet stable configurations with complex curvature through a vast array of local actuations.

Initial tests confirmed that a series of very simple rectangular wooden elements fastened to a larger sheet of timber can be deployed as local actuators. Each rectangular element is attached to a larger patch by four bolts, one in each corner. While two of the bolts in opposite corners are permanently fixed and thereby define the length of the diagonal line between them, the other two bolts remain adjustable. Tightening these two bolts increases the distance between the element's corners and the patch begins to bend. As each larger patch is covered with arrays of elements, the incremental induction of curvature results in a global (de)formation. Detailed investigations of the correlation of element and patch variables such as size, thickness and fibre orientation, actuator locations and torque lead to taxonomy of geometric patterns and generated system behaviour. This data enabled scripting of the parametric definition, assembly sequence and actuation protocols for a large prototype construction.

The configuration tested as a large-scale prototype consists of initially flat, identical timber patches onto which equal elements with actuator bolts are attached on one side. According to the particular distribution of actuator positions, the elements are connected to the patches and the patches are assembled into a larger structure with different orientations of the element's clad sides. The resulting material system consists of 48 identical patches, 1920 equal elements and 7680 bolts. After assembly, the structure is initially entirely flat. Through the subsequent incremental actuation of fastening delineated bolts it then rises into a stable, self-supporting state with alternating convex and concave curvature. Changes to variables within this actuation protocol allow for articulating and testing multiple emergent states and their inherent performative capacity. As the patches are perforated by drilled hole-patterns, the performative modulation of porosity and the adjustment of structural capacity through curvature are intrinsically correlated with the manipulation of the system's material and geometric behaviour. Developing an integral technique of form generating and making based on the material capacity and local actuation of the system enabled a variable, complex morphology derived through the materiality, geometry and interaction of amazingly simple material elements.

Joseph Kellner and David Newton,
(supervised by Michael Hensel and
Achim Menges), Protoarchitecture
Studio Rice School of Architecture
2004. Differential surface actuation,
Metapatch prototype at the *Modulations*
exhibition, Rice School of Architecture,
Houston US, November 2004 and
close-up view of actuation elements
and patches. Photograph Chad Loucks.
© Achim Menges/Chad Loucks.

Component Differentiation and Proliferation: Paper-Strip Experiment

A third approach towards polymorphous material systems is component differentiation and proliferation. While the experiment explained above relied on the differential actuation of equal components, the following morphogenetic technique is based on parametric components defined through geometric relationships. The proliferation of different instantiations of a parametric component generates a material system with differentiated sublocations. I developed such a design process through an experiment[7] based on very simple material components, namely twisted and bent paper-strips.

In this project, a digital component is defined as an open and extendable geometric framework based on the 'logics' of a material system that integrates the possibilities and limits of making, and the self-forming tendencies and constraints of the material. Through elaborate physical studies of the behaviour of twisted and bent paper-strips, the essential geometric features, such as points of curvature, developability of the surface and tangency alignments were captured in a digital component. This component describes the nonmetric geometric associations of a single paper-strip as part of a component collective and thereby anticipates the process of assembly and integration into a larger system. In other words, through parametric geometric relationships the digital component ensures that any morphology generated can be materialised as strips cut from sheet material.

A larger system can then be established through a process of proliferating components into polymorphic populations. For this, a variable 'proliferation environment' is defined to provide the constraints for the accretion of components as well as stimuli/inputs for their individual morphologies. An algorithm drives the distribution of components with three possible modes of proliferation: first, an outward proliferation of a component into a population that increases in number until the environment's boundaries are reached, second, an inward proliferation within the initial system's setup and, third, a hierarchical proliferation based on environments/inputs for secondary, tertiary, etc, systems. These three proliferation modes can also be deployed in combination, leading to nested populations of component systems.

The resulting system remains open to 'local' manipulation of individual components, 'regional' manipulation of component collectives and 'global' manipulations of the component system, proliferation environment and distribution algorithm. The parametric associations of and between components, collectives and the overall system allow the rapid implementation of these manipulations, leading to a multitude of self-updating system instances. Situated in a simulated environment of external forces, the system's behavioural tendencies then reveal its performative capacity. For example, exposing multiple system instances to digitally simulated light flow enables the registration of interrelations between parametric manipulations and the modulation of light levels upon and beyond the system.

Additional digital structural analyses of the same instances reveal the related load-bearing behaviour of the system. These behavioural tendencies of the system interacting with external forces and modulating transmitted flows can be traced across various parametrically defined individual morphologies. The resulting patterns of force

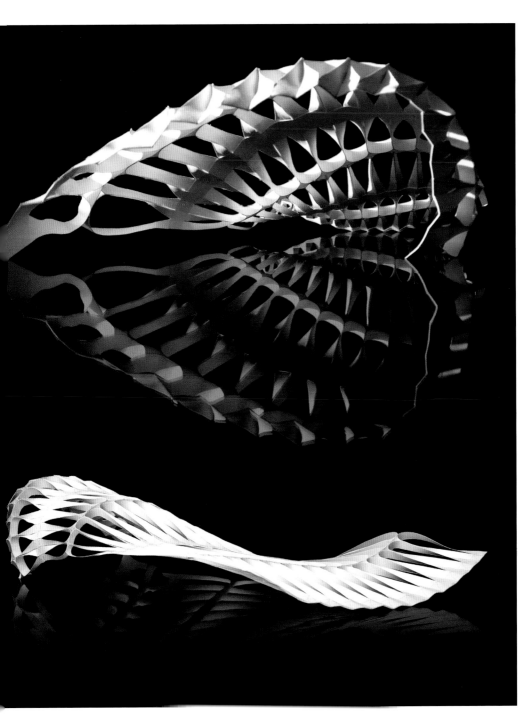

Achim Menges, component differentiation and proliferation. Physical test model of paper-strip system derived through a parametric process embedding the material characteristics, manufacturing constraints and assembly logics observed in physical tests. Photograph © Achim Menges.

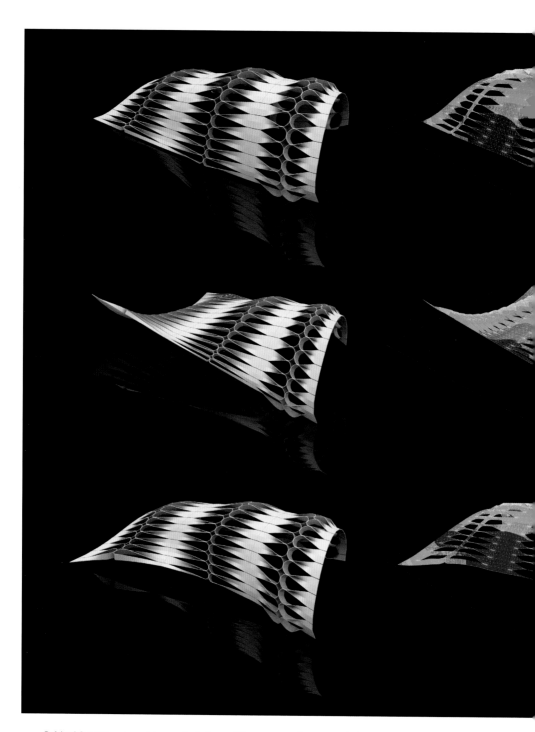

Achim Menges, geometric manipulations of the parametric system (left) and related patterns of structural behaviour (centre: contour plots of finite element analysis under gravity load) and modulation of light conditions (right: geographically specific illuminance analysis on the system and a register surface for an overcast sky). Illustrations © Achim Menges.

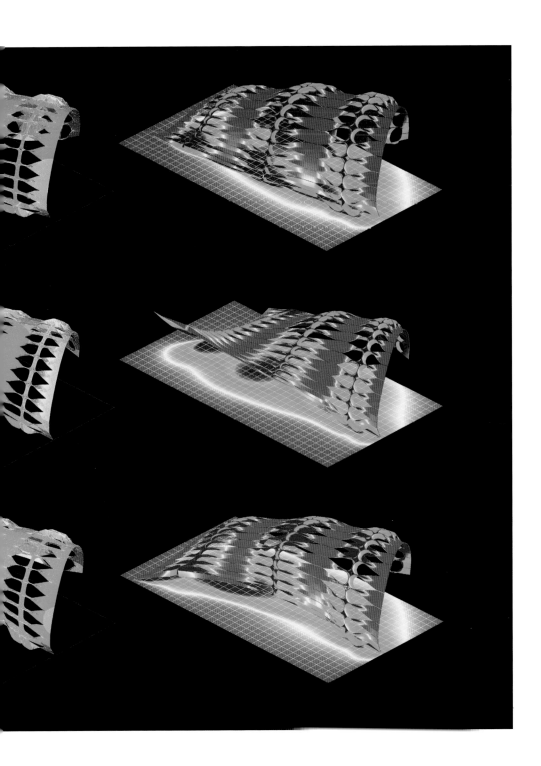

distribution and conditions of varying luminous intensity can inform further cycles of local, regional and global parametric manipulations. Continually informing the open parametric framework of component definition and proliferation yields an increasing differentiation with the capacity for negotiating multiple-performance criteria within one system. The important point is that the outlined parametric design technique permits the recognition of patterns of geometric behaviour and related performative capacities of the polymorphous component population. In continued feedback with the external environment, these behavioural tendencies can then inform the ontogenetic development of a specific system through the parametric differentiation of its sublocations. And these processes of differentiation will always remain consistent with the constraints of materialisation, fabrication and assembly of the paper-strips.

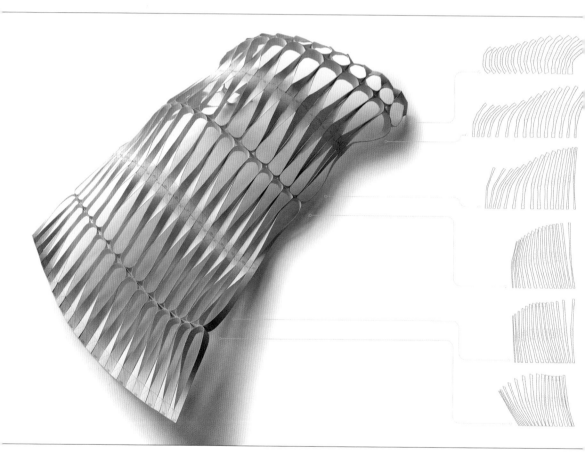

Achim Menges, physical test model of a
population of 90 paper-strip components
and related strip-cut patterns.
Photograph © Achim Menges.

Generative Algorithmic Definition: Honeycomb Morphologies

Another technique for the development of a polymorphous cellular structure has been researched by Andrew Kudless for his Masters dissertation[8] as part of the AA Emergent Technologies and Design programme led by Michael Weinstock, Michael Hensel and myself. While in the paper-strip experiment the material, manufacturing and assembly logics were embedded in a digital component corresponding to the physical element to be proliferated into a larger population, the focus in this project is to algorithmically generate a coherent honeycomb system able to colonise variable geometric envelopes within the limits of fabrication.

Standard honeycomb systems are limited to planar or regularly curved geometry due to their equal cell sizes resulting from the constraints of industrial mass-production. However, computer-aided manufacturing (CAM) processes allow for a greatly increased range of

Master-project by Andrew Kudless, EmTech (Michael Hensel, Achim Menges, Michael Weinstock), Architectural Association. Generative algorithmic definition, algorithmically derived honeycomb prototype in which each cell is unique in shape, size and depth, allowing for changing cell densities and double-curved global geometry. Photograph © Achim Menges.

geometries if the production logics become an integral part of the form-generation process. In this particular case, the embedding of manufacturing constraints in the rules of deriving the system required the consideration of three aspects for the construction of a large-scale prototype. First, to ensure topological continuity all generated cells need to remain hexagonal and tangential with the adjacent cell walls. Second, folded material strips of which the system consists are cut from planar sheet material with a laser, therefore the possible generation of elements must be linked to the constraints of the related production technique, namely two-dimensional cutting of limited size and the specific material properties such as, for example, the folding behaviour. The third important point is the anticipation of required assembly logistics through labelling all elements and inherently defining the construction sequence by the uniqueness of each pair of matching cell walls.

Based on these aspects, the resultant digital generation process comprises the following sequence. In order to define the eventual vertices of the honeycomb strips, points are digitally mapped across a surface that is defined by the designer and remains open to geometric manipulations. The parametrically defined correlation of point distribution and geometric surface characteristics can also be altered. An algorithmic procedure that connects the distributed points creates the required folded strip lines. Looping this algorithm across all points forms the honeycomb mesh, and this procedure is repeated across an offset point distribution to generate a system wire-frame model. In a following step the defined honeycomb strips are unfolded, labelled and nested to prepare for subsequent production.

This integral form-generation and fabrication process can create honeycomb systems in which each cell can be unique in shape, size and depth, allowing for changing cell densities and a large range of irregularly curved global geometries. The resultant differentiation in the honeycomb has considerable performance consequences, as the system now carries the capacity for adaptation to specific structural, environmental and other forces not only within the overall system, but locally across different sublocations of varying cell size, depth and orientation. Embedding the possibilities and constraints of material and production technology, the form-generation technique and its parametric definition become, per se, the main interface of negotiating multiple-performance criteria.

Master-project by Andrew Kudless, EmTech (Michael Hensel, Achim Menges, Michael Weinstock), Architectural Association. Generative algorithmic definition, close-up views showing planar connection tabs between honeycomb layers (left) and double-curved global surface articulation (right). Left: Photograph © Sue Barr/AA; Right: Photograph © Achim Menges.

Digital Growth and Ontogenetic Drifts: Fibrous Surfaces

The final project synthesises the presented methods of component differentiation and mapped propagation with digitally simulated growth.[9] This collaborative project,[10] developed by Sylvia Felipe, Jordi Truco and myself together with Emmanuel Rufo and Udo Thoennissen, aims to evolve a differentiated surface structure consisting of a dense network of interlocking members from a basic array of simple, straight elements. To achieve complexity in the resultant material system the exploration focuses on advanced digital generation techniques in concert with relatively common computer numerically controlled (CNC) production processes.

The basic system constituent is defined as a jagged, planar strip cut from sheet material on a three-axis CNC router. In a parametric software application a generic digital component is established through the geometric relationships that remain invariant in all possible instances of the material element and the variable production constraints of the intended machining technology and process. Each particular implementation of the parametric component in the system to be digitally constructed is then based on three interrelated inputs. Primary input influencing the particular geometry of a specific system type is given by a Gestalt envelope that describes the system's overall extent and shape. This envelope is defined by a geometric surface grown in a digitally simulated environment of forces. The digital growth process employed for the generation of the surface is based on extended Lindenmayer systems (L-systems), which produce form through the interaction of two factors: a geometric seed combined with rewriting rules that specify how elements of the shape change, and a process that repeatedly reinterprets the rules with respect to the current shape.

In this particular case the surface is represented by a graph data structure constituted by a set of edges, vertices and regions. Since all edges are constantly rewritten during the digital growth process, all parts of the surface continuously change until the ontogenetic drifts[11] settle into a stable configuration. Based on the growing surface, another input for the implementation of the material elements is generated. In response to particular geometric surface features such as global undulation and regional curvature, a variable distribution algorithm establishes a network of lines on the surface indicating the position of each element and the related node type. Digital components then populate the system accordingly and construct a virtual solid model. In the resultant organisation, crossing members only intersect if they are perpendicular due to the embedded manufacturing constraints. If not, they pass under or over crossing elements, not dissimilar to a bird's nest, and thereby form a geometrically defined, self-interlocking, stable structure.

This complex correlation of geometric definition, structural behaviour and production logics does not only remain coherent in a single system, such as the tested prototype with almost 90 members and 1000 joints, but is integral to the generation process itself. This is of particular importance if one considers that the surface defining the critical morphogenetic input is constructed through a bottom-up process in which all parts respond to local interactions and the environment. As these internal and external interactions are complex and the interpretation of the L-systems is nonlinear, the outcome of the growth process remains open-ended. This continual change, combined with the long-chain dependencies of the subsequent generation

Achim Menges, digital growth and ontogenetic drifts. Diagram: the surface
geometry generated through a digital growth process based on extended
Lindenmayer systems (bottom) provides the geometric data for an algorithmic
distribution of parametric components (centre), which results in a complex
network of self-interlocking straight members (top) that are immediately
ready for production. Illustrations © Achim Menges.

methods, enables the growth of different system types of member organisation, system topology and consequent performative capacity. Such an integral design approach begins to expand the notion of performative polymorphic systems towards digital typogenesis.

While the five experiments presented here remain in a proto-architectural state awaiting implementation in a specific architectural context, the related morphogenetic design techniques and technologies allow for the rethinking of the nature of currently established design processes. A design approach utilising such methods enables architects to define specific material systems through the combined logics of formation and materialisation. It promotes replacing the creation of specific shapes subsequently rationalised for realisation and superimposed functions, through the unfolding of performative capacities inherent to the material arrangements and constructs we derive. Most importantly, it encourages the fundamental rethinking of our current mechanical approaches to sustainability and a related functionalist understanding of efficiency.

Notes
1   Homologous systems share an evolutionary transformation from the same 'ancestral' state.
2   Polytypic species are species that comprise several subspecies or variants.
3   The organisational potentialities of complex built environments have been outlined in Achim Menges, 'Morpho-ecologies: Approaching Complex Environments', *Emergence: Morphogenetic Design Strategies, AD* 74, No 3, 2004, pp 48–53.
4   'Membrane Morphologies' Morphogenetic Design Experiment 04, April 2004 to Sept 2005. Phase 01: Physical and Digital Form-Finding Developments (Michael Hensel and Achim Menges, with Giorgos Kailis and Nikolaos Stathopoulos). Phase 02: Exhibition installation at the AA School of Architecture, London, 2004 (Michael Hensel and Achim Menges, with Tiffany Beriro, Edouard Cabay and Valeria Segovia). Phase 03: Exhibition installation at Rice School of Architecture, Houston, 2004 (Michael Hensel and Achim Menges).
5   See 'Frei Otto in Conversation with the Emergent and Design Group', *AD Emergence: Morphogenetic Design Strategies*, pp 19–25.
6   Joseph Kellner and David Newton, 'Metapatch' project, Generative Proto-Architectures Studio, Rice School of Architecture, Houston, September to December 2004. Visiting professors: Michael Hensel and Achim Menges. Visiting staff: Neri Oxman and Andrew Kudless.
7   'Paper-Strip Morphologies' Morphogenetic Design Experiment 03, April 2004 to April 2005. Phase 01: Physical and Digital Form-Finding Developments (Achim Menges with Andrew Kudless, Ranidia Leeman and Michuan Xu). Phase 02: Parametric Set-Up and Proliferation (Achim Menges); Finite Element Analysis (Nikolaos Stathopoulos).
8   Andrew Kudless, 'Manifold – Honeycomb Morphologies', MA dissertation project, Emergent Technologies and Design Masters programme, AA Graduate School of Architecture, London, 2004. Programme directors: Michael Hensel and Michael Weinstock. Studio master: Achim Menges.
9   See Dr Una-May O'Reilly, Martin Hemberg and Achim Menges, 'Evolutionary Computation and Artificial Life in Architecture', *AD Emergence: Morphogenetic Design Strategies*, pp 48–53.
10 'Fibrous Surfaces' Morphogenetic Design Experiment 05, June 2004 to October 2005. Phase 01: 'Integral Envelopes' Workshop (Sylvia Felipe, Achim Menges, Jordi Truco, Emmanuel Rufo and Udo Thoennissen), ESARQ International University of Catalunya, Barcelona. Phase 02: Algorithmic Distribution and Material Tests (Emmanuel Rufo, Sylvia Felipe, Achim Menges, Udo Thoennissen and Jordi Truco). Phase 03: Material Prototype (Emmanuel Rufo, Sylvia Felipe, Achim Menges and Jordi Truco).
11 Ontogenetic drifts are the developmental changes in form and function that are inseparable from growth.

Achim Menges, 'Polymorphism', Michael Hensel, Achim Menges, and Michael Weinstock (guest-editors), *Techniques and Technologies in Morphogenetic Design, AD* Profile 180, *AD* 76, March–April 2006, pp 78–87.
© 2012 John Wiley & Sons Ltd.

Scripting (2006)

Malcolm McCullough

Malcolm McCullough, the first Autodesk product manager for architecture in the mid 1980s, offers an insider's view of the history of digital design, from early design computing to the recent revival of architectural interest in software scripting and coding (which this 2006 *AD* Profile both reflected and catalysed). In the age of shape grammars and early (non-visual) parametricism, computers operated on relatively simple geometrical data, following sets of alphabetic or algorithmic instructions; image manipulation, when it occurred at all, was derived from rule-based scripts.

Then came cheap, ubiquitous and almost unlimited processing power, and with that, new graphic interfaces that enabled users to manipulate some kinds of forms directly onscreen. This was the age of the blob, and, technically, of spline modellers, that used advanced mathematics to convert all kinds of doodles into calculus-based geometrical objects, editable on the screen via vectors and control points – that is, without using any script or mathematical notation. This is when digital designers stopped being coders (with some notable exceptions), and computer-based design started to effectively change the history of architecture.

There are many reasons why architects may need or choose to go back to scripting. Designers who resent the limits of the software they use may try to tweak or bend its rules; open-source software is an interesting case in point, but increasingly even mainstream commercial software allows for so much leeway in user interaction and customisation that, McCullough concludes, given the better visual interfaces of today's software, designers may now be coding and scripting without even knowing.

20 Years of Scripted Space *AD* July–August 2006

The Invitation: Rules and Two-Part Design

You have to get free of the grind. It is just too much work to construct every design element uniquely, directly and without regard for what knowledge it represents. Now that technology lets us treat abstract schemas as objects for manipulation, it makes no more sense to design by drawing each line and modelling every surface than it does to drive an aeroplane down a highway. The more kinds of representation that software lets us manipulate, the more opportunity we have to take design to a higher level. After all, the very essence of software is to represent problems abstractly, through the use of variables, conditionals, iterations and procedures. All of this has now been made accessible to nonspecialists via user-friendly, shrink-wrapped design software. The disciplined programming work has been done by the professionals behind all this gear: all you need is the will to improvise.

Indeed you must. For as the coders in Silicon Valley would be the first to admit, while their knowledge of shapes and data structures and usable interfaces naturally surpasses anything some casual tinkerer (or headstrong academic) could come up with on his or her own, such knowledge stops at the border between the theory and the application of form. They know how to process forms, but only the design professional knows which forms, when, where and why. Thus every discipline must bring its domain knowledge to the question of software representation. The software part has been made as easy as possible by new scripting languages. Architects, engineers, fabricators – any domain whose knowledge depends on form – have all begun to adapt and extend generic software tools to the specifics of their disciplines. It is no longer so rare for a design firm to have a few people writing code – not the kind of code that requires a degree in computer science to get right, but the kind that can be crafted one line at a time on top of commercial software while working on form. No need to learn how to link headers or throw exceptions. This kind of code is by you, for you – and it is fun.

This is because it lets you game the rules of play. The amazing part of scripting is how it adds a whole extra level to design thinking. First you set up some rules for generating forms, then you play them to see what kind of design world they create, and then you go back and tweak the rules. With a bit of interface technology, even just a few simple button sliders, you can tweak almost as quickly as you play.

This does require some change in outlook. Many designers, or at least most design students, believe that any constraints on the character and construction of form will just hamper their creativity. This is wrong as wrong can be. Any expressive medium has its idioms, types and genres, and the better established of those are often where the richest expressions occur. Meanwhile, many technologists and managers also believe that computer usage is serious work, and that play is just distraction or, worse, entertainment. This too is wrong. Even before computers, tangible speculation was the heart of design work. Software just articulates and accelerates that conjecture. We can ask 'What if?' more often, and about more abstract kinds of assumptions.

But consider one last misconception, namely the old ambition (especially prevalent in the 1980s) towards the computability of all knowledge. To understand the limits of this, it is a degree not in computer science but in philosophy that is necessary. Any sage should know that some things are easier done than said, that an approximation is almost always enough, that convenience of measurement should not be mistaken for completeness of truth, that logic is so cumbersome that humans seldom use it, and so on. Therefore the role of computers in design is seldom one of automation. There are few sets of design rules that can be set up to be interesting enough to run on their own. Once the design world has been set up, it still needs to be explored, played and mastered with finesse.

At least that is what they were saying in the 1980s. I'm old enough, and fortunate enough, to report some of this first-hand.

Some Basic History and Theory of Design Computing
Twenty years ago, in 1986, you couldn't just noodle with spline surface models all day. No online chat idled in some nearby window – nor shopping nor shooter game. No gargantuan operating system was there to interrupt you with security alerts, nor to push you unwanted software, nor to cram your 'personal' computer with 10,000 needless things. Back then there was no presumption that anyone but the computer was dumb. You could almost still hear yourself think.

That year is significant in terms of today's interest in scripting because it was the year Autodesk took over the personal computer design-software market – mainly, I still think, because of its new advantages in scripting language. When a desktop PC was the world's idea of a 'microcomputer', the field was still wide open: and while the big architecture firms were still breaking the bank on a Vax or a Prime, something had to give. The company's AutoCAD was the first of the PC computer-aided design (CAD) programs to record command-line sequences of its drawing operations (which remains essential to the craft aspect of this culture) within the variable structures and flow constructs of an interpreted programming language. And even if the vast majority of its users never fully rose to this, there was remarkable promise in that this language was Lisp, the usual preference among the artificial intelligence (AI) community of the day. If we define 'scripting' as coding one line at a time on an interpreter that belongs to a powerful host program, then it is difficult to find an earlier popular instance in design graphics, nor one that expanded the constituency for design computing so far, so rapidly. (Among my own responsibilities as the company's architecture product manager in 1986 was reviewing proposals from dozens of new businesses to be included in Autodesk's catalogue of such scripted 'third party' software.)

The universities were aiming much higher, of course. Also coming of age in the 1980s was a knowledge representation that has long remained an academic focus in architectural computing: shape grammars. (At Autodesk we read all the papers of the theory's inventor, George Stiny, with whom I had just studied briefly at UCLA.) Everyone knew that the discrete entity-and-layer structure of early CAD systems was not enough. Theoretically, grammars were a powerful way beyond this towards substitutions and subdivisions in articulating form. It was expected that these could become very practical expert assistants on well-formed classes of design problems. Unfortunately, the level of codification was high. Early applications operated within very specific architectural motifs, the most famous example of which was Wrightian Prairie-style houses. Even for applications in rote architectural production – say, laying out a set of hotel rooms – these better formal structures had less ready application to everyday architectural problem-solving.

The more accessible next step in knowledge representation was instead a dimensionally driven approach that became known simply as 'parametrics'. This is mainly a matter of expressing design problems or, more specifically, formal types, computationally in terms of a short set of independent design variables, especially dimensions. From the values of these few independent dimensions, software can derive a particular instance in that type of form. The essence of the type is implied in the parameterisation, the circumstances of the instance are specified in the arguments given to the dimensional variable, and the two-level process of design begins. Although some classes of form can be codified to a single size variable, such as is designated for a hat or a pair of shoes, most cannot. Although many more arbitrary classes of form can be constructed if the number of independent variables is sufficiently large, the parametric process is more valuable if that set of variables is kept manageably low. The value is in the use of dependent variables to generate relatively detailed instances from relatively few inputs. This is especially true if those inputs can couple the generation of form to the ranges and constraints of the machine processes by which they are to be fabricated.

'The essence of the architectural type' quickly became good subject matter in design education using the new computational medium. In 1989, a healthy few years in advance of the wave that would reduce us all to teaching freeform direct manipulation with the latest spline surface modeller, Harvard introduced what may have been the first programming course required for all professional degree candidates in a leading school of architecture. The software basis for this initiative was a program called TopDown, written mainly at UCLA, by Robin Liggett and William Mitchell. This had been inspired in part by shape grammars, and in part by the existing pedagogy of teaching design theory through programming, and in part by recent improvements in ready-made interface widgets. TopDown provided a visual and dynamic way to combine substitution and dimensional variations on a compositional motif. To make a beginning artefact in it involved in the order of 20 lines of Pascal code. Even this was alien, however.

A self-conscious and sleep-deprived Harvard architecture student was often not the best casual coder. Furthermore, much of the faculty then still believed that gentlemen did not operate machinery. It is an understatement to say that this course met with resentment.

The Direct Manipulation Boom

As the 1990s wore on, the graphical user interface did so much to make computing accessible to nonspecialists that it quickly became the only form of computer use that most people had ever known. Perhaps the most essential principle of this interface remained that 1980s breakthrough of 'direct manipulation'. Tool-like operations modified visual objects of design in real time onscreen. Dense continuous notation became available for modelling, illustrating and orchestrating in time. Density was a matter of response time and resolution.

Between any two states of a digital artefact, there was effectively another. This made it much easier to achieve design states by discovery through manipulation rather than derivation through formulas. Nevertheless, a notation was effectively kept in software standard file formats. In other words, unlike any previous medium that was dense and fluid enough to allow continuous coaxing into conformity with whatever was held in the designer's mind's eye, this new medium had reproducible documentation. It also allowed a proliferation and management of versions without loss of quality. No longer 'just a tool' (in the apologetic sense of not influencing one's intentions), design computing rapidly matured as a medium in which bias, appreciation, expression and new genres were inevitable.

Alas the great rush to the seductions of all this new technical possibility effectively drowned most existing agendas in designers' programming culture. For the first time, the majority of computer users were noncoders. Improvisation prevailed over composition.

The theoretical prospects raised were of an open and bottom-up morphology rather than closed and top-down. Deleuzian difference-and-repetition spread through the discipline like an invasive species. So by 1996, not only did noodling with spline surfaces all day work comfortably in practice: it also worked in theory.

Of course there were other, more fundamental reasons why programming played out better in other form-giving disciplines than in architecture. The course of parametrics seems significant in this regard. Parametrics work better in domains whose subject matter is engineered form itself – especially in mechanical components for complex assemblies such as vehicles. Parametric design works less well where physical configuration and performance are just the means, and a more emergent usage pattern is the end. Or, to put it the other way round, when the subject matter of design is more the social arrangements and less the mechanical assemblies used to house them. Parameterisation breaks down when the design problems are wickedly under- or overconstrained, or where the design variables are less obvious. Compared with an aeroplane part, even the aforementioned rote hotel room is less computable.

Then, of course, the spirit of casual improvisation in code moved on – and struck gold with the World Wide Web. Accomplishments in scripting interactivity (for example using Java, Lingo and Perl) at least temporarily drew attention away from the prospect of scripting pure form. Indeed, it could make a million for you overnight.

Among those who did not abandon built form for more visual pursuits, code seemed unnecessary. Especially among architects preoccupied with radical novelty in autographic form – a pursuit now made so accessible by software that any fool could do it – the more immediate technical possibilities of direct manipulation were the order of the day. The most favoured genre of improvised objects became known as 'blobs'.

Nevertheless, the flame continued to burn for design education through programming. In 1996, John Maeda launched a Java-based design fundamentals pedagogy amid the gizmo-centrism of MIT, and the results were instantly stunning. As documented in *Design By Numbers*,[1] *Creative Code*[2] and the former's progeny online at dbn.media.met.edu, there is a lot to be said for the role of simple algorithmic beauty in aesthetic education. It is beyond the scope of this essay to document this landmark work, which is mentioned here mainly to set the historical context.

For one thing, the purity of Maeda's approach let aspiring designers step right outside the increasingly bloated commercial software standards. In the 1980s, the PC had been hailed as the first machine that someone might look forward to using, but by the late 1990s it was no longer so personal, nor pleasant, due to the disfiguring bloat of its operating system. Where any theory of abstract craft broke down was on the stability of the personal tools and medium. There wasn't any.

Architecture Rediscovers Programming

Even in the most delusional hours of the blobmeisters' boom, not all was the vagaries of fashion. And as the smoke cleared from the dotcom crash, many transformations in design work remained. Seemingly on the basis of such advances, programming culture has been rediscovered in architecture. Consider some reasons why.

Advances in digital fabrication must be first among these motives. Simply put, there is now far more incentive to express design in terms of a few variables based on the machining process. Whether in the schools, design-build practices or new niches in the just-in-time supply chain for a rapidly building world, rapid prototyping and computer-numerically controlled (CNC) machining have become competitive necessities.

Second, the theoretical basis of cultural expression in form is increasingly informed by a domain of knowledge that appears relatively comfortable with notions of generative algorithmic beauty: namely biology. Especially with respect to growth and emergence, but also with respect to the harmonies and recursions of static biomorphic objects, this present fashion in architecture has a greater need for coded formulations.

In addition, more people (and most management gurus) know that information technology and organisational change are just two sides of the same coin. Task automation gives way to strategic reconfiguration that legitimises creative work in more circles, and creates niches for new kinds of practice in the delivery of customisable design.

And finally, and perhaps most widespread culturally, the crafts of personalising one's workspace and scripting one's intellectual pleasures have become far more distinct in the generation of designers who grew up with computing. The bloat does not seem to bother so many of them, and the interruptions and multitask, fragmented attention may actually be felt as an advantage. Some of these designers have excellent training in algorithmic structures, even.

Given the visual interfaces of better software today, with the right process mindset, you might not even know when you are coding. The trick is to see patterns, and then to find the free play within the structures of them. Surely this is a form of intelligence.

Notes
1 John Maeda, *Design By Numbers*, MIT Press (Cambridge, MA), 1999.
2 John Maeda, *Creative Code: Aesthetics and Computation*, Thames and Hudson (New York), 2004.

Malcolm McCullough, '20 Years of Scripted Space', Mike Silver (guest-editor), *Programming Cultures: Art and Architecture in the Age of Software*, *AD* Profile 182, *AD* 76, July–August 2006, pp 12–15. © 2012 John Wiley & Sons Ltd.

Collective Intelligence (2006)

Christopher Hight, Chris Perry and Philippe Morel

In the autumn of 2006 *AD* Profile 183, *Collective Intelligence in Design,* marked the architectural debut of the nascent Web 2.0 environment – the term Web 2.0 itself, which appears to have been coined in 2004, is not mentioned in the issue, but Christopher Hight and Chris Perry's introduction outlines many of the arguments which were then central to the debate on the web's participatory turn. Due to technical improvements (and particularly to the diffusion of affordable high-speed, always-on Internet connections), early in the 21st century the Internet began to resemble the digital pioneers' vision of a flat and shareable platform for information exchange, where every node can upload and download data at will, and every participant can be at the same time a consumer and a provider of content. Digitally supported interactivity and collaboration became technically conceivable as well as socially acceptable, in ways that in many cases defied centuries-old traditions, and new and disruptive paradigms for the creation and distribution of content quickly began to emerge.

Hight and Perry's introduction emphasises the dual nature of digital participation – bureaucratic and democratic, global and local, and seen potentially both as an emanation of late-capitalist corporations and market forces and as an expression of social activism and self-organising communities. The essays collected in the issue focus on interactive technologies, responsive environments, and software and interface design, but also on new forms of design practices based on enhanced collaboration through digital communication technologies, which in turn anticipate a new generation of digital design tools specifically meant for information exchange and collaborative decision making (see pages 226–39).

Philippe Morel's essay discusses the rise of grid computing and its potential to bring to fruition one of the premises of the digital turn: cheap, ubiquitous and theoretically unlimited processing power (at the time of writing, in 2012, similar arguments are being made with regard to 'cloud computing' and 'big data', which however are based on proprietary services rather than on distributed participatory networks; earlier technologies of grid computing are now embedded in mainstream commercial software, such as Skype, currently owned by Microsoft). As an example of this 'quantitative shift' in design computing, Morel shows his own Bolivar Chair, a genetic notation supported by distributed computing, which includes expert structural feedback (the chair's stability is calculated through finite element analysis) and file-to-factory fabrication technologies.

CHRISTOPHER HIGHT AND CHRIS PERRY **Introduction to**
Collective Intelligence in Design AD September–October 2006

Collective intelligence is not purely a cognitive object. Intelligence must be understood here in its etymological sense of joining together (interlegere), as uniting not only ideas but people, constructing society.[1]

The alchemy of collaboration does not merge the two authors into a single voice but rather proliferates them to create the chorus of a multitude.[2]

That digital technology has transformed the forms and spaces of what we design has become commonplace. Its transformative potential for forms of design practice and spaces of knowledge has remained less examined, but is ultimately more radical in its implications. With the shift from the second machine age to that of information, the reflexive network has replaced the assembly line as a pre-eminent model of organisation even as media infrastructures have augmented physical transportation at multiple scales stretching from discrete sites of production and consumption, to economic, political and even social institutions. This nexus of computation, telecommunications and new organisations of economic and political power suggest that the 19th-century division of design into distinct professions might now be displaced by different organisations of knowledge and practices. The texts and projects contained in this issue demonstrate how networks of international, transdisciplinary, decentralised practices are emerging to reposition and retool design practice to engage today's unconventional problems, site briefs, clients and manufacturing processes.

'Collective intelligence', as both a concept and a term, has its roots in a number of historical and contemporary contexts. In the 1960s Marshall McLuhan noticed the emergence of new social organisations based on principles of decentralisation and collectivity. Enabled in part by the advent of telecommunication technology, McLuhan quaintly referred to this model as 'the global village'.[3] Computing pioneer Douglas Englebart went further by suggesting that communication technology does not simply augment pre-existing social orders, but is instead a mechanism for augmenting the human intellect with nonhumanist modes of production.[4]

Telecommunications have proved even more transformative than imagined, whether the rapid decentralisation of international corporate enterprise or the grassroots phenomenon of the peer-to-peer network (such as open-source software communities like BitTorrent, as well as alternative political organisations like smart mobs, moveon.org, and so on). Some are seen as ominous and dystopic forms of globalisation, while others lend themselves to a utopic and liberatory reading of communication technologies. In either case, collective intelligence is not simply technical, but also explicitly social, political and, by extension, professional. As Pierre Lévy has argued, these technologies increasingly dematerialise the closed boundaries of disciplines, making knowledge a 'larger patchwork' in which one field can be enfolded with another.[5] Moreover, for Michel Serres,

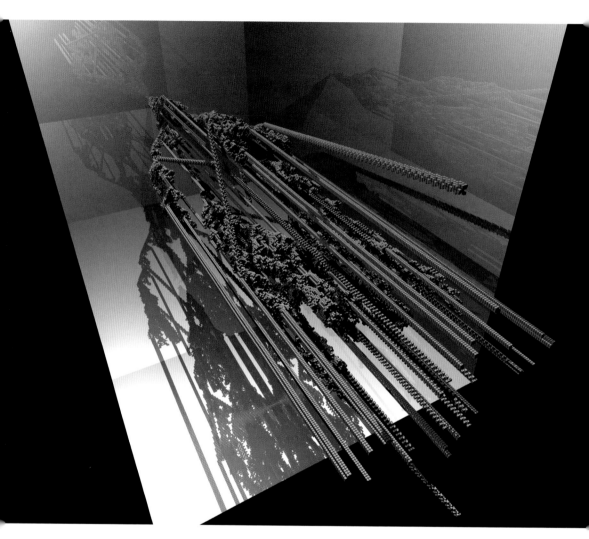

Frank Buss, Symmetric Rabbits, 2003. As seen in this
rendering of a cellular automaton, relying on local rules
that govern the behavioural logics of individual cells
or elements, cellular automata allow for larger patterns
of organisation to emerge over time, demonstrating
certain degrees of collective artificial intelligence
through basic programming and principles of self-
organisation. © Frank Buss.

knowledge and its techniques of electronic production and recombination become a new kind of infrastructure as disciplinary specificity is opened to practices of collaborative exchange. Thus, *Collective Intelligence in Design* attempts to map the reconfiguration of discrete design practices and disciplines into hypercommunicative technosocial networks.

Biopolitics and New Forms of Practice

> *The multitude is diffident of representation. … The people is always represented as a unity, whilst the multitude is not representable, because [it] is a singular multiplicity, a concrete universal. The people constituted a social body; the multitude does not … it is an active agent of self-organization.*[6]

The first way this is manifested is the relationship of design practice to the telecommunication technologies and their relationship to social power and order. With their influential books, *Empire and Multitude: War and Democracy in the Age of Empire*, the collaborative writing team of Michael Hardt and Antonio Negri have provided a lens through which to focus an analysis of the destructive as well as the productive effects of the shift from a disciplinary society to a biopolitical ordering of power. In brief, the term 'disciplinary society' (stemming from the work of Michel Foucault) describes a social ordering that relies primarily on physical and spatial mechanisms for instituting power. This is epitomised by Foucault's iconic description of the Panopticon prison. This disciplinary society differs dramatically from what Gilles Deleuze termed the 'control society', in which power is instituted from within and at the scale of the body. Combined, Foucault and Deleuze's work suggested a biopolitics that marks an important shift in the nature of power exercised upon general classes of society via physical space (and by extension architecture, at least as constituted in modernity) to the use of information at the scale of the individual subjects as a virtual controlling mechanism. For the sake of our argument, the economic corollary is often called post-Fordism, in which mass production is replaced by mass customisation, and rigid labour and productive practices are replaced by mobile and global markets.

What Hardt and Negri call 'Empire' uses the phenomena and technologies of our biopolitical power to produce increasingly centralised and integrated networks of international and intercorporate power – for example, in the form of pre-emptive wars and international markets rather than democratic control. In contrast, Hardt and Negri's reinvigoration of the concept of the 'Multitude' is a way of imagining the emergence of new forms of social, economic and political power enabled by the very same communication and information technologies, wherein a common space is constructed by linking an infinitely diverse set of individual interests through shared projects or desires in a more responsively democratic biopolitical ordering.

Prototypical examples of the Multitude include political organisations fostered by networking technologies, such as the highly distributed moveon.org and the partially Internet-coordinated World Trade Organization (WTO) resistance movement, but also user-generated organisations like the file-sharing communities of myspace and flickr or the online encyclopaedia network Wikipedia, open-source movements and peer-to-peer platforms. In these communities, participants operate from a variety of discrete locations spanning massive geographical distances via intensively reflexive feedback loops of communication and exchange. Dispersed and horizontal communication allows multiple agents to participate in the development of a particular material or technology via the Internet and its decentralising effects. The participants are at once geographically and culturally *apart from* one another while also a part of a common space of endeavour.[7]

Furthermore, these communities not only rely on communication, but produce communicability, that is to say the generation of new information as a product, and platforms for exchange.[8] Such multitudes operate according to a collective intelligence at the scale of practice. Such practices are inclusively political projects in so far that the resulting design becomes a site through which to configure the relationships between subjects and technologies. Indeed, their spaces may be the 21st century's biopolitical equivalent of the 19th century's architectural figuration of disciplinary power, as found in the Panopticon or, in a more liberatory way, the modern metropolis.

A number of design practices, as well as research groups, have started to learn from these models of distributed exchange and production, extending their logics to reconfigure the design office or research lab format by recasting it as an international, intergeographic, inter-institutional design-based file-sharing community. Examples featured in this issue include professional design practices such as servo, OCEAN net, United Architects (UA) and Open Source Architecture (O-S-A), as well as various inter-institutional research groups that integrate both academic and professional forms of design knowledge (the MIT Media Lab's OPENSTUDIO, RMIT's SIAL department, the Architectural Association's DRL, Cornell's Responsive Systems Group and the Columbia-based research practice CONTINUUM).

Intelligent Technologies and New Forms of Design

In computers everything becomes number: imageless, soundless, wordless quantity ... any medium can be translated into another ... a total connection of all media on a digital base erases the notion of the medium itself. Instead of hooking up technologies to people, absolute knowledge can run as an endless loop.[9]

---

top: Josh On, screenshot of theyrule.net, 2006. The website provides a database of various companies and institutions, allowing the user to map connections between those companies and institutions by way of shared executives and investments.

bottom: NASA, Mars Rover, 2003. The Mars Rover is an example of the vast and sophisticated assembly of emerging sensory, computation and behavioural technologies, combining to give the machine partial intelligence. While the rover relies on its human counterparts (users located back on earth) for strategic decision-making, its various sensing technologies allow it to make local decisions. © NASA.

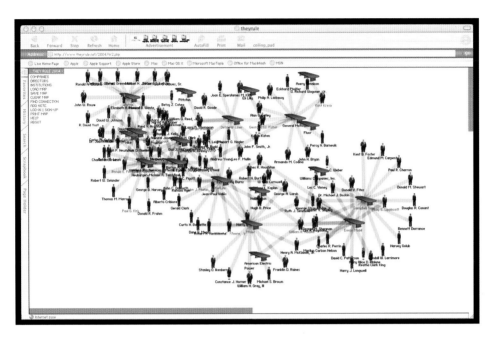

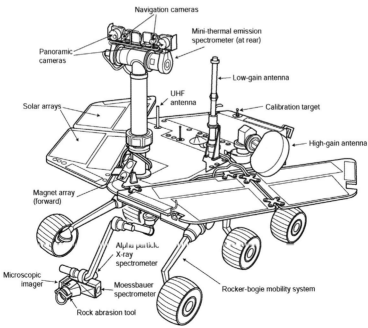

National Oceanic and Atmospheric Administration (NOAA), composite satellite photo of lights in North America, 1994–95. The image shows settlement patterns via infrastructure: the Internet provides a similar infrastructure for social geographies of the 21st century. Courtesy of NOAA/DMSP.

The second aspect of collective intelligence in design lay within the relationship of design technology and design products to emerging technological and material systems, specifically those concerned with the development of smart, or intelligent – or perhaps at this relatively early stage of development, simply adaptable – modes of behaviour. Examples in which intelligence is embedded in a given technological or material system range from genetic and nano engineering, to the development of new and increasingly adaptable organic LED display systems and amorphous alloys, as well as the burgeoning field of programmable matter (material systems in which fundamental properties of that material – for example, its rigidity or flexibility – can be altered via information). Such technologies integrate the predictive capacity of humans with the sophisticated computational and operational abilities of a technological apparatus. Such hybrid assemblages are more profound than wholly artificial intelligence, suggesting a nonhumanist understanding of agency and collective intelligence based on connectivity and molecular biotechnical power.

Many of the projects and practices featured in this issue are investigating such hybrid intelligent technological and material systems, whether as a site for professional practice or as research for interinstitutional groups. This includes the development of design environments that incorporate new software in connection with interaction technologies (such as information and motion sensing), as well as material systems in the form of adaptable surface structures and responsive machinic assemblies.

Cooperative Association for Internet Data Analysis (CAIDA), Walrus rendering of Internet, 2003. Image of an Internet 'map' using the Walrus software currently being developed by the collaborative network visualisation organisation CAIDA. © 2003 The Regents of the University of California. All Rights Reserved. Used by permission.

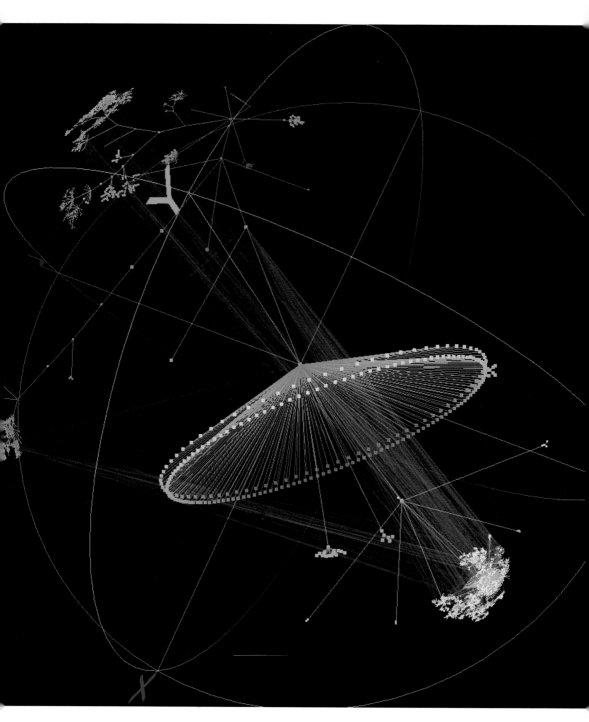

Cooperative Association for Internet Data Analysis (CAIDA), Walrus rendering of Internet, 2003. Image of an Internet 'map' using the Walrus software currently being developed by the collaborative network visualisation organisation CAIDA. © 2003 The Regents of the University of California. All Rights Reserved. Used by permission.

Design Synthesis and New Forms of Transdisciplinarity

The social network is a form of heterogeneous engineering comprised not only of people, but also of machines, animals, art and discourse, currency, architecture – the stuff of the social therefore, isn't simply human but a vast network of objects, human and non-human alike[10]

While we have located two primary scales of collective intelligence – the first generally regarding the scale of design *practice*, the second the scale of design *technology* and *product* – both are, of course, always integral to one another. Traditionally, design practice may appear as primarily social in nature, and thus analysed via loosely sociological terms, while the design product is regarded as primarily *material* or *technological* and therefore interpreted as an artefact representing cultural production. Our argument is that whether one is looking at the scale of society (its various institutional organisations and, by extension, the individual and collaborative behaviours of the agents and actors that make up those organisations), or the machines and technologies that are an extension of that social body, one cannot differentiate practice from product, or a notion of the human or social from the technological or the natural. Rather, one finds a much more ambiguous and synthetic set of conditions.

Embodied and embedded in a variety of material forms and scales, intelligence can be seen as at once a form of material matter and of organising and ordering those materials, a kind of 'heterogeneous engineering' in which bits and pieces from the social, the technical, the conceptual and the textual are connected and translated into a set of equally heterogeneous scientific (or, in our case, design) products.[11] Social relations shape machines as much as machines or new forms of technology shape social relations. Indeed, Bruno Latour has recently reiterated that rather than see the social as a distinct thing or domain, it is nothing more or less than the topologies of connectivity between a multitude of agencies, from the human to the material. Even science does not, in the first instance, investigate nature; nor do social forces determine knowledge. Rather, what is at stake is the design of network collectives of people, machines, technologies of communication and production.

Opening the Fields

We are seeing the combination of network communications and social networks. Whenever a new communications technology lowers the threshold for groups to act collectively, new kinds of institutions emerge.[12]

Understood in this way, collective intelligence requires a transdisciplinary approach to the built environment. Hence, this publication features a number of design fields including architectural design, interaction and information design, product design, sound design, software and interface design, motion graphic and typography design, set and exhibition design, and lighting design.

Rather than offer a stabilising or interpretive grid of explanation for these practices, we have attempted to install a collective intelligence within the issue itself, one the reader can engage with at a variety of levels, speeds, modes and angles of approach, from the pragmatic to the erudite, from media and programming to construction details. Instead of presenting an in-depth analysis of a few practices we could pretend represent 'collective intelligence', we have tried to map out a heterogeneous network of interconnected practices and their concerns. Furthermore, this issue of *AD* is itself an example of collective intelligence, written and edited collaboratively through Internet technologies (blogs, wikis, ftp sites and email), from several cities and multiple institutional and intellectual contexts, and through distributed forms of production and identity. Moreover, during the nine-month editorial process, some of the featured collaborations reconfigured, dissolved or gained new interconnectivities. To this extent, the issue is a historical cross section of nodes within an evolving network of agents, projects and ideas. Like a map of the Internet, it is accurate as a representation only for the fleeting moment; its enduring usefulness lies in its triangulations of potential trajectories into the future.

Ultimately, innovative design does not concern the novel appearance of objects, but rather constructing new manifolds for the production of knowledge that transform the objects given by known tools and sets of practices. The first design problem, therefore, is the construction of a precise and synthetic commons of exchange across previously separate and distinct areas or fields of design. Such trandisciplinarity requires and precipitates the construction of a collective intelligence through the design process itself. All design is the production of techniques of connectivity. The result is not so much a product of this process as it is a platform for it, inseparable from its continual unfolding of new technosocial lifeworlds.

Notes
1 Pierre Lévy, *Collective Intelligence: Mankind's Emerging World in Cyberspace*, Perseus Books (London), 1997, p 10.
2 'The Theory & Event Interview: Sovereignty, Multitudes, Absolute Democracy: A Discussion between Michael Hardt and Thomas L Dumm about Hardt's and Negri's Empire', in Paul A Passavant and Jodi Dean (eds), *Empire's New Clothes: Reading Hardt and Negri*, Routledge (London), 2004, p 163.
3 Marshall McLuhan, *Understanding Media: The Extensions of Man*, MIT Press (Cambridge, MA), 1964.
4 Pierre Lévy, *Collective Intelligence*.
5 For more on the concept of patchwork, see Lévy, *Collective Intelligence*.
6 Antonio Negri, 'Approximations: Towards an Ontological Definition of the Multitude', *Interactivist Info Exchange*, 12 November 2002.
7 See Manuel Castells, *The Rise of the Network Society*, Blackwell Publishers (Oxford), 1996.
8 Jodi Dean, 'The Networked Empire: Communicative Capitalism and the Hope for Politics', in Passavant and Dean, *Empire's New Clothes*, p 163.
9 Friedrich Kittler, *Grammophon Film Typewriter*, Bosomann (Berlin), 1986
10 John Law, 'Notes on the Theory of the Actor Network: Ordering, Strategy, and Heterogeneity', www.comp.lancs.ac.uk/sociology/papers/Law-Notes-on-ANT.pdf, Centre for Science Studies, Lancaster University, 1992 (2003), p 3.
11 Bruno Latour, *Reassembling the Social: An Introduction to Actor-Network-Theory*, Oxford University Press (New York), 2005, pp 220–21.
12 Howard Rheingold, 'How the Protesters Mobilized', interview with Jennifer Lee, *New York Times*, 23 February 2003.

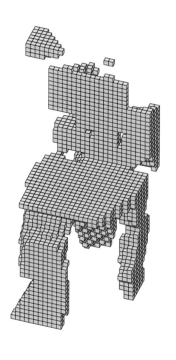
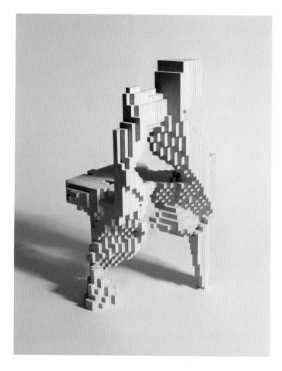

top left: EZCT Architecture & Design Research with Hatem Hamda and Marc Schoenauer, studies on optimisation: computational chair design using genetic algorithms, 2004. The 'Bolivar' model is evaluated for a multiple load strategy (it is always stable, whatever way the seat is positioned). This model (prototype and drawings) is part of the Centre Pompidou Architecture Collection. © Philippe Morel (original drawings © Centre Pompidou).

top right: Philippe Morel/EZCT Architecture & Design Research, chair 'Model T1-M', after 860 generations (86,000 structural evaluations). Courtesy Philippe Morel © Ilse Leenders.

above: EZCT Architecture & Design Research with Hatem Hamda and Marc Schoenauer, Studies on optimisation: computational chair design using genetic algorithms, 2004. Data analysis, 'Bolivar' model, Mathematica drawings. Because the data was structured for mutations and evaluation via finite element methods, it needed to be rearranged for fabrication. Mathematica was therefore used for writing different algorithms in order to ease pricing, cutting and assembling. The drawings are part of the Centre Pompidou Architecture Collection. © Philippe Morel (original drawings © Centre Pompidou).

PHILIPPE MOREL **Computational Intelligence:**
The Grid as a Post-Human Network *AD* September–October 2006

Indeed, today, it has sadly become very fashionable to reject, in an obscurantist way, many more things in the subconscious than is necessary: it is much nicer to adore the 'primitives' and to note, happily, a 'bankruptcy of the rationalist mind' … than to realize, once and for all, without equivocation, that the age of physics, far from becoming extinct, is just beginning!

Arno Schmidt, 'Calculus I'[1]

The scientific man is the ulterior development of the artistic man.

Friedrich Nietzsche, *Human, All Too Human*[2]

'Distributed' Paradigm

During the past five years, most of my (post-) 'critical-political time' has been spent dealing with a new idea of collective intelligence that replaces the one implicitly defined, a century ago, by Gabriel Tarde[3] or, explicitly, 10 years ago, by Pierre Lévy.[4] This intelligence first evolved from communication networks ranging from the newspaper to the telephone, the fax to the Internet. Today, it finds its fullest expression in grid computing, the distributed computing paradigm *par excellence*. Grid computing is a protocol for linking discrete but geographically dispersed machines into a distributed parallel processing network. Grid computation has given rise to a distributed computational intelligence that renders the classical concept of singular and autonomous intelligence obsolete.

As important as the technology itself are the consequences of this phenomenon, namely the rise of a new kind of people – geographically isolated scientific farmers who exchange their postpolitical concepts in symposia[5] – and the rise of a posturban environment that I call the 'Ambient Factory'. What are the constituents of this factory? An early example, SETI@home, participated in deciphering extraterrestrial radio signals for signs of extraterrestrial intelligence. And this experiment has recently been transformed into a new model of industrial production with projects such as Folding@Home, Evolutionary@Home, XPulsar@Home, Fightaids@Home, Genome@Home, Models@Home and HIWTNI (Home is where the network is).[6] All these examples of grid computing use the downtime of geographically dispersed PCs (at the moment often running as screensavers, but there is no doubt that computation power per se will become a global market – take, for example, the polluting rights market and the recently created Powernext Carbon)[7] to process the immense amounts of data involved in investigating a scientific research problem. Through a home PC, which becomes a piece of e-laboratory equipment, any user therefore participates in a community of scientists and nonscientists in producing knowledge. This effectively creates a carpet constructed of autonomous but interconnected 'farms': computer farms, energy farms and so on. The term 'farm' may seem anachronistic, but it is appropriate because it connotes the sorts of new living practices these networks produce.

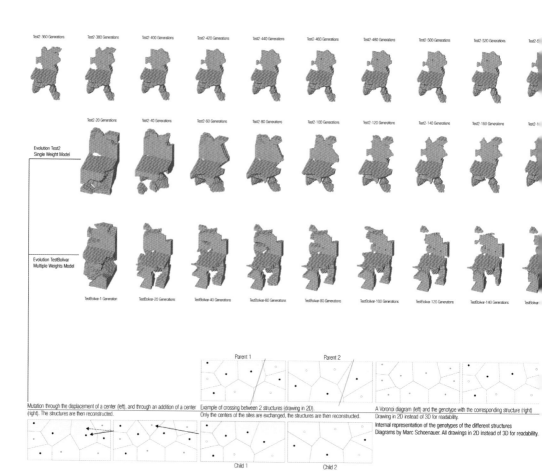

Test2-360 Generations | Test2-380 Generations | Test2-400 Generations | Test2-420 Generations | Test2-440 Generations | Test2-460 Generations | Test2-480 Generations | Test2-500 Generations | Test2-520 Generations | Test2-5...

Test2-20 Generations | Test2-40 Generations | Test2-60 Generations | Test2-80 Generations | Test2-100 Generations | Test2-120 Generations | Test2-140 Generations | Test2-160 Generations | Test2-1...

Evolution Test2
Single Weight Model

Evolution TestBolivar
Multiple Weights Model

TestBolivar-1 Generation | TestBolivar-20 Generations | TestBolivar-40 Generations | TestBolivar-60 Generations | TestBolivar-80 Generations | TestBolivar-100 Generations | TestBolivar-120 Generations | TestBolivar-140 Generations | TestBolivar...

Parent 1   Parent 2

Mutation through the displacement of a center (left), and through an addition of a center (right). The structures are then reconstructed.

Example of crossing between 2 structures (drawing in 2D). Only the centers of the sites are exchanged, the structures are then reconstructed.

A Voronoi diagram (left) and the genotype with the corresponding structure (right). Drawing in 2D instead of 3D for readability.

Internal representation of the genotypes of the different structures
Diagrams by Marc Schoenauer. All drawings in 2D instead of 3D for readability.

Child 1   Child 2

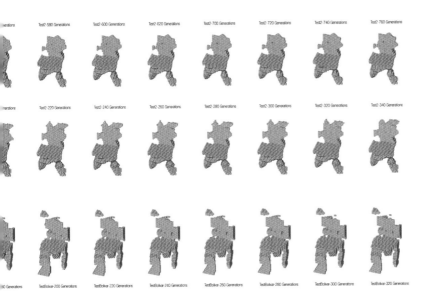

Test2-580 Generations Test2-600 Generations Test2-620 Generations Test2-700 Generations Test2-720 Generations Test2-740 Generations Test2-760 Generations

Test2-220 Generations Test2-240 Generations Test2-260 Generations Test2-280 Generations Test2-300 Generations Test2-320 Generations Test2-340 Generations

TestBolivar-200 Generations TestBolivar-220 Generations TestBolivar-240 Generations TestBolivar-260 Generations TestBolivar-280 Generations TestBolivar-300 Generations TestBolivar-320 Generations

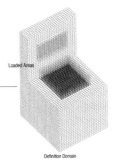

Loaded Areas

Definition Domain

above: EZCT Architecture & Design Research with Hatem Hamda and Marc Schoenauer, studies on optimisation: computational chair design using genetic algorithms, 2004. The process sheet shows seven chairs optimised through a mono-objective optimisation strategy, two chairs optimised through a multi-objectives strategy, and the optimisation process for Model 'Test2'. The sheet shows the crossing-over internal representation based on Voronoi diagrams. This high-level representation strategy, developed by Marc Schoenauer, allows for a better correspondence between the genotype representation and the phenotype of the real chairs. © Philippe Morel.

left: Philippe Morel/EZCT Architecture & Design Research, preliminary structural studies for a lounging chair (unrealised). © Philippe Morel.

The questions such projects raise for (a-)spatial and (a-)social organisations of production for the present are as significant as Ludwig Hilberseimer's recognition of the electrical power grid in 1955 as 'the real force toward [urban] decentralization', since 'even the smallest settlement can be supplied with water, electricity, heat and light'.[8] Today, grid-computing networks not only allow the multitudes to communicate and to give an existence to the 'world brain', they allow computers to communicate in autonomous ways as a pure infrastructure that is at once global, abstract and standardised. This infrastructure allows a new kind of distributed computational and linguistic production, revealing what previously was called human production[9] as what it truly was all along: reproduction. Indeed, because of the growing complexity of all production (for example, in biotechnology, material science, pharmaceutics and computer sciences), all that is left for human labour is conceptual work. Everything else, in any field, is done by computers or numerically controlled machines.

'Quantitative' Shift

Why use ideas of industrial production, post-human networks or disappearing cities in reference to bionetworks and the multitude? Contemporary production seems to be driven by scientific rather than social forces. If so, understanding science means understanding real characteristics of our civilisation driven by 'quantitative concepts' such as numbers, statistics, approximation tools and methods, and mathematical precision. Quantity sounds abstract if, in the field of architecture, we consider Hilberseimer's diagram *H Bomb on Chicago*, dated 1946, but it also appears as a very practical concept if we listen to Max Planck's comment on the same nuclear power problem (1947): 'An appropriate calculation has shown that the quantity of energy liberated in this way in a cubic meter of uranium oxide pulverized in a hundredth of a second would be enough to raise a load of a billion metric tons to a height of some 18,000 meters (59,055 feet). Such a quantity of energy could replace the combined production of all the world's most powerful plants for a good many years.'[10]

Here, quantity is a concrete problem, as concrete as Robert Musil's definition of the traditional newspaper – 'filled with a measureless opacity' that 'goes far beyond the intellectual capacity of a Leibniz'[11] – a definition often envisioned for our contemporary information overload. In this respect, thinking about collective intelligence means thinking about the way it works and the way problems are solved. Quantitative questions in fact pose their problems and their solutions simultaneously. Algorithms solve searching problems, peer-to-peer storage problems, open-source collaborative practices' problems[12] and open technologies standardisation and communication problems. An answer to a technological problem is always a technological answer. Then, what is grid computing if not an appropriation, for industrial purposes,[13] of a new kind of productive paradigm? Is not SETI@home, which processes each year the equivalent of 400,000 years of computing time by a single processor, the new paradigm for industrial production, for 'collaborative computational practice' in any field, including architecture? It seems that corporations have already answered positively to this with their employment of the SETI@home model,[14] and I believe that grid computing is the next step for collective intelligence – an infrastructure-based computational intelligence.

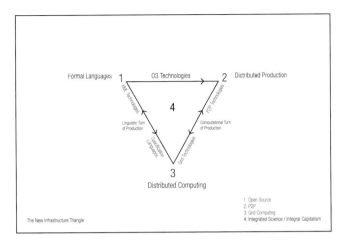

Formal Languages 1 OS Technologies 2 Dictributed Production

XML Technologies

Linguistic Turn
of Production

4

P2P Technologies

Computational Turn
of Production

Specification
Languages

Grid Technologies

3
Distributed Computing

1: Open Source
2: P2P
3: Grid Computing
4: Integrated Science / Integral Capitalism

The New Infrastructure Triangle

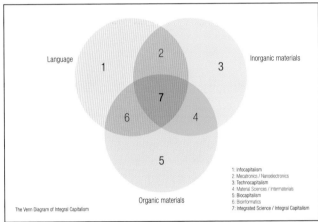

Language 1 2 3 Inorganic materials

7

6 4

5

Organic materials

1: Infocapitalism
2: Mecatronics / Nanoelectronics
3: Technocapitalism
4: Material Sciences / Intermaterials
5: Biocapitalism
6: Bioinformatics
7: Integrated Science / Integral Capitalism

The Venn Diagram of Integral Capitalism

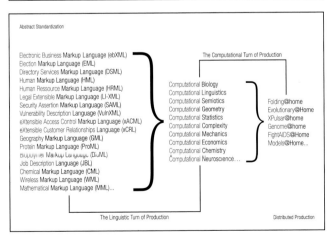

Abstract Standardization

Electronic Business Markup Language (ebXML)
Election Markup Language (EML)
Directory Services Markup Language (DSML)
Human Markup Language (HML)
Human Ressource Markup Language (HRML)
Legal Extensible Markup Language (LI-XML)
Security Assertion Markup Language (SAML)
Vulnerability Description Language (VulnXML)
eXtensible Access Control Markup Language (xACML)
eXtensible Customer Relationships Language (xCRL)
Geography Markup Language (GML)
Protein Markup Language (ProML)
Biopolymer Markup Language (BioML)
Job Description Language (JBL)
Chemical Markup Language (CML)
Wireless Markup Language (WML)
Mathematical Markup Language (MML)...

The Computational Turn of Production

Computational Biology
Computational Linguistics
Computational Semiotics
Computational Geometry
Computational Statistics
Computational Complexity
Computational Mechanics
Computational Economics
Computational Chemistry
Computational Neuroscience...

Folding@home
Evolutionary@Home
XPulsar@home
Genome@home
FightAIDS@Home
Models@Home...

The Linguistic Turn of Production Distributed Production

Philippe Morel/EZCT Architecture & Design Research, integral capitalism diagrams, from 'The Integral Capitalism', Philippe Morel Masters thesis, 2001–02. The diagrams are part of a global analysis of contemporary science-based capitalism – through the linguistic/computational turn of contemporary production – developed by Philippe Morel over the past four and a half years. This study insists on the merging of three inseparable forms of capitalism (infocapitalism, technocapitalism and biocapitalism) into an integrative economy: the Integral Capitalism. The study has to be considered as a post-Koolhaas (as well as postSassen) analysis of globalisation.
© Philippe Morel.

Tools and Concepts

The integration of concepts like distributed partial machine intelligence within the design process is an integral component of EZCT Architecture & Design Research's work. However, the practice not only refers to ideas of technology and science in their analyses of technology, but makes use of them. Architects should not metaphorically depict technology but use it, in a flat model, beyond any representation. Finally, because EZCT is part of the multitudes whose work concerns the 'ultimate production of human imagination' – that is, concepts – the practice also builds proofs for these concepts as design projects constructed through computers and programming languages.

For example, the practice has recently moved towards a grid model of design conceptualisation and production, extending its long-standing use of Mathematica, software normally oriented towards scientific communities, as a design tool, by using its grid-computing variant. GridMathematica leads to more efficient collaborative practice while alleviating the constraints of a single computer's calculation power. Its use has allowed EZCT to reinforce its long-term collaboration with physicist Bruno Autin (author of the Geometrica software package, formerly of CERN) and mathematician Maryvonne Teissier (Paris VII University). Of course, GridMathematica is not the only way to achieve distributed computing. During the summer of 2004, EZCT led a project wherein a series of chairs were computed using genetic algorithms for optimisation using a cluster of 12 computers from the École Polytechnique in Paris. They were controlled by Hatem Hamda, from a geographically distinct lab (INRIA), using a Linux platform and open-source libraries and software including Evolving Objects (an evolutionary computation library) and xd3d (a scientific visualisation tool). In this process, first a human collaborative practice was evidently implied in the previous development of the open-source libraries, software and so on, and second a computational and 'post-human' collaborative practice became the paradigm since a very limited number of people were able to appropriate a vast amount of computational resources.

Thus we should not underestimate the fact that collaborative practice does not necessarily mean a human collaborative practice, and take into account newly emerging concepts; for example, that of productive autonomy.

Notes

1   Arno Schmidt, 'Calculus I' (Berechnungen I), in *Texte und Zeichen*, No 1, 15 January 1955, reprinted in Rosen & Porree, Stahlberg (Karlsruhe), 1959.
2   Friedrich Nietzsche, *Human, All Too Human: A Book for Free Spirits* (Menschliches, Allzumenschliches. Ein Buch für freie Geister), trs Marion Faber and Stephen Lehmann, Penguin Classics (London), 1994.
3   Gabriel Tarde, *Les lois de l'imitation: étude sociologique*, F Alcan (Paris), 1890.
4   Pierre Lévy, *Collective Intelligence: Mankind's Emerging World in Cyberspace*, Perseus Books Group (New York), 1997.
5   Those who are not scientists, who are, by implication, in marketing or business, exchange their ideas in trade shows or technology conferences, places where, following Nietzsche's sublime prediction, our whole civilisation affords 'buying or selling as a luxury of our sensibility'. Friedrich Nietzsche, *The Gay Science* (*La Gaya Scienza*), 1882.

6   I used this HIWTNI abbreviation, developed by the McKinsey quarterly, in my work 'Living in the Ice Age' (2001–02), which is an explicit theorisation of what I only evoke in the present article.

7   Due to the Kyoto Protocol, companies and countries now trade polluting rights on this dedicated marketplace (Powernext Carbon).

8   Ludwig Hilberseimer, *The Nature of Cities*, Theobald (Chicago), 1955. The Ambient Factory concept actualises not only Hilberseimer's but also Mies' parallel comment: 'There are no cities, in fact, any more. It goes on like a forest. That is the reason why we cannot have the old cities anymore; that is gone forever, planned cities and so on. We should think about the means that we have to live in a jungle, and maybe we do well with that.' Ludwig Mies van der Rohe, Interview with J Peter, in Phyllis Lambert (ed), *Mies in America*, CCA, Whitney Museum & Harry N Abrams (New York), 2001.

9   The classical one theorised by Adam Smith then Karl Marx.

10 Max Planck, 'The Meaning and Limits of Science', 1947. Lecture given at the Harnack-Haus, Berlin-Dahlem.

11 Robert Musil, *The Man Without Qualities* (*Der Mann ohne Eigenschaften*), first edition, Rowohlt (Hamburg), 1930.

12 Open source is an answer from contemporary capitalism to itself: 'I've worked for IBM in Linux for more than six years, and it has become big business for us, it's a fundamental part of IBM's business. We're not into Linux and open source because it's cool. It's nice that it's cool, but it's good business. We're making billions.' Daniel Frye, 'From Open Source Software to Open Technology: How a Phenomenon is Turning Into an Exciting New Industry', InnoTech Conference, Portland, Oregon, 9 March 2005.

13 Keep in mind that everything is industrial – it is pharmaceutics, high-energy physics experiments, education, and so on – and that some distinctions between laboratories on one side and transnational corporations on the other do not really hold any more.

14 Arcelor or AstraZeneca [*sic*]: 'Large-scale clusters allow us to manage and share computing resources across the entire Discovery Function, accelerating drug discovery, design and time-to-market, and realize our investment in hardware. Platform LSF has more than proved itself so far and is now the preferred solution for managing computer farms in AstraZeneca.' Sandra McLaughlin, AstraZeneca's senior systems administrator for physical and structural sciences, in 'Platform to Accelerate Drug Discovery, Design at AstraZeneca', *HPCwire*, 3 January 2002.

Christopher Hight and Chris Perry, 'Introduction', Christopher Hight and Chris Perry (guest-editors), *Collective Intelligence in Design*, *AD* Profile 183, *AD* 76, September–October 2006, pp 5–9. © 2012 John Wiley & Sons Ltd.

Philippe Morel, 'Computational Intelligence: The Grid as a Post-Human Network', Christopher Hight and Chris Perry (guest-editors), *Collective Intelligence in Design*, *AD* Profile 183, *AD* 76, September–October 2006, pp 100–03. © 2012 John Wiley & Sons Ltd.

above and overleaf. Ali Rahim and Hina Jamelle/Contemporary Architecture Practice, Residential Tower, Dubai, UAE, 2005–. The tower overlooks the city of Dubai and the Persian Gulf on one side and the desert on the other. The project attempts to engage in Dubai's status as a regional economic hub and as a haven for foreign nationals seeking to invest abroad and to escape political unrest at home. © Ali Rahim and Hina Jamelle/Contemporary Architecture Practice.

Elegance (2007)

Ali Rahim, Hina Jamelle and Mark Foster Gage

AD Profile 185, *Elegance*, the first *AD* issue of 2007, signals the transition from the first to the second generation of digital blob-makers, reaffirming and redefining the style of continuous lines and smooth curving surfaces which has characterised digital design and fabrication since its beginnings in the early 1990s. Guest-edited by Ali Rahim and Hina Jamelle, the issue includes essays by, among others, Manuel DeLanda, Ben van Berkel and Caroline Bos, Preston Scott Cohen, Kivi Sotamaa, Hani Rashid, Patrik Schumacher, Benjamin Bratton and Hernan Diaz Alonso, with frequent reference to the works and theory of Greg Lynn throughout the volume. The editors' introduction and other essays, particularly Joseph Rosa's (not reproduced here), announce a second age of digital smoothness, an age of maturity and self-confidence, where the theoretical emphasis and radical experimentation of the first generation of digital designers are abandoned in favour of practice and 'elegant' making; as such, the issue also marks the conflation of digital design and post-critical thinking, which digital design theory had in many ways anticipated and heralded.

The editors' own project, a residential high-rise designed for the city of Dubai, itself an icon of the rise of globalised finance in the years immediately preceding the banking crash of 2008, features prominent folding and bulging smooth surfaces, both for core structures and for the curved glazing of the curtain walls. Emphasising the availability, affordability and cost-effectiveness of the technologies they employ, the authors present design variability and the customisation of residential units as a tool to devise new marketing strategies and suitable real estate sale models.

Mark Foster Gage's essay argues for aesthetics as the keystone of a new theory of digital formalism to follow the demise of the linguistic mandate in architecture, which he ascribes both to Post-Modernism and to 'critical modernism'. Linguistics and semiotics are concerned with what buildings mean, regardless of how they look, and indifferent to beauty. Foster Gage pleads for a new scopocentric approach to design, to replace the logocentric and logicocentric interests of Modernists, Post-Modernists and Late Modernists; he also claims that a new architectural aesthetics must be based upon some form of intuitive ('visceral', 'precognitive') visual intelligence, hence on some empathy with the body, sensations and desire. (Some of these arguments are also developed in *Log* 17, 2009, guest-edited by Mark Foster Gage and Florencia Pita). Foster Gage concludes, the mathematics of continuity, in its new and multifarious digital applications, provides a new standard and almost a common expression for contemporary design, and a system within which the dialectic between rule and anomaly, or prediction and invention, can create elegance and beauty – just like in the centuries-old history of the classical tradition.

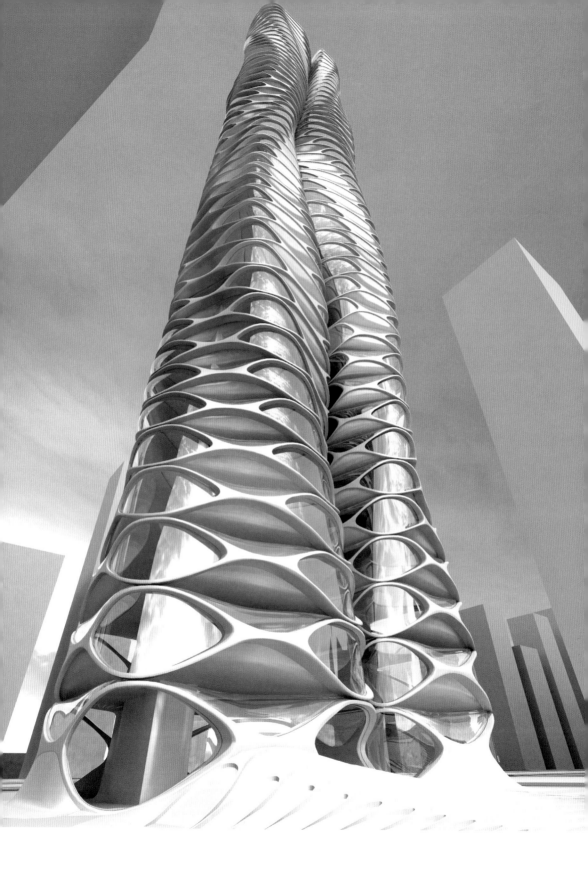

ALI RAHIM AND HINA JAMELLE The Economies of Elegance, Migrating Coastlines: Residential Tower, Dubai *AD* January–February 2007

This 45-storey, 41,800-square-metre (450,000-square-foot) residential tower incorporates multiple levels of architectural complexity in its design, manufacturing and assembly. The design of the structure is based on a transformation of four tubes – three interior and one exterior – which integrates all of the mechanical and electrical systems. As it transforms, it opens to allow light to penetrate to the interior. The integration continues in the development of techniques that enable the fabrication and assembly of all building systems. Through its capacity to be adjusted and fine-tuned interactively, the design creates varied unit types that provide opportunities for new real-estate sales models based on qualities and potentialities of spaces rather than simply square footage. Economy at the scales of assembly and manufacturing, combined with the provision for innovative approaches to unit sales, allow for the development of elegance in a cost-effective way.

The building overlooks the city of Dubai and the Persian Gulf on one side and the desert on the other. Located on Sheikh Zayed Road – the main thoroughfare connecting Dubai and Abu Dhabi – the project attempts to engage Dubai's status as a regional economic hub and as a haven for foreign nationals seeking to invest abroad and to hedge political unrest at home. By catalysing exchanges with both its residents and the larger city, it aims to facilitate a series of migrations, whether human, economic or architectural.

To incorporate the myriad economic factors and site relationships into the design, the goal was to activate the middle section of the building, which from a real-estate perspective is typically considered least desirable. Each floor of the structure needed to respond to three desirable conditions: privacy between units, maximisation of views to the surrounding landscape, and the provision of several emergency exit paths. Twisting generated the tower's undulating profile – a vertical coastline marking the flows and migrations within the system that generated it. In addition, the middle floors of the building were compressed or shorter in height. As these new organisational patterns were guided by the decision-making process, new possibilities for the economic development of the middle section of the tower were developed.

By increasing exchanges with both its residents and the larger city, the building aims to facilitate a series of migrations whether human, economic or architectural. Several features at the base of the tower may serve to draw commerce away from the main street towards the desert, possibly increasing the value of land behind the building. © Ali Rahim and Hina Jamelle/Contemporary Architecture Practice.

The tower consists of two contiguous 45-storey buildings that fuse, shedding their individual identities. Each storey is developed into a variable module of concrete, glass and portions of a concrete structural core, an elevator shaft and emergency exit stairs. In aggregate, the variations between the modules produce the dynamic shape of the overall tower. The exterior glass walls are inflected, some curving outwards, the others remaining flat. The windows are clad in heat-sensitive low-iron glass that exhibits differing qualities depending on the location of the sun and amount of heat on its surface. The structural modules also twist over the height of the building, altering the load-bearing capacities of each floor. The elevator core stays roughly in the same position between floors, but the emergency stairs are torqued to maximise their potential utility.

The inflections in the building's envelope and cores cause the interior spaces to compress and expand from floor to floor, and the plan of each level is unique. On floors where the emergency stairs and elevator core are close together, the space in between may be used for storage; on the floors above, as the two cores move further apart, the interstitial area becomes larger and may create space for dining. The compression of the middle levels leads to units that have lower ceiling heights and are generally smaller and more affordable, alleviating the potential undesirability of the apartments on these floors.

The units in the tower thus avoid the repetition and sameness typical of high-rise residential buildings. Apartments range from studios to four-bedrooms and vary in size from 93 square metres (1,000 square feet) to 465 square metres (5,000 square feet). However, the complex inflections of spaces, room sizes, ceiling heights and apartment organisations make it impossible to standardise marketing descriptions (for example, 'two-bedroom'). Instead, each apartment affords[1] a range of conditions and possibilities for occupation that expands the developer's options for marketing the units.

The relationships between structure, emergency stair core and unit change not only between floors, but also in response to the unique effects of each user. For example, the curvature of the exterior glass windows generates effects that change in relation to the perspective of inhabitants and passers-by moving within or past the building. As the building's envelope and spaces shift, twist and rotate, they produce migrating effects in perception and use. At a larger scale these perceptual and occupational effects may attract other foreign nationals to purchase units in the building. Hence the formation has the potential to inflect local migration patterns and to be transformed by changing occupancies.

The migration is also developed into interrelational models of the fabrication of the systems that are done off site. The model developed with the collaboration of glass manufacturers and concrete fabricators in Guangdong, China, is responsive and specific to the cost of glass and its curvature. The glass is linked to the overall building form, and as the form is changed so is the glass. In addition to this change in the direct relationship, the relationship of all of the other glass pieces also changes. This zone of influence of a particular change is designed to be gradual to maintain the aesthetic elegance of the project while also modulating the tower and the curvature of glass to make it affordable.

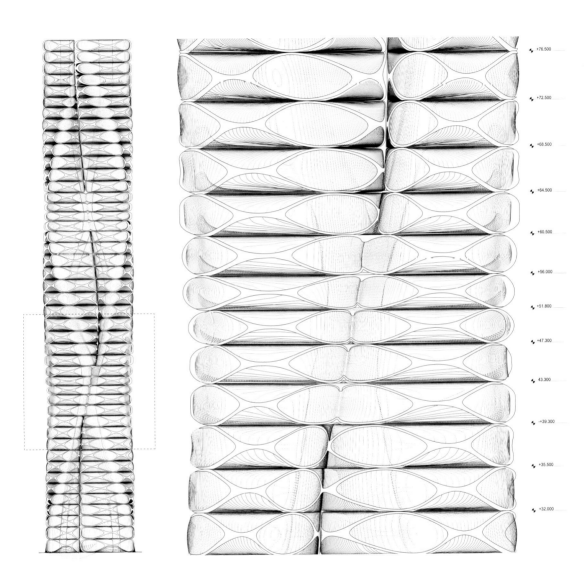

+76.500
+72.500
+68.500
+64.500
+60.500
+56.000
+51.800
+47.300
43.300
-+39.300
+35.500
+32.000

The building consists of two contiguous
buildings that fuse, shedding their individual
identities. © Ali Rahim and Hina Jamelle/
Contemporary Architecture Practice.

right: The transformation of
an accumulative strategy
of variations changes in
kind when it transforms
into the floor surface as
well as into the structural
tubes containing the
stairs and elevator cores.
© Ali Rahim and Hina
Jamelle/Contemporary
Architecture Practice.

below: The glazing panels
variation and fabrication
is developed in one
integrated interrelational
model that transforms
and adjusts, making
modulations at all scales
from floor-to-floor heights
to the glass curvatures,
and relating it directly to an
updated building cost. This
is done by collaborating
directly with the concrete
fabricators and glass
manufacturers, yielding a
cost for each trade as well
as for the entire project.
© Ali Rahim and Hina
Jamelle/Contemporary
Architecture Practice.

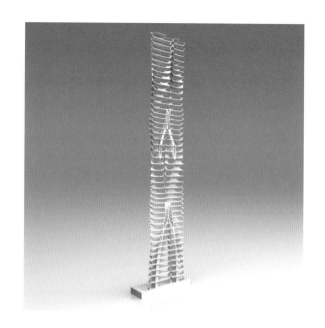

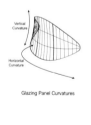

Glazing Panel Curvatures

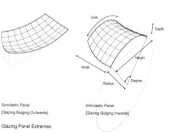

Synclastic Panel
[Glazing Bulging Outwards]

Anticlastic Panel
[Glazing Bulging Inwards]

Glazing Panel Extremes

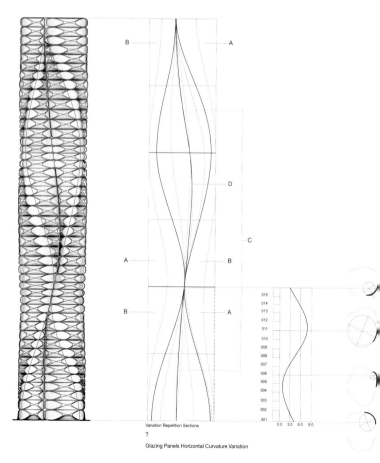

Variation Repetition Sections

Glazing Panels Horizontal Curvature Variation

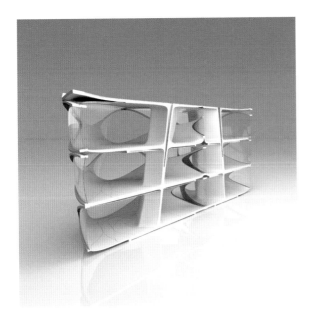

A close-up view of the section of the project reveals the mutation of surface from interior to the exterior shells which are porous to allow light to penetrate the structural skin. © Ali Rahim and Hina Jamelle/Contemporary Architecture Practice.

The building also contains effects in relation to its site. Several features at the base of the tower may serve to draw commerce away from Sheikh Zayed Road and towards the desert, possibly increasing the value of the land behind the tower and producing another migrating coastline. Amenities at the base include ponds that create a cool environment and power outlets that may facilitate the gathering of markets. The exact outcomes generated by such affordances depend on the specific behaviours of users. The intention, however, is to provide the potential of shifting economic exchanges and openness towards the desert.

By suggesting a new approach to selling real estate – in terms of quality and the potentials of space rather than just square footage – the design of the tower may influence how developers build and market condominiums in the future. The formation includes a series of migrating coastlines that reflect and shape the resettlement patterns of its residents – specifically, their attempts to gain residency in the UAE by purchasing real estate in Dubai. And the tower inflects the local economic conditions of Sheikh Zayed Road, potentially shifting the relationship between the desert and the city.

Note
1 Ali Rahim, *Catalytic Formations, Architecture and Digital Design*, Routledge (New York), 2006, pp 138–9.

Ali Rahim and Hina Jamelle/Contemporary Architecture Practice, 'The Economies of Elegance, Migrating Coastlines: Residential Tower, Dubai', Ali Rahim and Hina Jamelle (guest-editors), *Elegance*, AD Profile 185, *AD* 77, January–February 2007, pp 66–75. © 2012 John Wiley & Sons Ltd.

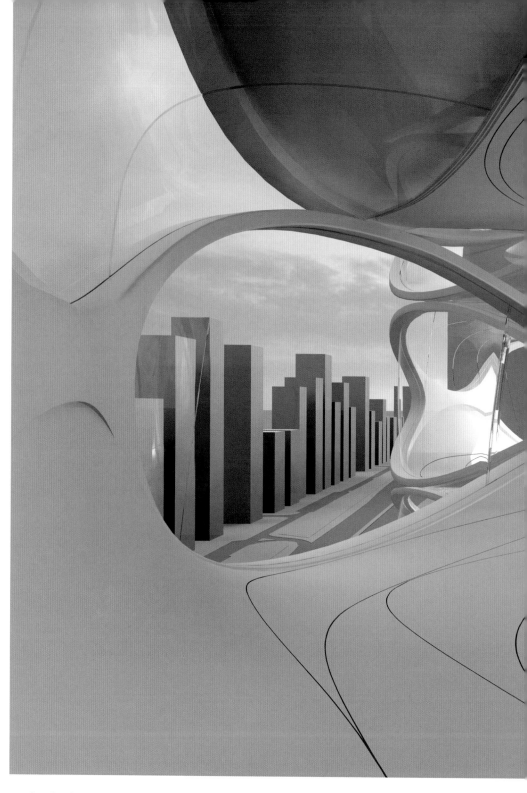

Interior view of the integration of lighting and floor pattern in a transforming surface.
© Ali Rahim and Hina Jamelle/Contemporary Architecture Practice.

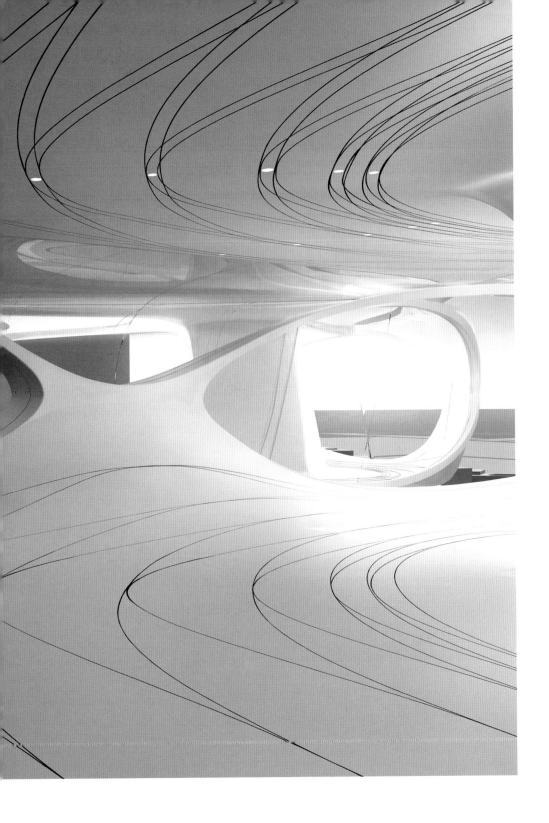

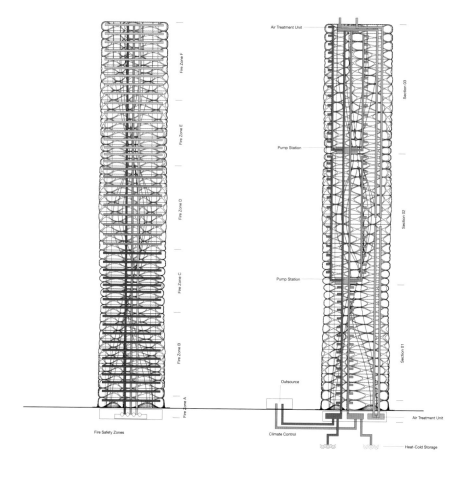

Fire Zone F

Fire Zone E

Fire Zone D

Fire Zone C

Fire Zone B

Fire Zone A

Fire Safety Zones

Air Treatment Unit

Section 03

Pump Station

Section 02

Pump Station

Section 01

Outsource

Climate Control

Air Treatment Unit

Heat-Cold Storage

MARK FOSTER GAGE Deus ex Machina: From Semiology to the Elegance of Aesthetics *AD* January–February 2007

Architecture has had its share of aesthetic design theories in the past – so why elegance, and why now? Modernism and its successors even seem at odds with the elegant as, for most of the 20th century, they rarely dabbled in the loquaciousness of adjectives. Instead, under the guise of supposed conflicts, architecture has lovingly endured decades of both Postmodernism's and critical Modernism's myopic interest in signification and semiotic content, whether indexical, iconic or symbolic.[1]

Choked with this need for signification, and bound by demands of economic and performance-based efficiencies, architecture has been excluded from the discourses of the aesthetic for nearly a century. It seems unlikely that digital technologies would be responsible for a 21st-century rebirth of aesthetics as a discourse, and even less likely that one of the first aesthetic judgements to emerge from this hiatus would be the historically aureate elegance – if for no other reason than its previously, and even distasteful, historical associations with the elite.

However, for the project of architectural formalism, a new aesthetic elegance is a clear and understandable direction. The supple surfaces, flowing vectors and allusions to movement enabled through topological and animate modelling techniques point clearly to a novel sensuousness of form, an eroticism of plasticity awaiting some future critical encounter. But surely it cannot be enough to desire only the smooth[2] sensuousness of continuously undifferentiated surfaces – and even structures that are 'continuously connected and intertwined through fine-grain local linkages'[3] that emerged from the pivotal discourse of 'Animate Form'[4] and were elaborated in that of 'Intricacy'[5] seem to crave a more encompassing narrative of aesthetics for their continuing enrichment.

Architecture now needs qualifiers, such as elegance, less as descriptors and more as aspirations enlisted for the production of new effects.[6] An increasingly architecturally savvy public has been misled by the guise of a false contemporaneity in what Charles Jencks plainly terms 'Iconic Buildings'.[7] Like gremlins, art museums, libraries and concert halls, with their star-studded pedigrees, continue to propagate in every metropolis as a fictional relief from generations of aesthetically and effectually inert development. As an antidote to satisfying such a hunger with mere optical[8] novelty, or as Peter Eisenman observes the 'saccharine confections'[9] that these icons tend to become, there must be a larger visual discourse under which this new work is subsumed.

---

top: Exterior view showing a gradient of transformation that migrates in the form of the tower as well as across the facade of the tower, producing elegant sensations. © Ali Rahim and Hina Jamelle/Contemporary Architecture Practice.

bottom: Fire safety and mechanical systems integration. The distribution of the engineering systems will locate a primary plant on each of the technical floors. In this way the central plant is broken down to enable it to be sized for improved part-load performance and thereby increase its overall annual efficiency. © Ali Rahim and Hina Jamelle/Contemporary Architecture Practice.

This initial premise, put forth by elegance and, by extension, a contemporary aesthetics, is that there is another objective emerging, like a literary *deus ex machina*,[10] from the retirement of the semiological – one larger and more encompassing than what would otherwise be dismissed as a mere formalist paroxysm. This new intent dismisses the need for semiological content, and replaces it with a new species of visual intelligence, sophisticated and nuanced, and designed towards the production of new aesthetically enabled effects,[11] such as elegance, aimed not at semiological satisfaction, but instead obsessed with the intricacies of aesthetic legibility and its affiliated production of desire.

The effect of elegance, with this ambition in mind, is not merely a contemporary substantive aesthetic judgement.[12] It is also a didactic and digestible architectural recipe. The production of elegance in this scenario requires not only techniques, but a visual and formal expertise. A truly expert and contemporary elegance cannot be generated from simple allusions to movement, sensuousness or fluidity, but also requires the production of desirable, yet sometimes mutant, anomalies that are curated to further exaggerate these, and other, aesthetic effects. Continuously variable forms provide degrees of sameness and difference, though rarely, without expert intervention, produce new emergent figural mutations within the system. This ability to curate mutation, and the production of emergent figures at multiple scales, is fundamental to contemporary elegance.

Elegance requires differentiation, but flourishes on mutation. Mutation, at its base level, is an evolution technique for the production of potentially useful anomalies. It exists when an offspring has a genetic trait produced by a new DNA sequencing that does not exist in the parent.[13] Unfortunately, 'mutation' is also one of the most debased terms within the glossary of contemporary architecture, being mistakenly used as a synonym for individuation. A clarification of the term reveals that mutation enables future differences between species, while individuation identifies individuals within a subspecies or group. Different markings on the wings of butterflies provide a means for individuation, a mutation of those wings, which unlike a mere individuation can lead to the production of an entirely new species of butterfly. Differentiated components, coupled with isolated and extreme mutations resulting in new figures, produce the aesthetic effect of elegance.

Architectural mutation, in the absence of true evolutionary influences and detached from its misuse as individuation and differentiation, requires an anticipatory intervention on the part of the designer to produce a desirable anomaly distinct enough to be legible as a mutation and not merely read as individuation. In this light, animation software easily enables changes in degree within successive components, or individuation, within a family. Elegance requires extreme differentiation or, rather, a change in degree that verges on, or commits to, a change in type – a mutation. Continuously differentiated components are legible as variations of a primitive form, but do not produce the emergence of new figures and traits and cannot therefore produce architectural elegance. That is to say, their similarities overcome their differences. The assembly of different types of components results only in collage – or a circumvention of sameness through excessive difference. Contemporary elegance requires the expert calibration of these two extremes to produce figural mutations that become legible as sensuous effects. The perfection of the hermetically sealed topological system then allows these mutations to be registered as a new species of emergent figure, not component and not whole, but existing as an ephemeral fugitive in between the two extremes.

The consensus use of surface modelling software authorises the legibility of the mutation. Such design systems include an implicit mathematical framework that provides for a common standard of architectural production not available to architects since the early 20th-century extermination of the classical.[14] The renewed adoption of such a consensus based approach to design is critical for the production of contemporary elegance as it alone provides the datum against which an expertly curated anomaly can be recognised. The establishment of such a datum, combined with an expert use of techniques, allows for not only the recognition of the parts as individual components, and their intricate assembly as wholes, but also enables a vast range of intermediary scale effects – vis-à-vis these mutations. These elegant effects exist between clear readings of parts and wholes, and between distinctions such as surface articulation and mass. Elegant design effects produce a new family of intermediary tropes that augment the limited aspirations of both efficient assemblies of standardised parts and talented compositions of complete wholes.

The interest of elegance, as one of a new generation of charismatic and contemporary[15] effects, relies on the presence of figuration. As such, a critical aspect of defining elegance is determining the type of figures that result in its realisation. Other emerging positions, such as the techno-romantic and the horrific, rely on the extreme production of figural geometries that disempower a formational legibility of wholeness. In both cases the means of viewership is cinematic, allowing for a sequential reading of figure through figure, and figure against figure. Elegance requires the topological framework against which a figure can be read. It is not cinematic in its ambitions, but rather curated through isolated views and expertly calibrated moments. Unveiled not through the movement of the body, but rather through the long caress of a continuous visual appraisal, elegance is statuesque in its retrieval and delicate in its aesthetic presumptions.

Because of its reliance on the visual and aesthetic, as opposed to the conceptual and semiological, contemporary elegance is a localised occurrence. Only a retreat from reading a building as a complete conceptual entity allows for the emergence of elegant effects. A building may exhibit elegance at a variety of scales, but it is always, and only, accessible as a locally specific occurrence. It is therefore permanent, but not omnipresent, always available yet experientially fleeting. This is the sacrifice of all sensate-based interests – and like all good sacrifices it enables the possibility of an alternate, and better, opportunity. Its potency is generated not through its eternal conceptual legibility, but rather through a visceral precognitive and momentary realisation.[16] It is a 'flash in the pan',[17] a powerful observation made all the more persuasive precisely because of its brevity. Elegance is reproducible at any scale, in any topological scenario, but it cannot be everywhere, always. It is, in this sense, an ephemeral effect, but one that can be rehearsed. Architecture is uniquely poised to capitalise on this rehearsal as part of its disciplinary specificity which has historically relied on an implicit assumption of permanence and stasis – allowing elegance to be perceptually fleeting yet architecturally predictable through curating views with expert manipulations of form.

These emerging aesthetic desires of architecture provide a new and common denominator for the discourse not available to architects since the early 20th century. Also emerging from this aesthetic consensus, as well as the unified use of tools and techniques, is the reintroduction of nuance and an extreme degree of individual sophistication. After its disappearance for decades, we now realise that formal nuance is impossible without group expertise that allows for its recognition. These emerging aesthetic tendencies and consensus use of tools demand a new aesthetic discourse. Elegance, as the ability to expertly integrate dissonant mutations towards the production of effect, expands the previously limited aesthetic range of digital formalism. In this capacity it is an important initial direction within the nascent discourse of aesthetics and architectural affects.

It is *en vogue* now for architects to study infrastructure, globalisation, marketing, branding and systems of commerce. It seems only fitting that a continuation of this research would inevitably lead back to the study of the architectural agency of desire, of which a significant portion must be aesthetic, as the driving force behind a significant percentage of this commercial and corporate activity. The study of aesthetics, including elegance effects, is not a careless disregard for conceptual semiological thinking, but rather heralds the production of a new and entirely contemporary species of intelligence – one not beholden to historical models of signification, but liberated and enabled by the ability to produce, control and understand a crucial aspect of the judgement and consumption of an architecture of irrefutable contemporaneity.

Notes

1   Peter Eisenman writes: 'In the early 20th century, American pragmatist philosopher Charles Sanders Peirce put forward an articulate, three-part typology of signs: the icon, the symbol and the index. The icon is distinguished by a similitude; it looks like its object, ie, the hot dog stand that looks like a hot dog. The symbol is understood by convention or rule, like words in a sentence, or a classical facade symbolising a public building … The last of Peirce's categories, the index, is understood as a record of a process or event.' Peter Eisenman, 'Duck Soup', in Cynthia Davidson (ed), *Log 7*, 2006, p 140.

2   Smoothness suggests a physical lack of articulation, but has also been enlisted architecturally as a theoretical distinction opposed to, but always in the presence of, the striated – architectural translations of the sedentary and nomadic. See Gilles Deleuze and Felix Guattari, *A Thousand Plateaus: Capitalism and Schizophrenia*, Athlone Press (London), 1988, p 478.

3   Greg Lynn, 'Intricacy', in *Intricacy: a Project* by Greg Lynn FORM, Institute of Contemporary Art (Philadelphia, PA), 2003, p 8.

4   See Greg Lynn, *Animate Form*, Princeton Architectural Press (New York), 1999.

5   See Greg Lynn, 'Intricacy', pp 8–10.

6   Jeffrey Kipnis notes that: 'To distinguish post-critical from pre-critical sensibilities and to call attention to the fact that the emotional impact of the work emanates not from the representations of the architecture but from the formal structures themselves, Eisenman termed these new sensations collectively as ''affects''.' Jeffrey Kipnis, 'P-TR's Progress', in Todd Gannon (ed), *The Light Construction Reader*, Monacelli Press (New York), 2002, p 151.

7   See Charles Jencks, *The Iconic Building*, Rizzoli (New York), 2005.

8   Eisenman, 'Duck Soup', p 140.

9   A reference by Peter Eisenman to the merely optical qualities of Santiago Calatrava's work. Ibid, p 41.

10 A '*deus ex machina*' is a literary device whereby an unexpected, artificial or improbable character, device or event is suddenly introduced to resolve a situation or untangle a plot – as in the final battle sequence of *Monty Python and the Holy Grail* which is suddenly halted by the appearance of

the modern-day police who arrest the entire cast of medieval characters for murder. See William Morris, *The American Heritage Dictionary*, Houghton Mifflin (Boston, MA), second college edition, 1982.

11   Sylvia Lavin has provided perhaps the finest description of effects and their role in contemporary discourse. See Sylvia Lavin, 'In a Contemporary Mood', in Zaha Hadid and Patrik Schumacher (eds), *Latent Utopias: Experiments Within Contemporary Architecture*, Steirischer Herbst (Graz), 2002, p 46.

12   For a description of the differences between substantive and verdictive judgements, see Nick Zangwill, *The Metaphysics of Beauty*, Cornell University Press (Ithaca, NY), 2001, pp 9–10.

13   Morris, *The American Heritage Dictionary*.

14   For an articulate record of the threats to which classicism ultimately succumbed in the early 20th century, see the 'fallacies' in Geoffrey Scott, *The Architecture of Humanism: A Study in the History of Taste*, Norton (New York), 1914, 1999.

15   Lavin, *Latent Utopias*, pp 46–7.

16   Kant, in the first two moments of his 'Critique of Judgment', presents the requisite for this as 'subsuming under concepts', the critical switch that, at its base level, requires aesthetic judgement to occur independently of the act of cognition by the subject. Immanuel Kant, *The Critique of Judgment*, James Creed Meredithf (tr), Clarendon Press (Oxford), first edition 1952, pp 41–60.

17   Sylvia Lavin aptly defines the fleeting aspects of the contemporary through the analogy of the 'flash in the pan'. Sylvia Lavin, 'Introduction', in Sylvia Lavin and Helene Furjan (eds), *Crib Sheets*, Monacelli Press (New York), 2005, pp 9–10.

Mark Foster Gage, 'Deus ex Machina: From Semiology to the Elegance of Aesthetics', Ali Rahim and Hina Jamelle (guest-editors), *Elegance*, *AD* Profile 185, *AD* 77, January–February 2007, pp 82–5. © 2012 John Wiley & Sons Ltd.

Building Information Modelling (2009)

Richard Garber

The generic term Building Information Modelling, or BIM, came into use in the early 2000s to designate software for building and construction management and cost control. More recently, under a variety of proprietary names, BIM software has been developed into a fully-fledged tool for design and construction; this *AD* Profile takes stock of this evolution, assessing the implications of BIM for contemporary design, professional practice and, more generally, for design theory and history.

BIM software evolved for the most part independently from the more formal and tectonic experimentations in digital design of the last 20 years. The recent interest it has generated among the design professions may be due to a crucial shortcoming of digital mass-customisation in architecture: file-to-factory technologies are easy to implement at the scale of fabrication, but less so at the scale of construction, because the making of full-size buildings requires plenty of information exchange and coordination among scores of different agents and actors, human and technical alike – each in charge of different parts or aspects of the project. BIM technology was developed partly as a solution to this informational predicament, and in its more recent developments BIM software increasingly serves as an interactive tool for collaboration and participatory decision-making.

Albeit to this day most BIM applications still pertain to optimisation, performance and efficiency in cost and delivery, Richard Garber emphasises the theoretical, as well as practical import of a new tool capable of 'closing the gap' between design intentions, architectural notations and material execution – a gap inaugurated in the Renaissance by the very invention of architectural design and of the architectural profession.

Optimisation Stories: The Impact of Building Information Modelling on Contemporary Design Practice AD March–April 2009

Over the last 25 years, the broad use of computer software has revolutionised the way we generate and document architectural design proposals. Much of this work has occurred either in visualisation or formal speculation (mainly academic concerns) or in conventional documentation and management (mainly professional preoccupations). This separation between theory and practice is amplified by the relationship between architects and those who build their design proposals. This formerly manual transfer of design documentation via the interpretation of others invites breaks, or gaps, in what should be a continuous and interrelated process of design development and building actualisation. However, these gaps are now closing as new possibilities emerging at either end of the spectrum demand the support of one another – advanced analysis software would not be necessary without design imagination.

Design computing has expanded in scope beyond representation-based documentation to now include analysis, simulation and digital fabrication. These new components allow architects to better understand and manage how their virtual ideas are realised, and to innovate or challenge traditional delivery and construction methods. The synthesis of such technologies and the need for better construction management has led to the emergence of building information models which close the gap and, in turn, promise to revolutionise contemporary design practice.

While current technologies are not sufficiently developed for full-scale buildings to be produced with computer numerically controlled (CNC) hardware, they do allow developed building information models to more precisely assist in the translation of a virtual construct into an actual one. Can a cost-effective paradigm shift be achieved using new computing technologies in architectural design?

The potential of building information modelling (BIM) is that a single, intelligent, virtual model can be used to satisfy all aspects of the design process including visualisation, checking for spatial conflict, automated parts and assembly production (CAM), construction sequencing, and materials research and testing. The model is shared, and contributed to, by all parties involved in the construction of the building, from architects to engineering consultants, contractors and subcontractors. This suggests a paradigm shift in design procedure and teaching that would involve time-based iteration and testing, not only of design potentials, but also of construction in a virtual environment. Indeed information models foster a kind of automatic coordination and collaboration that, partly due to the medium and partly due to the intentions of designers, has not been seen before in the broader building industry. However, this seems less likely to specifically enhance the architect's position as a central hub through which all things pass – a return to the status of master builder – during the design of buildings. Perhaps, more interestingly, these technologies allow for a medium in which notions of creativity and innovation merge through performance operations, cost efficiencies, and material and system simulations that are iterated digitally throughout the design process as opposed to in the field during construction, where finding errors or conditions not properly coordinated could lead to costly expenditures in terms of time and budget.

Information Models in Contemporary Design Practice

According to the US National Institute of Building Sciences (NIBS), BIM refers to 'the use of the concepts and practices of open and interoperable information exchanges, emerging technologies, new business structures and influencing the re-engineering of processes in ways that dramatically reduce multiple forms of waste in the building industry'.[1] The institute's work focuses mainly on the further development of integrated product delivery (IPD) and data translation for the streamlined sharing of information between architects and subcontractors, such as structural steel fabricators. Other areas in which it is developing standards include automated code compliance checking (AC3) and construction to operations building information exchange (COBIE).

Many firms are finding attractive information models based on their digital management capacity. As digital databases, these models can control and monitor construction events so as to streamline and refine the construction process itself. There are already numerous examples of how BIM has saved time and made the building process more efficient: one only needs to be reminded of how the geometrically complex Denver Art Museum by Daniel Libeskind was completed in 2005 by the Midwestern US contractor MA Mortenson three months ahead of schedule, and with no change orders during the construction process.[2]

Greg Lynn FORM, Garofalo Architects and McInturf Architects, Presbyterian Church of New York, Queens, New York, 1999. Greg Lynn's Presbyterian Church was 'stick-built'; that is, manually constructed of traditional construction materials that were fabricated and installed based on two-dimensional construction documents and shop drawings, much like a conventional project. However, it became a significant precedent for several of the architects represented in this issue of *AD* as the manual creation of construction documents in a CAD system required the measuring and rationalisation of the three-dimensional components of the virtual model. It was critical even at this early stage of the virtual construction to develop methods for the precise and accurate translation of three-dimensional geometries into a two-dimensional CAD document (profiles, plans, etc). The result is a stunning sanctuary space imagined in a virtual environment that, once actualised, spoke to the merit of such a design process while attracting the interest of a whole generation of young designers. © 2011 Jason Valdina/Received.com.

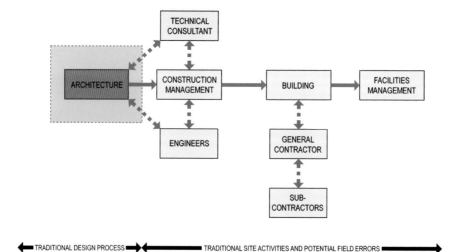

TRADITIONAL DESIGN PROCESS ◄►◄ TRADITIONAL SITE ACTIVITIES AND POTENTIAL FIELD ERRORS ►

above: GRO Architects, diagram showing the traditional architectural design process, 2008. In traditional architectural practice, a linear exchange of analogue information facilitated interpretation and the need for clarification on site. In this 'possible to real' paradigm, it was therefore necessary to transmit conventional documentation to others involved in the construction process. The manual translation of quantitative and qualitative building information (bills of materials, component quantities, as well as structural and environmental efficiencies based on rules of thumb) made full coordination of all the construction activities difficult. The result was a reality that was like the possible only through representation. © GRO Architects, PLLC.

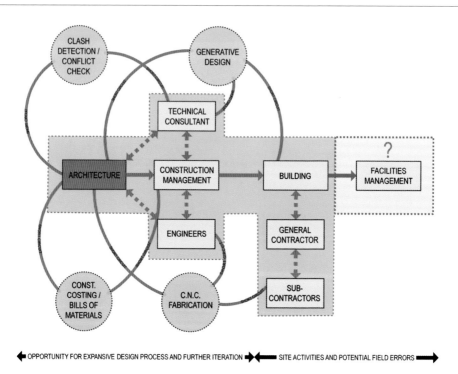

OPPORTUNITY FOR EXPANSIVE DESIGN PROCESS AND FURTHER ITERATION ◄►◄ SITE ACTIVITIES AND POTENTIAL FIELD ERRORS ►

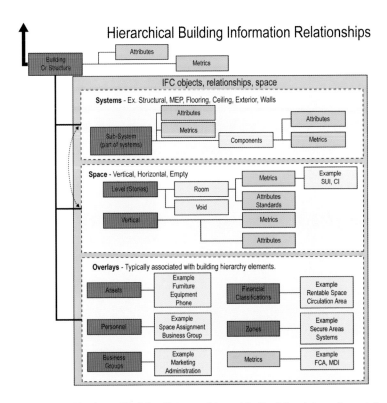

Hierarchical Building Information Relationships

above: National Institute of Building Sciences, hierarchical building information relationships, 2006. The National Institute of Building Sciences, based in Washington DC, has been instrumental in setting building information modelling (BIM) standards in the US and internationally. It has divided the BIM process into an object-based system of Industry Foundation Classes (IFCs): Systems represent the physical entities of the building and can be classified by form (high rise, suspension bridge) or function (single-family residence, courthouse); Space is tied to the physical structure or systems by a boundary definition; and Overlays are the abstract data – organisational, operational, functional, financial, non-fixed assets, resources, personnel, etc – tied to the Systems and Space classifications. Further definitions can be found on the institute's website (www.nibs.org). © Dianne Davis, CSI.

opposite bottom: GRO Architects, information modelling in architectural practice, 2008. In architectural practice augmented by information modelling, virtual translation of data and real-time performance testing become possible. In this new paradigm – the 'virtual to actual' – the virtual is already fully real and needs only be actualised by a process of translation from virtual matter to physical matter. Efficiencies of computer numerically controlled (CNC) fabrication, real-time generation of bills of materials and schedules, as well as construction sequencing occur. Through information modelling, the design process becomes augmented and more iterative, and allows for more in-depth collaboration between architects and allied design professionals such as engineers, technology consultants and subcontractors in a nonlinear fashion. Streamlined management of construction projects is not the only impact of these technologies as many information modelling packages contain generative design modules that promise further formal speculation tied to performance. Information models also lend themselves to the life-cycle management of a building, well beyond the conclusion of the design and construction process. © GRO Architects, PLLC.

The ability of an architect, engineer or contractor to simulate construction in a digital model has many merits and uses 4-D, or time-based, operations in what is seen as, perhaps finally, the use of animation for something other than the formal manipulations of the 1990s. Originally conceived of by Greg Lynn and others[3] for its capacity in the design process to allow all geometry to respond to a series of programmable (typically numeric) factors, animation became synonymous with the 'stopping problem'. This term was generally attributed to time-based geometric experiments in which the resulting forms were somehow imprecise because it was difficult to conventionally ascertain why one geometric frame was any more applicable than another: an arbitrariness that quickly branded certain architects and designers as not being grounded in the true problems of design and construction. However, these models were precise in that they were measurable (mass, volume, dimension, curvature) virtual constructs and represented a range of options. This notion of range forms the essence of the parametric experiments possible with BIM systems today: through optimisations of shape, cost, material, orientation and so on, an informed choice can be made from a family of related virtual solutions, and also serves to de-emphasise what perhaps was initially an interest in the formal aesthetic that also emerged from early studies of form generation and animation.

Material Simulation and Testing

Still other capacities of BIM systems, such as clash detection, the generation of bills of materials and real-time construction schedules, and the transfer of digital data to fabricators or subcontractors, are attractive in their potential to optimise the design and building process. If construction can now be controlled through a single model or, more appropriately, a database that can accept information from a variety of sources, design optimisations such as those listed above can be studied in the earlier stages of development. The ability to respond to material or geometric factors such as stress, weight, hardness, volume and area, as well as time-based concerns such as sequence, has allowed designers to apply virtual attributes that yield form. Buildings can be understood according to how they perform as opposed to what they look like.

While there is still work to be done on the translation of various types of data into such a model, it is important to recognise that not all information needs to be distributed to the entire construction team at any given time: for example, a CNC fabricator responsible, say, for custom steel connection plates need not be concerned with the size and orientation of supply ducts as long as he or she can be 'digitally assured' that the ducts will not interfere spatially with the plates.

External Pressures

One of the more curious occurrences in the last two decades has been the emergence of new building 'specialists' whose purpose it is to oversee the complex and messy construction process. The impact of these construction managers seems unclear and is in some ways ironic. They are essentially watchdogs employed by owners or contractors to ensure economic and production transparency, yet often make the

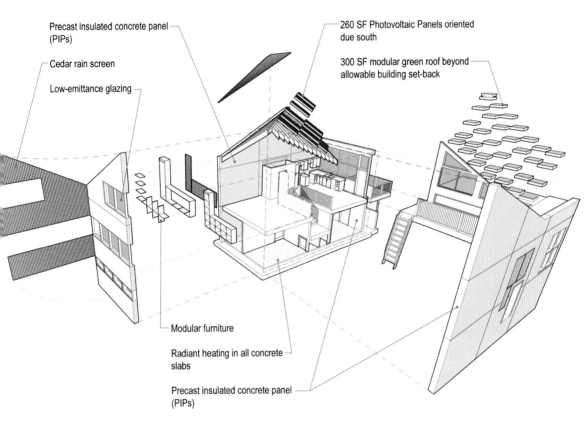

Precast insulated concrete panel (PIPs)

Cedar rain screen

Low-emittance glazing

260 SF Photovoltaic Panels oriented due south

300 SF modular green roof beyond allowable building set-back

Modular furniture

Radiant heating in all concrete slabs

Precast insulated concrete panel (PIPs)

GRO Architects, PREFAB House, Jersey City, New Jersey, 2008. BIM systems have two important and interrelated aspects. First, they allow all virtual geometry to be linked to real-time databases for the accurate costing of materials and for ensuring building components are properly integrated. Next, they allow for the smooth transfer of data to the software packages that enable simulation to occur. The PREFAB house was conceived as an economical yet environmentally responsive structure able to generate its own power and utilise efficient materials. In addition to developing a set of construction documents in a BIM system, the information model was translated into environmental analysis software to study criteria such as solar gain and heat loss in winter months, and also into a proprietary software to generate the 3-D formwork for the house's precast-concrete walls. The proprietary software also allows the virtual sequencing of the panel assembly prior to components being delivered to the site. © GRO Architects, PLLC.

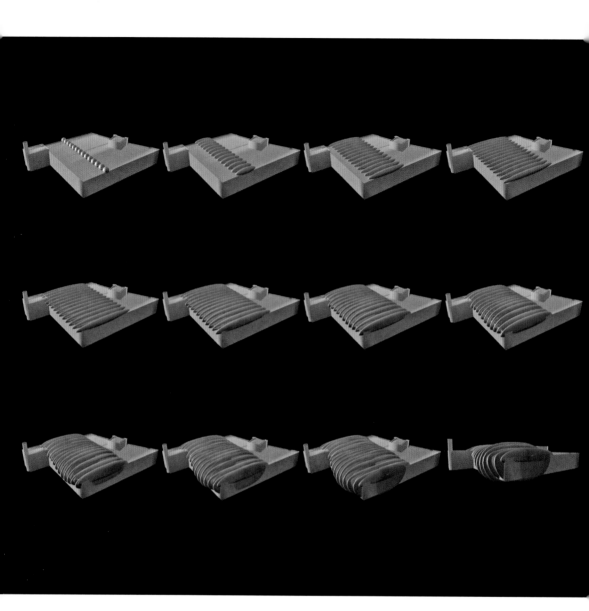

Greg Lynn FORM, Garofalo Architects and McInturf Architects, Presbyterian Church of New York, Queens, New York, 1999. The use of animation in early yet sophisticated modelling programs enabled designers to employ time-based operations in the design decision-making process. While these early modelling programs did not have the capability to link information such as material resistance to this form generation, virtual information such as mass and thickness could be extracted directly for material consideration. For the Presbyterian Church of New York, Greg Lynn FORM generated a virtual model that animated an interrelated series of forms for the main sanctuary space of the building. © Greg Lynn FORM.

GRO Architects, Best Pedestrian Route, Lower Manhattan, New York, 2007. As BIM systems allow designers to think through problems of construction sequence and assembly virtually, the relationship of design to fabrication becomes much more comprehensive. CNC fabrication from digital files enables different parts to be cut from materials as economically as standardised parts were machined in the 20th century. In the fabrication and assembly of Best Pedestrian Route, a digitally fabricated temporary construction walkway, a series of uniquely shaped aluminium gussets were required to resist the bending moment of the cantilevered roof of the walkway. The gussets were water-jet cut from pieces of 6-millimetre (0.25-inch) and 12.5-millimetre (0.5-inch) aluminium sheets and precisely positioned within pockets that were CNC-routed to the inside faces of the plywood rib geometry. The precision with which the rib assemblies fit together could not have been achieved manually. © GRO Architects, PLLC.

building management process more complex while also diverting fees away from those involved in the design of a building. The promotion of a more transparent process of checks and balances through information models would thus seem to be an important value-adding capacity of BIM.

The time-based, parametric and generational capacities of many information modelling softwares allow architects and designers to challenge conventional and outmoded construction methods while simultaneously introducing new techniques for organising and creating form and space. Parametric and organisational scripts for form generation take into account material attributes such as weight and maximum curvature so that the tedious process of translating one's design intentions into something buildable can become much more refined. This also offers the potential for the rationalisation of new building forms in much the same way that BIM packages can be used to optimise more conventional typologies or construction methods. Though the generational capacities of these tools are often overlooked, they nevertheless represent a real way of introducing the new organisations necessary to contend with increasingly complex, mixed and various programmes and building types to our constructed landscape.[4]

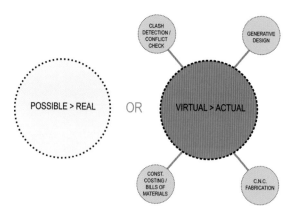

above: Interpretation, or at least discussion, on the project site of the Pavilion Zürichhorn, Switzerland, in 1960. In the possible to real paradigm, interpretation is necessary to construct an actual building from a set of design possibilities. As there is a gap in the transfer of static information between the architect and the general contractor, it is incredibly difficult to ensure the contractor has a comprehensive understanding of the design intent, and the architect of the construction techniques and methods. Interpretation leads to errors in the field, or situations where certain components or construction sequences need rethinking, both of which can be costly. This, unfortunately, has happened to the best of us! Pictured are Willy Boesiger, Editor of *Oeuvre Complète*, City Architect Adolf Wasserfallen, Le Corbusier, Inspector of Public Parks Pierre Zbinden, and the gallery owner Heidi Weber. © Rene Burri/Magnum Photos.

The Virtual to Actual Paradigm

Though instrumental in closing the gap between design and building, preliminary, or schematic, opportunities are often overlooked in the adoption of parametric building information models in professional practice. Design theorists such as Sanford Kwinter and Manuel DeLanda have both highlighted the paradigm shift, made possible by information models, whereby the previous method of architectural delivery, the 'possible to real', is being supplanted by a new and seamless one, the 'virtual to actual'. In the first, the formulation of the initial design intention was a necessarily cerebral operation.[5] The designer would dream up a form and then represent it as an architectural proposal to which would be attached information about materials, construction methods and so on. Because proposals were generally documented as two-dimensional abstractions of a possible building, they required interpretation by others than the designer to realise the building. As such it was impossible to guarantee that the intentions of the architect would be precise in the built project.

An example of this conventional model in digital architectural design is image mapping, in which representational as opposed to performance-based criteria are used in the selection of an appropriate design proposal. Three-dimensional modelling programs were first used to simulate what a building would look like via libraries of 'materials' (generally bitmapped images) that could be applied with relative ease to preconceived forms. These forms were primarily variations of non-eidetic geometries (planes, spheres, cubes) that had no relation or resistance to the representations of materials they would receive. The outcome of such operations was largely deemed successful if the applied image maps were adequate in texture and scale. Whether brick was a suitable material choice for such a form, or masonry construction appropriate, was usually given far less consideration.

This virtual reality further separated architects from the material process of building. When not linked to a database or library, the bitmapped brick (or grass, granite, or 'purple', for that matter) wall has no properties or attributes that architects must consider in its construction. It has no weight, is unaffected by its height to thickness, and displays no resistance if a second virtual object is placed on top of it. Consequently, it has no reference or attribute data to determine whether or not it can sufficiently behave like a wall.

Douglas Gauthier and Jeremy Edmiston, BURST* Project LLC, BURST*008, 'Home Delivery: Fabricating the Modern Dwelling', Museum of Modern Art, New York, 2008. Delivery and erection of the *BURST House's CNC-cut structurally insulated panels (SIPs) to the exhibition site where they were fastened together. This process is a different take on prefabrication, in that the house arrives on site as a series of parts that are put together like a jigsaw puzzle. It is important to note the difference between this process, in which many unique parts are cut by a CNC machine, and one of mass standardisation where the same parts are assembled by workers on site as a series of repetitive tasks. BURST*008 used CNC output for efficient mass-customisation, demonstrating how information models can be employed to optimise, simulate and make construction methods more efficient. © Douglas Gauthier, GA and BURST*LLC.

An often overlooked aspect of the introduction of computing to the design and management of buildings is the necessary break from traditional ideas and methods of teaching architecture. Though we are now some two decades into the digital, one senses that yet another gap between the teaching of new modes of practice using information models and traditional architectural education has been created. Lack of buildability and formal whimsy seem to inform the critique articulated by those who advocate more traditional methods of education. It is important to note, however, that the formal speculations of the last decade partially laid the foundations for the development and adoption of BIM systems in architectural design. When measured against performance or other optimising criteria, these speculations seem to intersect with the more pragmatic management tools and construction simulations proffered by information models.

In the contemporary virtual to actual paradigm, interpretation is no longer required because digital information models are already inherently real. As precise three-dimensional concepts are designed, tested, iterated and optimised in virtual space, they need only to be translated, or actualised, into physical media. A simple example would be a series of panels rationalised on a virtual sheet of plywood to be CNC-cut by a router.

Closing the Gap

The architects, engineers and academics who have contributed to this issue of *AD* have a broad and varied interest in the use of BIM technologies. The scope of the issue therefore covers architectural education, comparisons with historic models of practice, changes in contemporary design practice and the still newer opportunities for optimisation and CNC output. Rather than concentrating on a narrow or specific definition of BIM, the intention is instead to demonstrate how widespread and significant the impact of these technologies on the practice of architecture will be. As clever designers use BIM tools to better optimise, iterate and test their ideas, we will start to see design proposals and built projects that are not only integrated and precise, but truly new.

Notes

1 See http://www.nibs.org/newsstory3.html/.
2 I described this process in a lecture at the School of Architecture at NJIT on 19 September 2005.
3 See Greg Lynn, *Animate Form*, Princeton Architectural Press (New York), 1999.
4 See Chuck Eastman, 'Automated Assessment of Early Concept Designs', *Closing the Gap: Information Models in Contemporary Design Practice*, AD Profile 198, AD 79, March–April 2009, pp 52–7.
5 See Manuel DeLanda, 'Philosophies of Design: The Case for Modeling Software', in *VERB Processing: Architecture Boogazine*, Actar (Barcelona), 2002, pp 131–43.

A New Global Style (2009)

Patrik Schumacher

Patrik Schumacher of Zaha Hadid Architects defines parametricism as a 'solid new hegemonic paradigm' born of, and suited to, post-industrial society. Post-Fordism (and post-modernity) are based on customisation and complexity, just like industrial modernity was based on standardisation and economies of scale. The mathematics of parametricism, supported by today's electronic computing, appear as the best means to manage variability, hence to design and mass-produce variations.

This interpretation recapitulates a genealogy of digital thinking derived from early definitions of the Objectile – the generic, generative, open-ended notation that Deleuze and Cache hailed as the new technical object of post-modernity and of the digital age. Schumacher refers more particularly to Eisenman and Lynn's 'digital tectonics' of the early 1990s, and his generalisation of similar principles at the scale of urban design equally sums up tenets of Stan Allen's theory of 'field conditions', complexity theory, self-organisation, emergence and morphogenetics.

As Schumacher argues, sheer parametric processes and technologies do not necessarily lead to 'aesthetic recognisability'. As a style, however, parametricism must express its true 'sensibility', of which the visual hallmarks are 'the elegance of ordered complexity and the sense of seamless fluidity'. As is made evident by the examples featured in the essay, parametricism also aims for full authorial control of design at all scales, from the building to the city. Schumacher furthers some of these arguments in his noted monographs, *The Autopoiesis of Architecture* (John Wiley & Sons, 2011 and 2012).

Zaha Hadid Architects, Kartal-Pendik Masterplan, Istanbul, Turkey, 2006. Fabric study. The urban fabric comprises both cross tower and perimeter blocks. The image shows the morphological range of the perimeter block type. Blocks are split into four quadrants allowing for a secondary, pedestrian path system. At certain network crossing points the block system is assimilated to the tower system: each block sponsors one of the quadrants to form a pseudo-tower around a network crossing point. © Zaha Hadid Architects.

Parametricism: A New Global Style for Architecture and Urban Design AD July–August 2009

There is a global convergence in recent avant-garde architecture that justifies its designation as a new style: parametricism. It is a style rooted in digital animation techniques, its latest refinements based on advanced parametric design systems and scripting methods. Developed over the past 15 years and now claiming hegemony within avant-garde architecture practice, it succeeds Modernism as the next long wave of systematic innovation. Parametricism finally brings to an end the transitional phase of uncertainty engendered by the crisis of Modernism and marked by a series of relatively short-lived architectural episodes that included Postmodernism, Deconstructivism and Minimalism. So pervasive is the application of its techniques that parametricism is now evidenced at all scales from architecture to interior design to large urban design. Indeed, the larger the project, the more pronounced is parametricism's superior capacity to articulate programmatic complexity.

The urbanist potential of parametricism has been explored in a three-year research agenda at the AADRL titled 'Parametric Urbanism' and is demonstrated by a series of competition-winning masterplans by Zaha Hadid Architects.

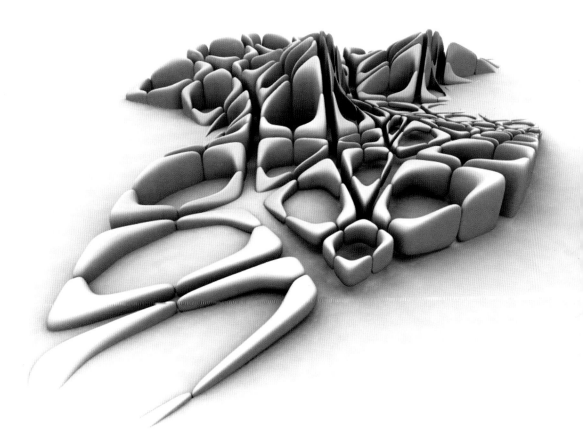

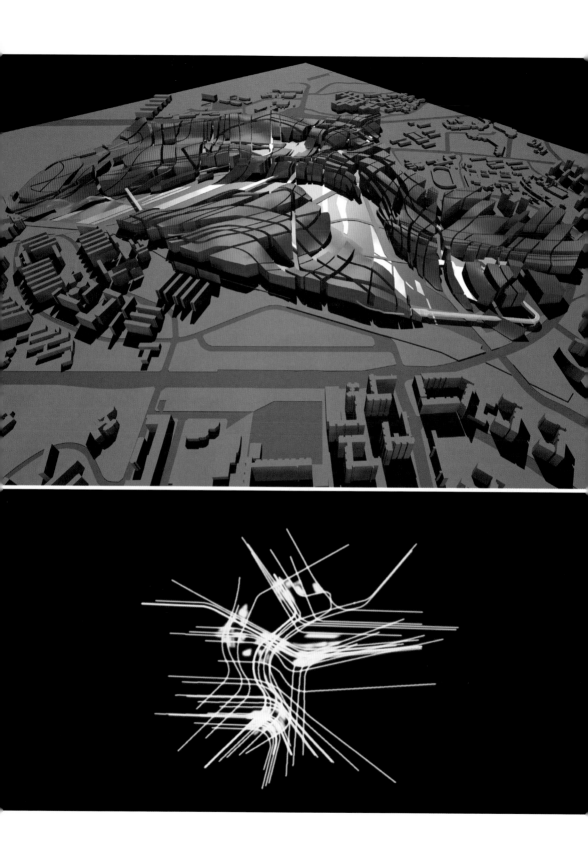

Parametricism as Style

Avant-garde architecture and urbanism are going through a cycle of innovative adaptation – retooling and refashioning the discipline to meet the socioeconomic demands of the post-Fordism era. The mass society that was characterised by a universal consumption standard has evolved into the heterogeneous society of the multitude, marked by a proliferation of lifestyles and extensive work-path differentiation. It is the task of architecture and urbanism to organise and articulate the increased complexity of our post-Fordist society.

Contemporary avant-garde architecture and urbanism seek to address this societal demand via a rich panoply of parametric design techniques. However, what confronts us is a new style rather than merely a new set of techniques. The techniques in question – the employment of animation, simulation and form-finding tools, as well as parametric modelling and scripting – have inspired a new collective movement with radically new ambitions and values. In turn, this development has led to many new, systematically connected design problems that are being worked on competitively by a global network of design researchers.[1] Over and above aesthetic recognisability, it is this pervasive, long-term consistency of shared design ambitions/problems that justifies the enunciation of a new style in the sense of an epochal phenomenon.[2] Parametricism is a mature style. There has been talk of 'continuous differentiation',[3] versioning, iteration and mass customisation among other things for quite some time now within architectural avant-garde discourse.

Not long ago we witnessed an accelerated, cumulative build-up of virtuosity, resolution and refinement facilitated by the simultaneous development of parametric design tools and scripts that allow the precise formulation and execution of intricate correlations between elements and subsystems. The shared concepts, computational techniques, formal repertoires and tectonic logics that characterise this work are crystallising into a solid new hegemonic paradigm for architecture.

Parametricism emerges from the creative exploitation of parametric design systems in the course of articulating increasingly complex social processes and institutions. That parametric design tools themselves do not account for this profound shift in style from Modernism to parametricism is evidenced by the fact that late Modernist architects are employing parametric tools in ways which result in the maintenance of a Modernist aesthetic, using parametric modelling inconspicuously to absorb complexity. The parametricist sensibility, however, pushes in the opposite direction, aiming for maximum emphasis on conspicuous differentiation and the visual amplification differentiating logics. Aesthetically, it is the elegance[4] of ordered complexity and the sense of seamless fluidity, akin to natural systems that constitute the hallmark of parametricism.

Zaha Hadid Architects, One North Masterplan, Singapore, 2003. Fabric and network. This masterplan for a new mixed-use urban business district in Singapore was the first of a series of radical masterplans that led to the concept of parametric urbanism and then to the general concept of parametricism. © Zaha Hadid Architects.

Styles as Design Research Programmes

Avant-garde styles can be interpreted and evaluated analogously to new scientific paradigms, affording a new conceptual framework and formulating new aims, methods and values. Thus a new direction for concerted research work is established.[5] Thus styles are design research programmes.[6]

Innovation in architecture proceeds via the progression of styles so understood: as the alternation between periods of cumulative advancement within a style and of periods of revolutionary transition between styles. Styles therefore represent cycles of innovation, gathering design research efforts into a collective endeavour. Here, stable self-identity is as much a necessary precondition of evolution as it is in the case of organic life. To hold on to the new principles in the face of difficulties is crucial for the chance of eventual success, something that is incompatible with an understanding of styles as transient fashions. Basic principles and methodologies need to be preserved and defended with tenacity in the face of initial difficulties and setbacks: each style has its hard core of principles and a characteristic way of tackling design problems/tasks.

The programme/style consists of methodological rules: some tell us what paths of research to avoid (negative heuristics), and others what paths to pursue (positive heuristics). Negative heuristics formulates strictures that prevent relapse into old patterns that are not fully consistent with the core; positive heuristics offers guiding principles and preferred techniques that allow the work to fast-forward in a particular direction.

Defining Heuristics and Pertinent Agendas

The defining heuristics of parametricism is fully reflected in the taboos and dogmas of contemporary avant-garde design culture:

· Negative heuristics (taboos): avoid rigid geometric primitives such as squares, triangles and circles, avoid simple repetition of elements, avoid juxtaposition of unrelated elements or systems.
· Positive heuristics (dogmas): consider all forms to be parametrically malleable; differentiate gradually (at varying rates), inflect and correlate systematically.

The current stage of development within parametricism is as much to do with the continuous advancement of the attendant computational design processes as it is due to the designer's grasp of the unique formal and organisational opportunities afforded by these processes. Parametricism can only exist via the continuous advancement and sophisticated appropriation of computational geometry. Finally, computationally advanced design techniques such as scripting (in Mel-script or Rhino-script) and parametric modelling (with tools such as GC or DP) are becoming a pervasive reality such that it is no longer possible to compete within the contemporary avant-garde architecture scene without mastering and refining them. However, the advancement of techniques should go hand in hand with the formulation of yet more ambitions and goals. The following five agendas seek to inject new aspects into the parametric paradigm and to further extend the new style's reach:

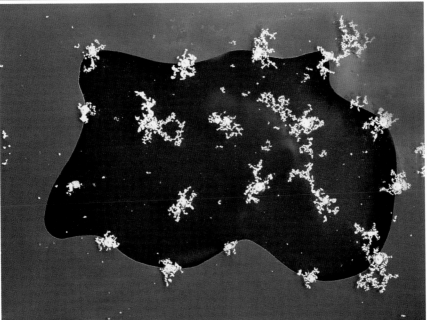

Frei Otto, occupation with simultaneous distancing and attracting forces, Institute for Lightweight Structures (ILEK), Stuttgart, Germany, 1992. Analogue models for the material computation of structural building forms (form-finding) are the hallmark of Frei Otto's research institute. The same methodology has been applied to his urban simulation work. The model shown integrates both distancing and attractive occupations by using polystyrene chips that cluster around the floating magnetic needles that maintain distance among themselves. © Frei Otto.

Zaha Hadid Architects, Kartal-Pendik Masterplan, Istanbul, Turkey, 2006. Maya hair-dynamic simulates minimised detour net. The path network was thus generated with a digital wool-thread model. The set-up registers the multitude of incoming streets and bundles them into larger roads affording larger parcels. © Zaha Hadid Architects.

1   *Parametric interarticulation of subsystems*
    The goal is to move from single system differentiation (for example, a swarm
    of facade components) to the scripted association of multiple subsystems –
    envelope, structure, internal subdivision, navigation void. The differentiation in
    any one system is correlated with differentiations in the other systems.[7]

2   *Parametric accentuation*
    Here the goal is to enhance the overall sense of organic integration by means of
    correlations that favour deviation amplification rather than compensatory adaptation.
    The associated system should accentuate the initial differentiation such that a far
    richer articulation is achieved and more orienting visual information made available.

3   *Parametric figuration*[8]
    Complex configurations in which multiple readings are latent can be constructed
    as a parametric model with extremely figuration-sensitive variables. Parametric
    variations trigger 'gestalt-catastrophes', that is, the quantitative modification
    of these parameters triggers qualitative shifts in the perceived configuration.
    Beyond object parameters, ambient parameters and observer parameters have to
    be integrated into the parametric system.

4   *Parametric responsiveness*[9]
    Urban and architectural environments possess an inbuilt kinetic capacity that
    allows those environments to reconfigure and adapt in response to prevalent
    occupation patterns. The real-time registration of use patterns drives the real-
    time kinetic adaptation. The built environment thus acquires responsive agency
    at different timescales.

5   *Parametric urbanism*[10] *– deep relationality*
    The assumption is that the urban massing describes a swarm formation of many
    buildings whereby the urban variables of mass, spacing and directionality are
    choreographed by scripted functions. In addition, the systematic modulation
    of architectural morphologies produces powerful urban effects and facilitates
    field orientation. The goal is deep relationality, the total integration of the
    evolving built environment, from urban distribution to architectural morphology,
    detailed tectonic articulation and interior organisation. Thus parametric urbanism
    might apply parametric accentuation, parametric figuration and parametric
    responsiveness as tools to achieve deep relationality.

Parametricist vs Modernist Urbanism

Le Corbusier's first theoretical statement on urbanism begins with a eulogy to the straight
line and the right angle as means whereby man conquers nature. Famously, the first two
paragraphs of *The City of Tomorrow* contrast man's way with that of the pack-donkey:

Man walks in a straight line because he has a goal and knows where he is going; he has made up his mind to reach some particular place and he goes straight to it. The pack-donkey meanders along, meditates a little in his scatter-brained and distracted fashion, he zig-zags in order to avoid larger stones, or to ease the climb, or to gain a little shade; he takes the line of least resistance.[11]

Le Corbusier admires the urban order of the Romans and rejects our sentimental modern-day attachment to the picturesque irregularity of the medieval city: 'The curve is ruinous, difficult and dangerous; it is a paralyzing thing;'[12] instead, he insists that 'the house, the street, the town … should be ordered; … if they are not ordered, they oppose themselves to us.'[13] Le Corbusier's limitation is not his insistence upon order but rather his limited conception of order in terms of classical geometry. Complexity theory in general, and the research of Frei Otto in particular,[14] have since taught us to recognise, measure and simulate the complex patterns that emerge from processes of self-organisation. Phenomena such as the 'pack-donkey's path' and urban patterns resulting from unplanned settlement processes can now be analysed and appreciated in terms of their underlying logic and rationality, that is, in terms of their hidden regularity and associated performative power.

Le Corbusier realised that although 'nature presents itself to us as a chaos … the spirit which animates Nature is a spirit of order'.[15] However, while his understanding of nature's order was limited by the science of his day, we now have the tools to reveal the complex order of those apparently chaotic patterns by simulating their 'material computation'. In this process, parametricist sensibility gives more credit to the 'pack-donkey's path' as a form of recursive material computation than to the simplicity of clear geometries imposed in a single, sweeping gesture.

Frei Otto's pioneering research on natural structures included work on settlement patterns. He started by focusing on the distinction/relation between occupying and connecting as the two fundamental activities involved in all processes of urbanisation,[16] his analysis of existing patterns paralleled by analogue experiments modelling crucial features of the settlement process. In a pioneering experiment, to simulate distancing occupation he used magnets floating in water, while to model attractive occupation he used floating polystyrene chips. A more complex model integrates both distancing and attractive occupations such that the polystyrene chips cluster around the floating magnetic needles that maintain distance among themselves.[17] The result closely resembles the typical settlement patterns found in our real urban landscapes.[18]

With respect to processes of connection, Frei Otto distinguishes empirically three scalar levels of path networks, each with its own typical configuration: settlement path networks, territory path networks and long-distance path networks. All start as forking systems that eventually close into continuous networks. In tandem, Otto distinguishes three fundamental types of configuration: direct path networks, minimal path networks and minimising detour networks. Again, he conceives material analogues that are able to self-organise into relatively optimised solutions. To simulate minimal path networks Otto devised the soap bubble skin apparatus in which a glass plate is held over water and the minimal path system forms itself from needles.[19] To capture the optimised detour networks the famous wool-thread models[20] are able to compute a network solution between given points that optimises the relationship of total network length and the average detour factor imposed. For each set of points, and for each adopted sur-length over the theoretical direct path, an optimising solution is produced. Although no unique optimal solution exists, and each computation is different, characteristic patterns emerge in different regions of the parametric space.

Frei Otto's form-finding models bring a large number of components into a simultaneous organising force-field so that any variation of the parametric profile of any of the elements elicits a natural response from all the other elements within the system. Such quantitative adaptations often cross thresholds into emergent qualities.

Where such an associative sensitivity holds sway within a system we can talk about 'relational fields'. Relational fields comprise mutually correlated sublayers, for instance the correlation of patterns of occupation with patterns of connection. The growth process of unplanned settlement patterns does indeed oscillate continuously between moments

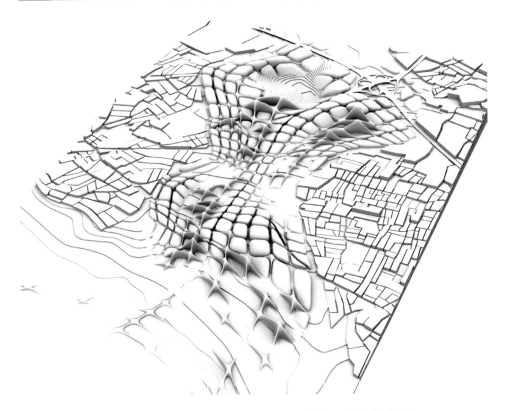

Zaha Hadid Architects, Kartal-Pendik Masterplan, Istanbul, Turkey, 2006. Global Maya model. The model features the interarticulation between cross towers and perimeter blocks as well as the affiliation to the surrounding fabric. The correlation of global width to global height can also be observed. © Zaha Hadid Architects.

when points of occupation generate paths and paths in turn attract occupation. The continuous differentiation of the path network – linear stretches, forks, crossing points – correlates with the continuous differentiation of the occupying fabric in terms of its density, programmatic type and morphology. The organising/articulating capacity of such relational fields is striking, particularly in comparison with the grid of the modern American city, which is undifferentiated and therefore non-adaptive. Its 'freedom' is now limiting: it leads to arbitrary juxtapositions that result in visual chaos.

Modernism was founded on the concept of universal space. Parametricism differentiates fields. Space is empty. Fields are full, as if filled with a fluid medium. We might think of liquids in motion, structured by radiating waves, laminal flows and spiralling eddies. Swarms have also served as paradigmatic analogues for the field-concept: swarms of buildings that drift across the landscape. There are no platonic, discrete figures or zones with sharp outlines. Within fields only regional field qualities matter: biases, drifts, gradients, and perhaps conspicuous singularities such as radiating centres. Deformation no longer spells the breakdown of order, but the inscription of information. Orientation in a complex, differentiated field affords navigation along vectors of transformation. The contemporary condition of arriving in a metropolis for the first time, without prior hotel

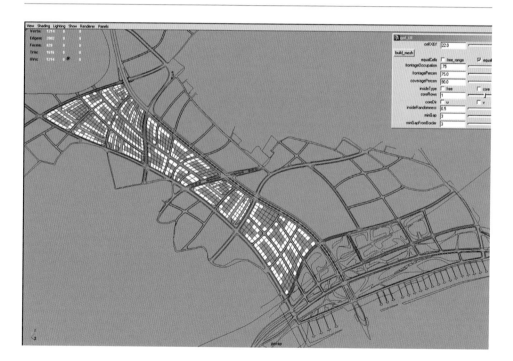

Zaha Hadid Architects, Kartal-Pendik Masterplan, Istanbul, Turkey, 2006. Scripting calligraphy block patterns. Various scripts were developed that configure the perimeter blocks depending on parcel size, proportion and orientation. The script also allowed for random variations regarding the introduction of openings within blocks. © Zaha Hadid Architects.

arrangements and without a map, might instigate this kind of field-navigation. Imagine there are no more landmarks to hold on to, no axes to follow, no more boundaries to cross.

Parametricist urbanism aims to construct new field logics that operate via the mutually accentuating correlation of multiple urban systems: fabric modulation, street systems, a system of open spaces. The agenda of deep relationality implies that the fabric modulation also extends to the tectonic articulation. Both massing and fenestration, if each in its own way, might be driven by sunlight orientation, producing a mutual enhancement of the visual orienting effect. Thus local perceptions (of the facade) can provide clues to the relative position within the global system of the urban massing. The location and articulation of building entrances might be correlated with the differentiated urban navigation system,[21] a correlation that might even extend to the internal circulation. This concept of deep relationality might also operate in reverse so that, for example, the internal organisation of a major institutional building might lead to multiple entrances that in turn trigger adaptations within the urban navigation system. It is important that such laws of correlation are adhered to across sufficiently large urban stretches.

Implementing Parametricist Urbanism

The urban implementation of parametricism is still in its infancy. However, Zaha Hadid Architects was able to win a series of international masterplanning competitions with schemes that embody the style's key features. The projects include the 200-hectare (494-acre) One-North Masterplan for a mixed-use business park in Singapore; Soho City in Beijing, comprising 2.5 million square metres (26.9 million square feet) of residential and retail programme; the mixed-use masterplan for Bilbao including the river's island and both opposing embankments; and the Kartal-Pendik Masterplan,[22] a mixed-use urban field of 55 hectares (136 acres) with 6 million square metres (64.6 million square feet) of gross buildable area comprising all programmatic components of a city.

The Kartal-Pendik project requires the design of a subcentre on Istanbul's Asian side to reduce pressure on the city's historic core. The site is being reclaimed from industrial estates and is flanked by the small-grain fabric of suburban towns. Respecting the parametricist taboo on unmediated juxtapositions, the adjacent context, in particular the incoming lines of circulation, was taken as an important input for the generation of the urban geometry. Maya's hair dynamic tool achieved a parametrically tuned bundling of the incoming paths into larger roads enclosing larger sites such that the resultant lateral path system exhibits the basic properties of Frei Otto's minimising detour network. The longitudinal direction was imposed via a primary artery with a series of subsidiary roads running parallel. The result is a hybrid of minimising detour network and deformed grid. At the same time, Zaha Hadid Architects worked with two primary fabric typologies, towers and perimeter blocks, each conceived as a generative component or geno-type that allows for a wide range of pheno-typical variation. The towers, conceived as cross towers, were placed on the crossing points to accentuate the path network. The perimeter block inversely correlates height with parcel area so that courtyards morph into internal atria as sites get smaller and blocks get taller. Blocks split along the lines of the secondary

Zaha Hadid Architects, Kartal-Pendik Masterplan, Istanbul, Turkey, 2006. New cityscape. The Kartal-Pendik plan incorporates a vast quarry that becomes the largest item in a system of parks that are spread throughout the urban field. The rhythmic flow of the urban fabric gives a sense of organic cohesion. © Zaha Hadid Architects.

path network, which together with the accentuating height differentiation, allows the block type to be assimilated to the cross-tower type. 'Pseudo-towers' are formed at some crossing points by pulling up the four corners of the four blocks that meet at such a corner.

Thus, an overall sense of continuity is achieved despite the entire process having started from two quite distinct urban typologies. In terms of global height regulation, and aside from local dependency of height on parcel size, the project correlates the conspicuous build-up of height with the lateral width of the overall site. Parametricist applications thus allow the rhythm of urban peaks to index the rhythm of the widening and narrowing of the urban field. The result is an elegant, coherently differentiated cityscape that facilitates navigation through its lawful (rule-based) constitution and through the architectural accentuation of both global and local field properties.

It may well be possible to implement this design for the Kartal-Pendik project assuming the imposition of strict planning guidelines using building lines and height regulation. Political and private buy-ins are also required. Moreover, all constituencies need to be convinced that the individual restrictions placed upon all sites really deliver collective value: the unique character and coherent order of the urban field from which all players benefit if compliance guidelines can be enforced. Ordered complexity here replaces the monotony of older planned developments and the disorienting visual chaos that marks virtually all unregulated contemporary city expansions.

To go further. In terms of the concept of deep relationality, Zaha Hadid Architects must extend its involvement from urbanism to architecture; only then can the desired accentuating correlations be intensified by involving the systematic modulation of tectonic features. For instance, in terms of the 'calligraphy blocks' (a third perimeter block variation that has been designed both to open up the interior of parcels and to cross parcels), a continuous facade differentiation that leads from the street side to the courtyard on the basis of an initial distinction between external and internal facades is used. Other moments of deep articulation are the coordination of landscape and public spaces, and the correlation of the secondary path system with the disposition of internal navigation systems.

Doubts may be experienced when confronted with the possibility of designing an urban field of up to 6 million square metres (64.6 million square feet) gross area with a single design team. Are we overstretching our capacity here? The answer is, no. The more often we are confronted with the task of designing large-scale developments of this kind, the more confident we become that the tools and strategies we are deploying under the banner of parametricism can indeed deliver something that produces a decisive surplus value when compared with the usual alternative of uncoordinated, arbitrary juxtapositions. The contemporary choice of typologies, construction options and styles is simply too wide to expect the underlying pragmatic logics to become legible. The result is a cacophony of pure difference. Parametricism is able to further coordinate pragmatic concerns and articulate them with all their rich differentiations and relevant associations while the danger of overriding real-life richness is minimised because variety and adaptiveness are written into the very genetic make-up of this new style.

Zaha Hadid Architects, Kartal-Pendik Masterplan, Istanbul, Turkey, 2006. Close-up of cross towers. The cross towers produce the urban peaks. Through their ground-level articulation these tower complexes participate in the creation of a continuous urban fabric that frames the streets and occasionally widens the street space into semi-public plazas. This is achieved while maintaining total continuity between the podium-like ground fabric and the shafts of the towers. © Zaha Hadid Architects.

Zaha Hadid Architects, Kartal-Pendik Masterplan, Istanbul, Turkey, 2006.
Calligraphy blocks – tectonic detail. The articulation of the facades is a function
of the location within the urban field. The exterior of the blocks is given a heavier
relief than the interior. Where a block opens up and the public space flows into the
private courtyard, a semi-private zone is articulated via the gradient transformation
between the outer and inner articulation. © Zaha Hadid Architects.

Notes

1 ZHA and AADRL together form just one node within this fast-growing network.

2 Also, we should not forget that the desire for an architecture marked by a complex, fluid, nature-like continuity was clearly expressed before the new digital tools had entered the arena: see Zaha Hadid's work of the late 1980s and Eisenman/Lynn's folding projects of the early 1990s. (This point also indicates that we are confronted with a new style and not merely new techniques.) Since then we have witnessed a conceptual radicalisation and increased formal sophistication along the lines previously set out, leading to the emergence of a powerful new style.

3 The credit for coining this key slogan goes to Greg Lynn and Jeff Kipnis.

4 For a pertinent concept of elegance that is related to the visual resolution of complexity, see Patrik Schumacher, 'Arguing for Elegance', in Ali Rahim and Hina Jamelle, *Elegance*, AD Profile 185, *AD* 77, January–February 2007.

5 This interpretation of styles is valid only with respect to the avant-garde phase of any style.

6 It is important to distinguish research programmes in the literal sense of institutional research plans from the meta-scientific conception of research programmes that has been introduced into the philosophy of science: whole new research traditions that are directed by a new fundamental theoretical framework. It is this latter concept that is utilised here to reinterpret the concept of style. See Imre Lakatos, *The Methodology of Scientific Research Programmes*, Cambridge University Press (Cambridge), 1978.

7 Parametricism involves a conceptual shift from part-to-whole relationships to component-system relationships, system-to-system relationships and system-subsystem relationships. Parametricism prefers open systems that always remain incomplete; that is, without establishing wholes. As the density of associations increases, so components may become associated in multiple systems. The correlation of initially independent systems implies the formation of a new encompassing system.

8 'Parametric figuration' featured in teachings at the Yale School of Architecture, the University of Applied Arts in Vienna and in the author's studio at the AADRL.

9 'Parametric responsiveness' was at the heart of our three-year design research agenda 'Responsive Environments' at the AADRL in London from 2001 to 2004.

10 'Parametric Urbanism' is the title of our recently completed design research cycle at the AADRL, from 2005 to 2008.

11 Le Corbusier, *The City of Tomorrow and its Planning*, Dover Publications (New York), 1987, p 5. Translated from the French original: Urbanisme (Paris), 1925.

12 Ibid, p 8.

13 Ibid, p 15.

14 Frei Otto might be considered as the sole true precursor of parametricism.

15 Le Corbusier, *The City of Tomorrow*, p 18.

16 Frei Otto, *Occupying and Connecting – Thoughts on Territories and Spheres of Influence with Particular Reference to Human Settlement*, Edition Axel Menges (Stuttgart/London), 2009.

17 Ibid, p 45.

18 Within the AADRL research agenda of 'Parametric Urbanism' we too always started with material analogues that were then transposed into the domain of digitally simulated self-organisation.

19 Frei Otto, *Occupying and Connecting*, p 64.

20 Marek Kolodziejczyk, 'Thread Model, Natural–Spontaneous Formation of Branches', in SFB 230, *Natural Structures – Principles, Strategies, and Models in Architecture and Nature*, Proceedings of the 2nd International Symposium of the Sonderforschungsbereich 230, Stuttgart, 1991, p 139.

21 This is what Zaha Hadid Architects imposed within the urban guidelines for the Singapore masterplan.

22 Zaha Hadid Architects, design team: Zaha Hadid, Patrik Schumacher, Saffet Bekiroglu, Daewa Kang, Daniel Widrig, Bozana Komljenovic, Sevil Yazici, Vigneswaran Ramaraju, Brian Dale, Jordan Darnell, Elif Erdine, Melike Altinisik, Ceyhun Baskin, Inanc Eray, Fluvio Wirz, Gonzalo Carbajo, Susanne Lettau, Amit Gupta, Marie-Perrine Placais, Jimena Araiza.

Patrik Schumacher, 'Parametricism: A New Global Style for Architecture and Urban Design', Neil Leach (guest-editor), *Digital Cities*, AD Profile 200, *AD* 79, July–August 2009, pp 14–23. © 2012 John Wiley & Sons Ltd.

Index

Figures in italics refer to captions.